The Identities of the Beast from the Sea and the Beast from the Land in Revelation 13

The Identities of the Beast from the Sea and the Beast from the Land in Revelation 13

JOSEPH POON

Foreword by James Crossley

☙PICKWICK *Publications* · Eugene, Oregon

THE IDENTITIES OF THE BEAST FROM THE SEA AND THE BEAST FROM THE LAND IN REVELATION 13

Copyright © 2017 Joseph Poon. All rights reserved. Except for brief quotations in critical publications or reviews, no part of this book may be reproduced in any manner without prior written permission from the publisher. Write: Permissions, Wipf and Stock Publishers, 199 W. 8th Ave., Suite 3, Eugene, OR 97401.

Pickwick Publications
An Imprint of Wipf and Stock Publishers
199 W. 8th Ave., Suite 3
Eugene, OR 97401

www.wipfandstock.com

PAPERBACK ISBN: 978-1-62564-445-9
HARDCOVER ISBN: 978-1-4982-8760-9
EBOOK ISBN: 978-1-4982-4449-7

Cataloguing-in-Publication data:

Names: Poon, Joseph.

Title: The identities of the beast from the sea and the beast from the land in Revelation 13.

Description: Eugene, OR: Pickwick Publications, 2017 | Includes bibliographical references.

Identifiers: ISBN 978-1-62564-445-9 (paperback) | ISBN 978-1-4982-8760-9 (hardcover)| ISBN 978-1-4982-4449-7 (ebook)

Subjects: LCSH: Bible. Revelation, XIII—Criticism, interpretation, etc.

Classification: LCC BS2825.A2 P75 2017 (paperback) | BS2825 (ebook)

Manufactured in the U.S.A. 03/09/17

Scripture quotations are from Revised Standard Version of the Bible, copyright © 1946, 1952, and 1971 National Council of the Churches of Christ in the United States of America. Used by permission. All rights reserved.

This book is dedicated to Blanche Yan

Contents

Foreword by James Crossley | ix
List of Abbreviations | xi

1 Introduction | 1
  A Review of the Scholarship on the Topic | 2
  Language and Imagery | 10
  Methodology | 14
  Significance of the Thesis | 15
  Structure of the Thesis | 16
  Assumptions, Scope and Limits | 17

**2 A Study of the Prominent Imagery in Daniel 7
  as It Relates to Revelation 13 | 20**
  The Chaoskampf Tradition in Recent Scholarship | 20
    The Ugaritic Myth Known as the Baal Cycle | 24
    Four Beasts Coming up out of the Sea | 50
  Conclusion | 56

**3 The Leviathan-Behemoth Motif
  in the Second Temple Apocalypses | 58**
  4 Ezra 6:49–52 | 59
  2 Baruch 29:4 | 65
  1 Enoch 60:7–10, 24ab | 68
  Apocalypse of Abraham 10:10; 21:4 | 76
  Ladder of Jacob 6:13 | 81
  Conclusion | 85

**4 An Examination of the Tripartite Ideology
  in Revelation 12 and 13 | 87**
  Revelation 12 and 13 | 88
    A Brief Review of the Structure of the Book of Revelation | 88

The Link between Revelation 12 and 13 | 95
　　The Hierarchical Relationship of the Three Figures
　　　　in Revelation 12 and 13 | 100
　The Tripartite Ideology in the Ancient World | 116
　　The Hypothesis of the Tripartite Ideology of Georges Dumézil | 116
　　Evidence for the Tripartite Ideology in the Structure of Roman Society | 118
　　Evidence for the Divine Triad in the Roman Pantheon | 122
　　The Great Temple of Capitoline Triad, Jupiter, Juno, and Minerva | 124
　　Capitolia: Shrines of Jupiter, Juno, and Minerva | 130
　Conclusion | 139

5 The Identities of the Two Beasts | 141
　The Identity of the Beast from the Sea | 141
　　The Date of Revelation | 149
　The Identity of the Beast from the Land | 157
　Conclusion | 166

6 Summary | 168

Bibliography | 173

Foreword

JOSEPH MAN-KIT POON IS a rarity among contemporary New Testament scholars in that he is prepared to challenge consensus thinking *as a historian* with no obvious theological line of attack or defense. Combined with his attention to detail, this independence of mind contributed to his much-deserved award as a PhD student at the European Association of Biblical Studies for the outstanding paper in New Testament studies (based on the topic of this book). But Poon does not provoke for provocation's sake. Rather, he always thinks long and hard about his research with honesty and integrity. It should not be forgotten that this study is a fitting testament to a scholar who has always shown dedication and has always worked hard.

In this book he looks beyond the conventional contexts for understanding Revelation 12 and 13 (Leviathan, Behemoth, Daniel 7) to combine them with issues surrounding hierarchical and tripartite structures in ancient ideological systems. As is well known, contemporary scholarly tendencies stress the importance of reading New Testament texts in the context of Roman imperialism but what studies such as Poon's do is to suggest that we need to go beyond situating texts as either pro- or anti-Empire and further examine the complex structural issues at play in ancient imperialism and how New Testament texts might have engaged with them. While there are broader issues at play for the study of Christian origins more generally, scholars of Revelation will find this book particularly fascinating as Poon combines his interdisciplinary thinking with traditional exegesis. Anyone working on a close reading of Revelation 12 and 13 in its ancient context will have to reckon with Poon's provocative reading.

James Crossley,
Professor of Bible, Society and Politics,
St Mary's University,
Twickenham, London

List of Abbreviations

ABD	*Anchor Bible Dictionary*. Edited by David Noel Freedman. 6 vols. New York: Doubleday, 1992.
AJA	*American Journal of Archaeology*
ANET	*Ancient Near Eastern Texts Relating to the Old Testament*. Edited by James B. Pritchard. 3rd ed. Princeton: Princeton University Press, 1969.
APOT	*The Apocrypha and Pseudepigrapha of the Old Testament*. Edited by R. H. Charles. 2 vols. Oxford, 1913.
BA	*Biblical Archaeologist*
BASOR	*Bulletin of the American Schools of Oriental Research*
Bib	*Biblica*
BMC	*British Museum Catalogue: A Catalogue of the Greek Coins in the British Museum*. Edited by R. S. Poole et al. 29 vols. London: British Museum Trustees, 1873–1927.
BT	*The Bible Translator*
CBQ	*Catholic Biblical Quarterly*
CIG	*Corpus Inscriptionum Graecarum*. Edited by August Boeckh. 4 vols. Berlin, 1828–1877.
CIL	*Corpus Inscriptionum Latinarum*. Berlin, 1862–.
CPJ	*Corpus Papyrorum Judaicarum*. Edited by Victor A. Tcherikover and Alexander Fuks. 3 vols. Cambridge: Harvard University Press, 1957–1964.

List of Abbreviations

CTA	*Corpus des tablettes en cunéiformes alphabétiques découvertes à Ras Shamra-Ugarit de 1929 à 1939*. Edited by Andrée Herdner. Paris: Geuthner, 1963.
EncJud	*Encyclopedia Judaica*. 16 vols. Jerusalem, 1972.
ETL	*Ephemerides Theologicae Lovanienses*
ExpTim	*Expository Times*
GRBS	*Greek, Roman, and Byzantine Studies*
HAR	*Hebrew Annual Review*
HSCP	*Harvard Studies in Classical Philology*
HTR	*Harvard Theological Review*
IEph	Wankel, Hermann, et al., eds. *Die Inschriften von Ephesos*. 8 vols. Bonn: Habelt, 1979–1984.
IGRR	*Inscriptiones graecae ad res romanas pertinentes*. Edited by René Cagnat et al. 3 vols. Paris: Leroux, 1906–1927.
IK	*Inschriften griechischer Städte aus Kleinasien*. Edited by Helmut Engelmann. Bonn: Habelt, 1972–.
ILLRP	*Inscriptiones latinae liberae rei publicae*. Edited by Attilio Degrassi. 2 vols. Biblioteca di studi superiori 23. Florence: La Nuova Italia, 1957–1963.
ILS	*Inscriptiones latinae selectae*. Edited by Hermann Dessau. 3 vols. in 5 parts. Berlin: Wiedmann, 1892–1916.
JAOS	*Journal of the American Oriental Society*
JAS	*Journal of Asian Studies*
JBL	*Journal of Biblical Literature*
JÖAI	*Jahreshefte des Österreichischen archäologischen Instituts*
JSJ	*Journal for the Study of Judaism in the Persian, Hellenistic, and Roman Periods*
JSNT	*Journal for the Study of the New Testament*
JSOT	*Journal for the Study of the Old Testament*
JTS	*Journal of Theological Studies*

List of Abbreviations

KTU	*Die keilalphabetischen Texte aus Ugarit.* Edited by Manfried Dietrich, Oswald Loretz, and Joaquín Sanmartín. AOAT 24/1. Neukirchen -Vluyn, 1976. 2nd enl. ed. of *KTU: The Cuneiform Alphabetic Texts from Ugarit, Ras Ibn Hani, and Other Places.* Edited by Manfried Dietrich, Oswald Loretz, and Joaquín Sanmartín. Münster: Ugarit-Verlag, 1995 (= *CTU*).
NovT	*Novum Testamentum*
NTS	*New Testament Studies*
NZ	*Numismatische Zeitschrift*
OGI	*Orientis graeci inscriptiones selectae.* Edited by Wilhelm Dittenberger. 2 vols. Leipzig: Hirzel, 1903–1905.
Or	*Orientalia*
OTP	*Old Testament Pseudepigrapha.* Edited by James H. Charlesworth. 2 vols. New York: Doubleday, 1983.
OTS	*Oudtestamentische Studiën*
RS	Ras Shamra
Sardis	*Sardis: Publications of the American Society for the Excavation of Sardis.* Edited by W. H. Buckler and David M. Robinson. Vol. 7. Greek and Latin Inscriptions. Part 1. Leyden: Brill, 1932.
SEG	Supplementum epigraphicum graecum
UF	*Ugarit-Forschungen*
UT	*Ugaritic Textbook.* C. H. Gordon. AnOr 38. Rome, 1965.
VT	*Vetus Testamentum*
ZNW	*Zeitschrift für die neutestamentliche Wissenschaft und die Kunde der älteren Kirche*
ZPE	*Zeitschrift für Papyrologie und Epigraphik*

1

Introduction

THE BOOK OF REVELATION is one of the most controversial biblical writings in the history of Christianity. This is not only because the composition of this literary piece is so unique that commentators can hardly reach a consensus on its structure and arrangement, but also because the fascinating and bizarre imagery and metaphors in the book always lead to opposing perspectives in interpretation. Within this work, chapter 12 has a unique role in particular, since the combat myth in the chapter points toward an ultimate divine battle in a cosmological context that appears to be central to the book. Chapters 12 and 13 are interrelated, however. Most commentators are aware of the relationship between the two chapters and see the dragon as the link between them. However, there is a more fundamental element of interrelationship between the two chapters that scholars rarely explore, that is, a tripartite hierarchical structure between the dragon and the beast from the sea and the beast from the land. In chapter 13, the dragon gives his power, throne and great authority to the sea beast, which in turn is allowed to make war on the saints and to conquer them. Similarly, the beast from the land exercises all the authority of the sea beast on its behalf and makes the world worship the sea beast. Thus, the land beast is subordinate to the sea beast, which in turn is subordinate to the dragon. This structure does not belong to biblical or extra-biblical traditions but to the Indo-European mythological tradition. In this structure, each figure is found in a specific context in accordance with its nature.

The present thesis aims to identify the beast from the sea and the beast from the land, employing the model of the tripartite ideology. Many recent scholars have studied the topic, and their advanced scholarship has resulted in a considerable level of accomplishment. In identifying the two beasts, commentators tend to focus on their characteristics, for instance, the "seven heads" (13:1), "mortal wound" (13:3), and the number "six hundred sixty-six" (13:18), as well as their parallels to Dan 7, for example, "a mouth speaking great things" and "forty-two months" (Rev 13:5; cf. Dan 7:8, 20, 25). This approach usually results in the conclusion that the sea beast symbolizes one of the Roman emperors and the land beast represents a figure relating to the imperial cult. While this approach contributes to identifying the two beasts, it cannot explain why the land beast is subordinate to the sea beast, which in turn is subordinate to the dragon. Using the template of the Indo-European tripartite ideology, the present thesis aims to demonstrate that the dragon, the sea beast and the land beast are arranged in accordance with the tripartite hierarchical structure, and that the three figures correspond to the three functions in that hierarchy. Thus, the thesis studies the topic through another trajectory that biblical scholars rarely explore on the one hand, and on the other, through this approach, it confirms the scholarship that they have brought to bear on the topic.

A REVIEW OF THE SCHOLARSHIP ON THE TOPIC

There is a long history of interpretation that holds that the sea beast and the land beast in Rev 13 represent the Roman Empire, or one of the emperors, and the imperial cult, respectively. Interpretation usually involves source critical analysis and allusions to Dan 7. As early as the nineteenth century CE, German scholars divided Rev 13 into two distinct sources with various degrees of cutting and pasting of different phrases depending on the scholar. Karl Erbes discerned in 13:1–18, along with 12:1–13, 18 and 14:9b–12, a Christian apocalypse that reflected Caligula's plan to establish his statue in the Jerusalem temple.[1] Friedrich Spitta, by removing a number of fragments in Rev 13 as well as adopting the reading 616 (v. 18),[2] restored in 13:1–8 a Jewish apocalypse describing the social conditions in Palestine in 39–41 CE during the reign of Caligula, with references to his critical illness (v. 3), his plan to set up his statue in Jerusalem (v. 6) and the worship

---

1. Charles, *Revelation*, 1:338.
2. Excising many clauses from vv. 3–18, see ibid.

offered to him (v. 8).³ Erbes identified the land beast as the Magi at the court of Caligula, whilst Spitta, taking up the reading ἑξακόσιοι δέκα ἕξ, "six hundred sixteen" (13:18),⁴ identified it as Simon Magus, a magician who was believed to have brought statues to life or at least to have made them speak.⁵

Wilhelm Bousset discerned in Revelation a number of sections that reflected existing fixed documents, such as 12:1–17 and 13:1–18. The vision in 12:1–17 was derived from eastern mythology. The visions of the two beasts in 13:1–18 were, on the whole, the work of the final redactor of the Apocalypse.⁶ In the formation of 17:1–18, the final redactor reworked the passages in vv. 1–7, 9–11, 15–18, which reflected an original Jewish source from Vespasian's time, by adding certain clauses in vv. 6, 9, 11, and contributed vv. 8, 12–14 to the chapter. The Jewish source and the redactor's contribution reflected two variants of the legend of Nero's return.⁷

According to Julius Wellhausen, the fragments in 13:1, 2, 4–7a, 10ab dealt with the desolation of the Jews after the destruction of Jerusalem in 70 CE,⁸ and said that the beast from the sea referred to the Roman Empire. And the texts in 13:11a, 12abc, 16b, 17, 18 were from another source of uncertain date there to introduce the legend of Nero's return (v. 18) and the beast from the land (v. 11a),⁹ who was the false prophet represented by the provincial state officials. The rest of the chapter (13:3, 7b–9, 10c, 11bc, 12d, 13–16a, 17b) were works of the final editor.¹⁰ For Wellhausen, instead of ἄλλο θηρίον, "another beast" (13:11), it read εἰκών, "image," since the beast and its image are mentioned together on many occasions later on in the book (14:9, 11; 15:2; 16:2; 19:20; 20:4).¹¹ He discerned two sources

---

3. Ibid.

4. This variant has support only from C, Tyc2, and some MSS reported by Irenaeus, who considered it a scribal error (*Haer.* 5.30.1). Aune notes that this variant "is clearly inferior" (*Revelation*, 2:722).

5. Charles, *Revelation*, 1:339. For the reference to Simon Magus, see Justin, *1 Apol.* 26; Irenaeus, *Haer.* 1.23; Eusebius, *Hist. eccl.* 2.13.1–8.

6. Bousset, *Offenbarung*, 379.

7. Ibid., 414–15.

8. Not including the second phrase in v. 1, ἔχον κέρατα δέκα καὶ κεφαλὰς ἑπτά, "having ten horns and seven heads."

9. Omitting the phrases, τὸ ὄνομα, "the name," and ἢ τὸν ἀριθμὸν τοῦ ὀνόματος αὐτοῦ, "or the number of its name," in v. 17.

10. Charles, *Revelation*, 1:339.

11. Ibid.

in 17:1–18. The first source consisted of vv. 3–4, 6b–7, 9, and 10, omitting some fragments.[12] The second source consisted of vv. 11–13, 16, and 17, leaving out some phrases.[13] The pieces of text in vv. 1b–3 belonged to either source.[14]

In Johannes Weiss' scheme, 13:1–2, 3–7 came from a Jewish apocalypse written in 70 CE. Since 12:18 was a redactional piece linking chapters 12 and 13 through the activity of the dragon, 13:2b and 4a belonged to the same redactional gloss as 12:18 as they went on to introduce the superiority of the dragon over the beast.[15] The vision in 13:11–18 originally dealt with a false prophet, but in the final form of the chapter, was transformed to represent the priesthood of the imperial cult symbolized by ἄλλο θηρίον, "another beast." By means of some additions, the final editor united the two sources and made the entire chapter refer to the Roman Empire, the legend of Nero's return and the imperial cult.[16]

Following the German scholarship, R. H. Charles' theory, though not recent, is still one of the most important works of English scholarship on the topic. According to Charles, there were two sources behind 13:1–10. The first source included vv. 1abd, 2, 4–7a, 10, and was a Jewish apocalypse originally written in Hebrew around 70 CE. Thus, the beast rising out of the sea (v. 1) represented the Roman Empire, the μῆνας τεσσεράκοντα [καὶ] δύο, "forty-two months," and σκηνὴ αὐτοῦ, "his dwelling" (vv. 5b–6b), referred to the siege of Jerusalem by the Romans and the woeful plight (v. 10) of the survivors.[17] The second gloss consisted of vv. 3c, 8, which were independent translations of the same Hebrew source. The fragments in vv. 3ab, 7b, 9 were the author's own works.[18] The sources behind 13:11–18 were more complicated. The materials in vv. 11, 12ab, 13–14a, 16b, 17a originated from the same source referring to the ψευδοπροφήτης, "false prophet," as the references found later in 16:13; 19:20; 20:10.[19] The two figures in this

---

12. Omitting καὶ κέρατα δέκα, "and ten horns" (v. 3), καὶ τὰ δέκα κέρατα, "and the ten horns" (vv. 6b–7), excluding the entire verse but αἱ ἑπτὰ κεφαλαί, "the seven heads" (v. 9), and omitting the initial καὶ, "and" (v. 10). See Charles, *Revelation*, 2:59.

13. Omitting καὶ τὰ δέκα κέρατα ἃ εἶδες καὶ τὸ θηρίον, "and the ten horns that you saw and the beast" (v. 16). See ibid.

14. Ibid.

15. Weiss, *Offenbarung*, 84–85.

16. Ibid., 93, 111, 115, 139–42.

17. Charles, *Revelation*, 1:340–41.

18. Ibid.

19. Ibid., 1:343.

gloss, however, ἄλλο θηρίον, "another beast" (v. 11), and τὸ θηρίον τὸ πρῶτον, "the first beast" (v. 12), were from the final apocalyptist, as well as the additions, οὗ ἐθεραπεύθη ἡ πληγὴ τοῦ θανάτου αὐτοῦ, "whose mortal wound was healed" (v. 12c), ἐνώπιον τοῦ θηρίου . . . ἀποκτανθῶσιν, "in the presence of the beast . . . to be slain" (vv. 14b–15), τοὺς μικροὺς . . . δούλους, "the small . . . slave" (v. 16a) and τὸ ὄνομα . . . ἑξήκοντα ἕξ, "the name . . . sixty-six" (vv. 17b–18).[20] By means of these additions, the false prophet was transformed into a secondary personage ἄλλο θηρίον, "another beast," which in the final form of the chapter referred to the priesthood of the imperial cult.[21] The legend of Nero's return is found in 13:12c, 14c, and 18.[22] On the other hand, like Wellhausen, Charles discerns two sources behind Rev 17. One source consists of vv. 1c–2, 3b–6, 7, 18, 8, 9, and 10.[23] This group of fragments identifies the sea beast with the Roman Empire. Another source consists of vv. 11–13, 16, and 17,[24] and reflects the legend of Nero returning from the east.[25] In his massive three-volume commentary, David Aune proposes that Revelation was written in three stages. The first stage was the formation of twelve self-contained textual units produced in approximately the 50s and 60s of the first century CE, well before their inclusion in the compilation with the visionary and prophetic narratives.[26] The second stage was the composition of the first edition of the Apocalypse from approximately 68 to 74 CE.[27] The third stage was the second edition of the work completed near the end of the first century during the reign of Trajan (98–117 CE).[28] The combat myth in 12:1–17 and the visions of the sea beast and land beast in

20. Ibid.
21. Ibid.
22. Ibid.
23. Omitting several phrases in vv. 6–10, καὶ ἐκ τοῦ αἵματος τῶν μαρτύρων Ἰησοῦ, "and with the blood of the martyrs of Jesus" (v. 6), ἦν καὶ οὐκ ἔστιν, καὶ μέλλει ἀναβαίνειν ἐκ τῆς ἀβύσσου, καὶ εἰς ἀπώλειαν ὑπάγει, "was and is not and is to ascend from the bottomless pit and go to perdition," ὅτι ἦν καὶ οὐκ ἔστιν καὶ παρέσται, "because it was and is not and is to come" (v. 8), ὧδε ὁ νοῦς ὁ ἔχων σοφίαν, "this calls for a mind with wisdom," ἑπτὰ κεφαλαὶ ἑπτὰ ὄρη εἰσίν, ὅπου ἡ γυνὴ κάθηται ἐπ᾽ αὐτῶν, "seven heads are seven mountains on which the woman is seated" (v. 9), and the first καὶ, "and" (v. 10). See Charles, *Revelation*, 2:59.
24. Omitting two phrases in v. 11, ὃ ἦν καὶ οὐκ ἔστιν, "that was and is not," and καὶ εἰς ἀπώλειαν ὑπάγει, "and it goes to perdition." Ibid., 2:60.
25. Ibid., 2:59–60.
26. Aune, *Revelation*, 1:cxxii.
27. Ibid., 1:cxxiii.
28. Ibid., 1:cxxxii.

13:1–18 as well as the vision of the whore of Babylon in 17:1–18 were works from the first stage.[29]

In agreement with Weiss, Aune concurs that 12:18 is a redactional link connecting chapters 12 and 13. Thus, the dragon in that link was not part of either of the two visions in 13:1–10 and 13:11–18 but was introduced into these visions in order to tie them more closely to chapter 12, where it is found eight times (vv. 3b, 4b, 7b [twice], 9a, 13, 16b, 17a).[30] With this link, the ensuing fragments referring to the dragon are redactional too, including καὶ ἔδωκεν αὐτῷ ὁ δράκων τὴν δύναμιν αὐτοῦ καὶ τὸν θρόνον αὐτοῦ καὶ ἐξουσίαν μεγάλην, "And to it the dragon gave his power and his throne and great authority" (v. 2b), καὶ προσεκύνησαν τῷ δράκοντι ὅτι ἔδωκεν τὴν ἐξουσίαν τῷ θηρίῳ, "And men worshiped the dragon, for he had given his authority to the beast" (v. 4a), ὡς δράκων, a phrase describing the land beast speaking (v. 11), as well as καὶ μίαν ἐκ τῶν κεφαλῶν αὐτοῦ ὡς ἐσφαγμένην εἰς θάνατον, καὶ ἡ πληγὴ τοῦ θανάτου αὐτοῦ ἐθεραπεύθη, "And one of its heads seemed to have a mortal wound, but its mortal wound was healed" (v. 3a). This last sentence reflects the legend of Nero's return.[31]

Again, in agreement with Weiss, Aune sees that the two references to the mortal wound, οὗ ἐθεραπεύθη ἡ πληγὴ τοῦ θανάτου αὐτοῦ, "whose mortal wound was healed" (v. 12c), and ὃς ἔχει τὴν πληγὴν τῆς μαχαίρης καὶ ἔζησεν, "which was wounded by a sword and yet lived" (v. 14c), are interpolations analeptically referring back to the beast from the sea.[32] On the other hand, the noun θηρίον, "beast," is found anarthrously only in 13:1 and 17:3; the first occurrence of the beast in each chapter. Following 13:1, the beast is found with the anaphoric article twenty more times before 17:3 (13:2, 3, 4 [thrice], 12 [twice], 14 [twice], 15 [thrice], 17, 18; 14:9, 11; 15:2; 16:2, 10, 13), which in turn is followed by the arthrous noun τὸ θηρίον, "the beast," on eight occasions in the chapter (17:7b, 8ac, 11a, 12b, 13, 16a, 17b). Aune sees this association as a seam between Rev 13–16 and Rev 17, which was the work of christianizing additions produced in the second stage of composition.[33] Finally, the gematria reference (v. 18) is an explanatory redactional addition.[34]

29. Ibid., 1:cxxii.
30. Ibid., 2:725.
31. Ibid., 2:726.
32. Ibid., 2:758, 762.
33. Ibid., 1:cxxxi-cxxxii.
34. Ibid., 2:769.

Introduction

It would be next to impossible to produce a thorough evaluation of the various source critical approaches to the topic in this introduction as there are as many treatments as there are commentators. This brief review highlights some relevant points, however. Scholars using source criticism are in general agreement that the two visions in 13:1–10 and 13:11–18 reflect two sources, each of which is, in turn, a compilation of different fragments, while they differ in how they analyze the materials. Of these bits and pieces, a group of fragments indicates the identity of the sea beast, while some others point to the land beast. The three references to the mortal wound of the sea beast (13:3a, 12c, 14c) are the sources used for identification. However, there are some minor problems. In 13:3a, μίαν ἐκ τῶν κεφαλῶν αὐτοῦ, "one of the heads of the beast," seemed to have a mortal wound, but ἡ πληγὴ τοῦ θανάτου αὐτοῦ ἐθεραπεύθη, "its mortal wound was healed." Thus, it was the beast, not its head, which recovered from the mortal wound,[35] since the second pronoun αὐτοῦ would normally be αὐτῆς, if it referred to μίαν ἐκ τῶν κεφαλῶν.[36] In 13:12c and 14c, it was the beast that suffered from the wound too. Taking up the wound upon the beast's head, some ancient writers identify the beast as Caligula.[37] Most modern scholars, however, identify it as Nero.[38] The 666 gematria (13:18) is an addition to the chapter. There is little argument among commentators that the best solution to the 666 gematria is the legend of Nero's return. The land beast is more complicated. On the one hand, it appears to come from the source of the false prophet as it is so expressed in three later passages (16:13; 19:20; 20:10). On the other, it is related to the beast's image as the beast and its image are mentioned together in many places (14:9, 11; 15:2; 16:2; 19:20; 20:4). In either case, commentators are roughly in agreement that, in the final form of the composition, this figure is primarily related to the imperial cult.

Furthermore, chapter 17, the seven-head conundrum (vv. 8–11) in particular, refers to the legend of Nero's return, probably from variant versions. The riddle has been understood as a clue to dating the book. Charles,[39]

---

35. Ibid., 2:736; Mounce, *Revelation*, 248; Beale, *Revelation*, 690.
36. Mounce, *Revelation*, 248 n. 26.
37. Suetonius, *Cal.* 14; Dio Cassius, *Hist. rom.* 59.8.
38. Aune, *Revelation*, 2:736–37; Charles, *Revelation*, 1:350–51; Roloff, *Revelation*, 156–57; Caird, *Revelation*, 164; Witherington, *Revelation*, 182; Beasley-Murray, *Revelation*, 210–11.
39. Charles, *Revelation*, 2:69.

Albert Bell,[40] Elisabeth Schüssler Fiorenza,[41] and George Beasley-Murray,[42] and many other scholars have used different systems to enumerate the twelve Roman emperors, from Julius Caesar to Domitian, in order to yield ἑπτά, "seven," the number of the emperors in the riddle.[43] Scholars, however, rarely reach a consensus concerning the way in which the seven heads are counted, since from antiquity, there had been two systems for enumerating the Roman emperors. Suetonius began his *Lives of the Caesars* with the biography of Julius Caesar.[44] Dio Chrysostom and Josephus counted Julius Caesar as the first emperor too, as the two ancients referred to Augustus as "the second Caesar" (*Or.* 34.7) and "the second emperor of the Romans" (*Ant.* 18.32) respectively. A possible rationale for this view is that since the term Caesar was derived from the name Julius Caesar, it was natural for ancients to consider him the first Roman emperor.[45] On the other hand, Tacitus began his *Annals* with Augustus, taking the title *princeps* as the major distinction between the emperors and all the earlier magistrates of the Roman state.[46] Claudius, too, began his history of Rome with the death of Julius Caesar, according to Suetonius (*Claud.* 41).[47]

If Suetonius' list is employed, the first five emperors, that is, the kings who have fallen as reported in 17:10, are Julius Caesar, Augustus, Tiberius, Caligula and Claudius. If this were the case, Nero would have been the emperor whom the verse refers to as ὁ εἷς ἔστιν, "the one who is," and hence the current emperor at the time Revelation was written. Galba would have been the subsequent emperor who would remain ὀλίγον, "only a little while," when he came. A number of scholars hold this view.[48] If Tacitus' scheme were at work, the five fallen emperors would have been Augustus, Tiberius, Caligula, Claudius, and Nero. Then, Nero would have been the fifth emperor, and Galba, the emperor described as "the one who is,"

---

40. Bell, "Date of John's Apocalypse," 93–102.

41. Schüssler Fiorenza, *Revelation*, 97.

42. Beasley-Murray, *Revelation*, 256–57.

43. In reality in dating Revelation there may be a problem to relate this passage to the passage in Rev 13:1–10. This is because this passage may be a later political interpolation (Rissi, *Time and History*, 75–83).

44. Suetonius, *Jul.* 1; *Lives of the Caesars*, 3–42.

45. Aune, *Revelation*, 3:946.

46. Tacitus, *Ann.* 1.1.

47. Momigliano, *Claudius*, 6–7.

48. Wilson, "Domitianic Date," 605.

and so the current emperor when the apocalyptist produced the work. The next would have been Otho. Some commentators take this view.[49] Other scholars even omit Galba, Otho and Vitellius, arguing that they were not emperors since their reigns were too short in order to make up the list that fits their dating.[50] Thus, historical interpretation of the present riddle rarely results in a non-controversial solution. Rather, many recent scholars argue that a symbolic interpretation seems to be more relevant here; the number "seven" symbolizes the totality of Roman emperors.[51]

In addition to source critical analysis, the allusion to Dan 7 and to the Leviathan-Behemoth tradition has been understood as an important issue in understanding Rev 13. Exegetes are in agreement that there are a number of parallels to Dan 7 in Rev 13. The sea beast had κέρατα δέκα, "ten horns"; it was like a παρδάλει, "leopard"; its feet were like a πόδες ἄρκου, "bear's"; and its mouth was like a στόμα λέοντος, "lion's mouth" (13:2). These characteristics are blended with the features of the four beasts in Dan 7:2–7. There, the four beasts are generally understood as representations of four different kingdoms, which are Babylon, Media, Persia and Greece.[52] Also, the beast was given στόμα λαλοῦν μεγάλα καὶ βλασφημίας, "a mouth uttering haughty and blasphemous words" (13:5a). It was allowed ποιῆσαι πόλεμον μετὰ τῶν ἁγίων καὶ νικῆσαι αὐτούς, "to make war on the saints and to conquer them" (13:7a). It was allowed to exercise authority for μῆνας τεσσεράκοντα [καὶ] δύο, "forty-two months" (13:5b). These features are allusions to the little horn in Dan 7. The little horn is generally believed to refer to Antiochus IV. His hostility towards Jerusalem provides a historical background for understanding the use of these allusions in Revelation.

On the other hand, most commentators agree that in both Dan 7 and Rev 13 the ultimate mythic background is the *Chaoskampf* tradition, that is, the Ugaritic Baal Cycle. In both cases, the beast comes up from the sea. The allusion to Leviathan and Behemoth is particularly explicit in Rev 13 as

---

49. Ibid.; Bell, "Date of John's Apocalypse," 97–102; Rowland, *Open Heaven*, 405.

50. For instance, Beasley-Murray, *Revelation*, 256–57. In agreement with Bell, Wilson argues with solid evidence that since most ancient writers include Galba, Otho and Vitellius in their accounts of Roman history, it does not make sense to omit them in reckoning the Roman emperors just because they reigned only for a short term, as some commentators do (Bell, "Date of John's Apocalypse," 99–100; Wilson, "Domitianic Date," 600–602).

51. Aune, *Revelation*, 3:948; Caird, *Revelation*, 218–19; Mounce, *Revelation*, 315; Bauckham, *Climax*, 405; Harrington, *Revelation*, 172.

52. Collins, *Daniel*, 295; Caird, *Revelation*, 162; Mounce, *Revelation*, 245 n. 8.

in this chapter the beast coming up from the sea and the beast coming up from the land are clearly stated. Adela Yarbro Collins notes that Rev 12, 13 and 17 are the most noteworthy parallels to the combat myth.[53] Leviathan and Behemoth are also found together in several Second Temple apocalypses roughly contemporaneous with Revelation (*4 Ezra* 6:49–52; *2 Bar.* 29:4; *1 En.* 60:7–10, 24ab), in which the two beasts are described as food for the righteous at the end time. Unlike those accounts, however, the passage in Rev 13:1–18 contains little detail about Leviathan and Behemoth. Most commentators see the allusion to the two mythic figures in the passage. Aune notes that important features of the Leviathan-Behemoth myth are omitted in the chapter.[54] It appears that there is a basic difference between Revelation and those Second Temple writings in using the tradition.

LANGUAGE AND IMAGERY

Regardless of the complexity of the form of its main body, Revelation appears as a letter in its final form, since it opens with an epistolary address that strikingly resembles the openings of the Pauline epistles (1:4–8) and concludes with an ending that is customary in letters (22:21). Furthermore, its first main section (1:9—3:22) consists of seven letters addressed to seven specific churches in Asia.[55] At the beginning of the book (1:3), it is clearly stated in the first beatitude that the book was written to be read aloud in community worship as a prophetic word.[56] Thus, Revelation was written in the first place for hearers.[57] The apocalyptist truly emphasized the importance of hearing the Apocalypse (2:7, 11, 17, 29; 3:6, 13, 22; 22:7b, 18a).[58] Being a work to be read out loud to the assembled community, Revelation contains within it the characteristic common to anything that is performed which is, that through reading it out loud and hearing it read aloud, the hearers undergo a collective change in consciousness, which is a transformative experience.[59]

---

53. Collins, *Combat Myth*, 77.
54. Aune, *Revelation*, 2:728.
55. Bauckham, *Climax*, 3; Roloff, *Revelation*, 7.
56. Roloff, *Revelation*, 21.
57. Bauckham, *Climax*, 3.
58. Callahan, "Language of the Apocalypse," 459.
59. Ibid., 460.

Introduction

In terms of rhetorical mode, the book reflects the elements of all three classical types: forensic, deliberative and epideictic. Its epistolary framework and its calls to deliberation and decision function as deliberative rhetoric in the community assembly. Its visionary descriptions of the heavenly liturgy as well as its hymnic praises identify it as ceremonial rhetoric. Its indictments, warnings, divine judgments, as well as its promises of reward and punishment, qualify the book as forensic rhetoric.[60] Of the three modes, forensic rhetoric appears to be the dominant form in the book, as it follows the basic rhetorical pattern of persuasion.[61] The speaker's authority was first established with the audience in the commissioning vision in the introduction (1:1-2). Then, at the heart of the Apocalypse (chs. 4-21), John cited both the Hebrew Bible and the living Word of Jesus as the testimony of witnesses in a forensic setting described in the form of visions, to persuade his audience to heed his exhortations. Finally, the divine verdict is redemption (chs. 20-22).[62] The rhetorical function of these assertions is to change the audience's mind in the present.[63]

There are different perspectives on how to interpret the symbols and imagery in Revelation. Literary-critical reading has been one of the popular ways to deal with the issue in the latter decades of the twentieth century. Literary interpretation sees that the language of Revelation is not referential but polyvalent. Being polyvalent, the language does not appeal to logic but to the emotions, and so is expressive and evocative.[64] In interpreting the Apocalypse, scholars who hold this view tend to depoliticize and universalize the apocalyptic symbols and imagery, and to resort to archetypal approaches to articulating the deeper religious or theological meaning.[65] According to this school, the language of Revelation is also described as pictorial and non-objectifying as opposed to propositional.[66] And interpreters acknowledge the ambiguity, openness and indeterminacy of the literary vision and symbolic narrative of the Apocalypse.[67] For instance, exegetes using this approach do not see the number 666 (13:18) as a code

---

60. Schüssler Fiorenza, *Revelation*, 21, 26.
61. Witherington, *Revelation*, 15.
62. Ibid., 16-17.
63. Royalty, *Streets of Heaven*, 128.
64. Schüssler Fiorenza, *Revelation*, 19; Boring, *Revelation*, 54-55.
65. Schüssler Fiorenza, *Revelation*, 18-19.
66. Boring, *Revelation*, 51, 57.
67. Schüssler Fiorenza, *Revelation*, 19.

referring to a particular first-century Roman ruler. Instead, they argue that the number points to the prototypal conflict between the demonic and the divine, and that the call for wisdom is not a call to decipher the number but to recognize its deeper meaning and significance.[68] Likewise, from this perspective, "Babylon" (17:1–14), is not a univocal code-word simply identical with "Rome," though that was the meaning in John's situation, but embodies the essence of urban civilization and human empire.[69]

Schüssler Fiorenza is correct in pointing out that such an interpretation risks reducing the multiple layers of meaning in Revelation to a universalizing hard core of propositional truth, and that it is important to trace how an image or symbol works within the overall composition of the mythological symbolization in the Apocalypse.[70] She cites the "great city" references as evidence. In 11:8 the dead bodies of the two witnesses will lie in the street of the "great city" where their Lord was crucified, which was allegorically called "Sodom and Egypt." The "great city" is mentioned again in 16:19 in connection with Babylon and is identified explicitly as Babylon in 18:10, and 21. Here, Babylon is used as a code name for Rome, just as it was so frequently used in some biblical and extra-biblical writings (1 Pet 5:13; *Sib. Or.* 5.143.159). In 17:18, the "great city" is in turn identified with the woman who rides on a scarlet beast with seven heads (17:3), which is explicitly interpreted as the geographical city of Rome (17:9).[71] Thus, while the city is named and referred to allegorically, it still represents a specific location on earth. Also, it is highly likely that the number 666 (13:18) is best interpreted as gematria referring to the legend of Nero's return, as most scholars agree.[72] As a matter of fact, the polemics in forensic rhetoric concern real persons and entities.[73] Whilst the language in Revelation is not descriptive in a literal sense, it is nevertheless referential, which is also in keeping with the apocalyptic prophecy in this work.[74]

The letters to the seven churches in Rev 2–3 clearly indicate that the author was dealing with specific events in actual particular congregations on the western edge of the province of Asia, and that the author knew

68. Ibid.
69. Ibid.; Boring, *Revelation*, 55.
70. Schüssler Fiorenza, *Revelation*, 20.
71. Ibid.
72. See chapter 5.
73. Witherington, *Revelation*, 16.
74. Ibid.

his audience and their issues, and had a detailed knowledge of their geographical, historical, political and religious circumstances. In the letter to the Thyatira church (2:18–29), John mentions a woman who calls herself a prophetess and is teaching and beguiling Christ's servants to practice immorality and to eat food sacrificed to idols (2:20). John does not mention the figure's name. Instead, he provides a symbolic name for this person, namely, Jezebel,[75] a well known figure in Jewish tradition. According to 1 Kings (16:31; 18:1–19; 19:1–2), Jezebel converted King Ahab of the northern kingdom from worship of the Lord to worship of the Phoenician god, Baal. She had many Jewish prophets killed and became the enemy of Elijah. Here in Rev 2:20, Jezebel is accused of leading the church πορνεύω, "to practice immorality." The term πορνεύω usually means some kind of sexually promiscuous behavior.[76] In Jewish tradition, however, it is sometimes employed metaphorically to refer to idolatry. For instance, in Hosea, the prophet compares Israel with a whore as she has abandoned God, her metaphorical husband.[77] Since sexual metaphors are used elsewhere in the Apocalypse (e.g., 17:2, 5), it is likely that John intends a metaphorical meaning rather than a literal meaning for the term here.[78]

Secondly, Jezebel is accused of teaching the church to eat food sacrificed to idols. The same issue had been mentioned in 1 Cor 8–10, roughly a half-century before the composition of Revelation. The accusation refers to either consuming the meat bought at the local meat market, which in turn is sacrificial meat from the local pagan temples, or eating the meat sacrificed to the pagan deities at their festivals, or both.[79] In addition to the activity of the traditional pagan religion, it could refer to the newly ascendant form of idolatry in the imperial cult.[80] Here, John does not accuse his readers directly of doing this but he does accuse the uncommitted majority in the community of tolerating the behavior. Perhaps these people accepted the prophetic legitimacy of both John and Jezebel.[81] There seems to have been rivalry between John and Jezebel, since John, who considered himself a prophet (cf. 1:3; 22:18, 19), scoffed at Jezebel's illegitimate

75. Boring, *Revelation*, 92.
76. Duff, "Wolves in Sheep's Clothing," 66–67.
77. Ibid., 67 n. 4.
78. Ibid., 67.
79. Ibid.
80. Biguzzi, "Ephesus," 276–90.
81. Aune, "Social Matrix," 28–29.

self-claim to the prophetic office by saying that ἡ λέγουσα ἑαυτὴν προφῆτιν, "she calls herself a prophetess" (2:20). The problem of eating food sacrificed to idols is also mentioned in the letter to Pergamum (2:12–17). The church in Pergamum is commended for holding fast to the faith, like Antipas, "my witness, my faithful one," who was killed there (2:13). Some people in the audience, however, are accused of holding the teaching of Balaam (2:14). On the basis of Num 31:15–16, Jewish tradition had made Balaam into a false prophet, one of the paradigmatic ringleaders who tempted Israel to participate in idolatrous religion (Philo, *Mos.* 1.48–55; Josephus, *Ant.* 4.126). Both Balaam and Jezebel are understood as foreigners and agents of the foreign religion who seduced Israel into idolatry. In the present context, the two names are used symbolically to refer to John's opponents.[82]

According to Collins, the response to the opponents reflects the transference of aggression felt by the author or the hearers to another subject.[83] In 2:16, it is said that Christ will make war with the sword of his mouth against the Pergamenes who follow Balaam, as well as Nicolaitans, if they do not repent. In 2:22–23, it is said that the Son of God will throw Jezebel into a sickbed and those who commit adultery with her into great tribulation. In these cases, John's apparent hostility to his opponents is transferred to the one like a son of man.[84] Hence, the two cases indicate that what John was dealing with were actual events and people in the Christian community in Asia Minor, and that he chose sources with specific characteristics corresponding to what he wanted to say about his opponents.

METHODOLOGY

The methodology of the present thesis employs source criticism and literary comparative analysis with the support of archaeological and related ancient literary evidence. Beginning with a source critical analysis of the layers in Revelation and comparative analysis of Second Temple apocalyptic writings, the thesis seeks a justification for the broadly accepted identification of the beast from the sea, the beast from the land, and the dragon in Rev 12 and 13 by providing insight into the relevant passages in those two chapters through the lens of ancient literary texts and archaeological finds. This methodology could be called literary-archaeological.

82. Boring, *Revelation*, 93.
83. Collins, *Crisis and Catharsis*, 156.
84. Ibid.

Introduction

The methodology employed in chapter 2 is a mix of historical and literary criticism. Through an historical and literary critical study of the important imagery and motifs in Dan 7 that have parallels in Rev 13, the chapter seeks to demonstrate that John employs these sources to allude to events of the same nature in writing Rev 13. The methodology used in chapter 3 is literary comparative analysis. By comparing the literary arrangement in which Leviathan and Behemoth are found in several Second Temple apocalyptic writings, the chapter seeks to demonstrate that there is a general pattern in which the author then employs the Leviathan-Behemoth motif.

The methodologies used in chapter 4 include source criticism, literary criticism and a study of ancient literary texts and archaeological evidence. Through source critical analysis, the chapter first aims to demonstrate that the sea beast is derived from the same source as the dragon, and is arranged with the land beast in accordance with the Leviathan-Behemoth tradition in the final form of Rev 13. Then, by studying the archaeological evidence and related texts about the tripartite ideology, in particular the Capitoline Triad, the chapter seeks to demonstrate that the tripartite ideology is the dominant principal behind the putting together of the dragon and the two beasts. Chapter 5 employs historical criticism and archaeological evidence to seek justification for the broadly accepted identification of the sea beast and the land beast.

SIGNIFICANCE OF THE THESIS

There is general consensus that Revelation reflects an extensive employment of Scripture, in particular Daniel. Many scholars believe that Rev 13 is primarily dependent on Dan 7 in terms of imagery and motifs. Evidence for this dependence includes "making war on the saints" (Rev 13:7a; Dan 7:21), "a mouth uttering haughty and blasphemous words" (Rev 13:5a; Dan 7:20), and the period of "forty-two months" (Rev 13:5b; Dan 7:25). On the other hand, most commentators see that the ultimate mythological background of Dan 7 and Rev 13 is the tradition of *Chaoskampf*, since in both biblical passages the beasts are rising up from the sea. Based on this ultimate background, exegetes believe that the beast from the sea and the beast from the land in Rev 13 are allusions to Leviathan and Behemoth, the two monsters in the Canaanite myth. While Daniel and the *Chaoskampf* tradition have had an influence on Rev 13, the two sources cannot explain one significant element that commentators rarely explore, namely the link between Rev 12 and Rev 13.

There is a unique structure that explains the link between the dragon and the sea beast and the land beast in Rev 12–13 that biblical scholars have rarely examined. The three mythic figures are arranged in a hierarchical relationship. In the vision in 13:1–10, the dragon gives his power, his throne and great authority to the sea beast. With this endowment, the sea beast is allowed to make war on the saints and to conquer them. In the second vision in 13:11–18, the land beast exercises all the authority of the sea beast in its presence and makes the earth and its inhabitants worship the sea beast. Hence, the land beast is subordinate to the sea beast, which in turn is subordinate to the dragon. This tripartite hierarchical structure appears to be an underlying principal linking together both the three figures and the two chapters. This hierarchical relationship does not belong to the Leviathan-Behemoth motif, typically found in the Second Temple apocalypses, or to any biblical or extra-biblical sources, but to an Indo-European ideology, that is, the tripartite ideology. This tripartite ideology is an all-encompassing structural relationship underlying many Indo-European mythological traditions, including the Indic, the Iranian, the Scandinavian and the Roman. In this system, each figure carries a specific role and function corresponding to its hierarchical level. The dragon and the two beasts in Rev 12 and 13 are arranged in the same tripartite hierarchical relationship in which each figure has a specific function and role corresponding to its level in the hierarchy. Employing the details of the tripartite system, the present thesis aims to identify the beast from the sea and the beast from the land in Rev 13. This study is important because it demonstrates that the tripartite system, typically found in the Indo-European mythological traditions, can explain the underlying structure relating the dragon and the two beasts in Rev 12 and 13 which the biblical and extra biblical sources cannot explain.

STRUCTURE OF THE THESIS

Following this introduction, chapter 2 seeks to study the allusions from Dan 7 in Rev 13 by looking at the prominent imagery. The chapter begins with a review of recent scholarship on the *Chaoskampf* tradition, since this is the ultimate mythological background of both Dan 7 and Rev 13. Then, the chapter examines the imagery from Dan 7 that is paralleled in Rev 13, including "a mouth speaking great things" (7:8, 20), "made war with the saints" (7:21), and the period of "a time, two times, and half a time" (7:25). Since "one like a son of man" (7:13) is an important imagery in Dan 7 and is found in some Second Temple writings and Revelation, this section first studies this imagery. By studying these motifs, the chapter outlines the way Dan 7 is used in Rev 13. Chapter 3 examines the general pattern in which Leviathan and Behemoth are found in the Second Temple apocalyptic writings roughly contemporaneous with Revelation, including *4 Ezra*, *2 Baruch* and *1 Enoch*, and the pattern in which Leviathan is found alone in the *Apocalypse of Abraham* and the *Ladder of Jacob*. By so doing, the chapter aims to outline the formulaic pattern with which the apocalyptic author employs the tradition.

Chapter 4 is the central argument of the thesis. It contains two parts. The first part demonstrates how John divides the biblical Leviathan gloss into two figures, with one being the dragon in Rev 12 and the other being the beast from the sea in Rev 13, and then arranges the sea beast and the land beast in the latter chapter in accordance with the Leviathan-Behemoth tradition. This arrangement results in the fact that the three figures exist in a tripartite hierarchical structure, in which the dragon is superior to the sea beast, which in turn is superior to the land beast. The second part demonstrates that the structural relationship in which the dragon and the two beasts are arranged reflects a vestige of the tripartite ideology that is typically found in the Indo-European mythological traditions. This part first reviews the hypothesis of this theory. Then, it studies the related literary and archaeological evidence. Chapter 5 identifies the exact referents of the two beasts, employing the findings of the previous chapters. Chapter 6 is a summary of the thesis.

ASSUMPTIONS, SCOPE, AND LIMITS

There are three assumptions in the present thesis. Firstly, it accepts the general assumption of source criticism that Revelation is made up of different sources. The thesis does not discuss the process of how the different bits and pieces come together as a whole work and the way in which the final editor chooses and combines the sources available to him, since, obviously, this is a huge project that is more suitable for study elsewhere. This thesis, however, holds the assumption that it is the final editor who is responsible for the final form of Revelation, and that he integrated the different materials and glosses in accordance with the tradition he received.

Secondly, in line with the first assumption, the present thesis holds the majority opinion that Revelation is a post-70s CE work, written during the reign of Domitian. As the thesis will demonstrate, internal evidence supports a later date after 70 CE rather than an earlier date for the composition of the book.

Thirdly, the thesis assumes that Rev 12 and 13 are central to the book. Commentators are in general agreement, with nuanced perspectives in each case, that the two chapters describing the dragon and the two beasts are the center of the work because of the unique subject matter. The thesis will provide a brief review of this issue.

The scope of the present thesis is the identification of the sea beast and land beast in Rev 13. This is achieved by investigating the tripartite hierarchical structure underlying the two beasts and the dragon in Rev 12. The thesis has some limitations. Firstly, the tripartite hierarchical structure that this study assumes to have had an influence on the subject involves three constituents, with each having a specific role and function on its hierarchical level. In the case of the present study, the three constituents are represented by the two beasts in Rev 13 and the dragon in Rev 12. Since the study focuses on the sea beast and land beast, however, the examination in chapter 4 will not examine the dragon in as detailed a way as it does the two beasts but rather provides a contour of the mythological context of the dragon, which is, nevertheless, sufficient to indicate the primary nature of the dragon.

Secondly, the use of the Hebrew Bible in Revelation is not restricted to Daniel; the Apocalypse contains many themes and motifs that have parallels in other writings from the Hebrew Bible, for instance, Ezekiel. Since the thesis focuses on the two beasts in Rev 13, for which the source employed from the Hebrew Bible is predominantly Daniel, the examination of the related issue in chapter 2 will mainly cover the influence of Daniel. Likewise, although the ultimate mythological background of both Dan 7 and Rev 13 is the *Chaoskampf* tradition, chapter 2 will not examine the transmission of this tradition from the Canaanite myth to Daniel and to Revelation as there is a considerable time interval between the Canaanite myth and Daniel and Revelation. Instead, chapter 2 will review recent scholarship on the *Chaoskampf* tradition.

Introduction

Thirdly, in terms of the theory of the structure and arrangement of Revelation, there are as many perspectives as there are commentators working on the subject. In chapter 4, the section examining the structure of Revelation will only cover three major theories, namely, the recapitulation, chiastic and progressive approaches. This is because the section does not intend to study the structure of the Apocalypse but to indicate that different theories on the structure are in general agreement that Rev 12 and 13 are positioned in the center of the work.

Fourthly, most scholars argue that Revelation was written in the reign of Domitian, while a few are in favor of a date during the reign of Nero or a time in the pre-70s CE. The present thesis will not compare these assumptions because this is a huge topic more suitable for study elsewhere. Instead, it accepts the major argument for the Domitianic date since the evidence for this date appears to be more solid than the evidence for other dates, as many scholars believe. In chapter 5, the section concerning the dating of the Apocalypse will provide a list of evidence for the Domitianic date.

Fifthly, the present thesis will not be able to provide details concerning the function of the imperial high priest in the section discussing this office in chapter 5. This is because there is a dearth of knowledge about this office. However, there is enough inscriptional and archaeological evidence for the existence of this priesthood.

Finally, the central idea of the present thesis is the tripartite ideology, which will be introduced in a section in chapter 4. The tripartite ideology Georges Dumézil proposes involves a huge system of concepts since it aims to describe an all-encompassing structure of relationships that underlie most Indo-European mythological traditions. Like most influential ideas, the tripartite ideology raises much discussion in the related scholarship, in which while some scholars see the ideology as a comprehensive system that can explain the common nature of many different religious and mythological traditions, some scholars find it too flexible. In chapter 4, the section introducing this idea will not discuss these arguments, which constitute a huge topic more suitable to be examined elsewhere, but will provide a precise outline of the main elements of this theory.

2

A Study of the Prominent Imagery in Daniel 7 as It Relates to Revelation 13

IT IS CERTAIN THAT Revelation is influenced by Daniel. The relationship of Dan 7 to Rev 13 is an engaging topic, specifically because it leads many scholars to explore the particulars of the allusions to Dan 7 in Rev 13. This chapter aims to examine the prominent imagery in Dan 7 that has parallels in the beast from the sea in Rev 13. This imagery includes the distinctive features of the four beasts, that they resemble a lion, a bear and a leopard (7:2–7), respectively, as well as prominent motifs, including "a mouth speaking great things" (7:8, 20), "made war with the saints" (7:21), and the period of time described as "a time, two times, and half a time" (7:25). Since the motif "one like a son of man" is a particularly significant theme in Dan 7 and apocalyptic literature, this examination will also investigate references to "the son of man" in the related Second Temple apocalypses. Before studying this imagery, I will review the recent scholarship relating to the *Chaoskampf* tradition, since this tradition is the background of the combat myth in both Dan 7 and Rev 13.

THE CHAOSKAMPF TRADITION IN RECENT SCHOLARSHIP

In the nineteenth century, a pile of fragments of cuneiform tablets containing materials relating to the Babylonian myth was unearthed from the excavation of the palace of Ashurbanipal at Kuyunjík, ancient Nineveh.¹ Since George Smith recognized in the fragments a rough parallel between the Mesopotamian account of the deluge and the biblical story of Noah and the ark, the archaeological discovery led to a debate among biblical scholars as to how important these mythic materials were in understanding the Bible.² For the present study, the most important piece is the Babylonian cosmogony *Enuma Elish*. The myth describes divine creation as a result of a primordial combat between the goddess, Tiamat, and the young god, Marduk. Tiamat and her consort Kingu gathered their forces together in preparation for war with the gods. Knowing the threat, the gods were in panic. Marduk promised to vanquish Tiamat and her armies if the gods made him supreme among them. Having agreed to this, Marduk defeated Tiamat in the fight and hence was crowned supreme king among the gods.³ The discovery of the fragments first led George Barton to argue for parallels between the *Enuma Elish* and some biblical passages.⁴ However, there was no significant speculation on this topic in biblical scholarship until those of the German tradition historian and form critic Hermann Gunkel.

In his landmark work, *Creation and Chaos in the Primeval Era and the Eschaton*,⁵ Gunkel argued that the Babylonian myth of creation by divine *Chaoskampf* had considerable influence on the formation of the Bible by demonstrating traces of the *Enuma Elish* in a number of biblical passages.⁶ With his emphasis on the traces in Gen 1 and Rev 12, it is likely that Gunkel intended to use the two chapters as a symbolic *inclusio* bracketing the entire Christian Bible, in order to show the permeation of the *Chaoskampf* motif

---

1. Following the discovery of the palace of Sennacherib and the palace library at Kuyunjík by Austen Henry Layard during several excavations from 1847 to 1850, in 1853 Hormuzd Rassam, Layard's assistant, discovered the great library of Ashurbanipal in the area nearby. It included many cuneiform tablets dealing with literary, religious and historical subjects. Layard reported the expeditions and discoveries in his volumes, *Discoveries in the Ruins of Nineveh and Babylon* (London: John Murray, 1853), and *A Second Series of the Monuments of Nineveh* (London: John Murray, 1853). Although he was not officially credited with it due to many reasons then, Rassam was the one who discovered the site. For details, see Reade, "Hormuzd Rassam," 48–49.

2. The discovery was not a scholarly issue until in 1872 Smith presented his restoration and decipherment of the cuneiform tablet before the Society of Biblical Archeology at the British Museum. See Hoberman, "BA Portrait," 41–42.

3. For an English translation of the myth, see Heidel, *Babylonian Genesis*, 18–60.

4. Barton, "Tiamat," 1–27.

5. Gunkel, *Creation and Chaos*.

6. Ibid., 82–111.

throughout the biblical timeframe from the primordial beginning to the eschatological setting.[7] From these passages, he discerned two interrelated traditions that reflected the *Chaoskampf* motif.[8] One tradition preserved materials about a primordial sea, which was God's rival fashioned in a personified form.[9] The other was the dragon tradition,[10] which was reflected in materials about God's old rival in the divine combat variously called Leviathan,[11] Behemoth,[12] Rahab,[13] the serpent[14] or the dragon,[15] in different contexts and this was likely to be the source of the first tradition.[16]

Citing the related references to the creation context,[17] Gunkel argued that in biblical tradition *Chaoskampf* and creation are two interrelated motifs, and went further to explain that their interrelatedness indicated the influence of the Babylonian creation myth because the correlation of the two motifs was also found in the *Enuma Elish*, in which the defeat of Tiamat by Marduk was integral to his creation of the world from her carcass.[18] Due to these levels of interrelatedness, Gunkel surmised that the Babylonian creation myth circulated in Israel and this led to the development of the Hebrew *Chaoskampf* in which Yahweh defeated the marine monster in the creation context. His conjecture led to the conclusion that the creation

---

7. In his PhD dissertation, *Two Strange Beasts*, 1 n. 3, Whitney comments that in Gunkel's thesis, the function of Gen 1 and Rev 12 as a symbolic *inclusio* is reflected in the subtitle of his work, *Eine religionsgeschichtliche Untersuchung über Gen 1 und Ap Joh 12*, and that his purpose in demonstrating the permeation of the Babylonian myth in the biblical writings within the *inclusio* is reflected in the italicized line in the foreword, *vom ersten Capitel der Genesis an bis zu den letzten der Offenbarung.*

8. Whitney notices Gunkel's discernment at this point and according to which formats his translation, as shown in the following biblical references in the translation.

9. Gunkel, *Creation and Chaos*, 61–75.

10. Ibid., 21–66.

11. Ps 74:12–19; Isa 27:1; Job 40:25—41:26; 3:8; Ps 104:25f. (see Gunkel, *Creation and Chaos*, 27–38).

12. Job 40:19–24; Isa 30:6; Ps 68:31; see also *1 En.* 60:7–9; *4 Ezra* 6:49–52 (see Gunkel, *Creation and Chaos*, 39–43).

13. Isa 51:6f.; Pss 89:10–14; 87:4; 40:5; Job 26:12f.; 9:13; Isa 30:7 (see Gunkel, *Creation and Chaos*, 21–27).

14. Amos 9:2f. (see Gunkel, *Creation and Chaos*, 52–53).

15. Job 7:12; Ps 44:20; Ezek 29:3–6a; 32:2–7; Jer 51:34, 36, 42; *Pss. Sol.* 2:28b–34 (see Gunkel, *Creation and Chaos*, 43–52).

16. Gunkel, *Creation and Chaos*, 57–61.

17. For example, Job 41:17; 38:7; Ps 89:7.

18. Gunkel, *Creation and Chaos*, 75–77.

myth in the Hebrew Bible was ultimately dependent on the Babylonian creation myth.[19] This approach had been the major direction in studying the topic until new insight was gained from a discovery in the early twentieth century.

During a series of excavations between 1929 and 1939 at a site on the coast of northern Syria called Ras Shamra, ancient Ugarit, the French archaeologist Mons. C. F. A. Schaeffer discovered a large amount of material that shed light on our understanding of the cultic, social and political life of Canaan in the second millennium BCE. Of primary interest is a series of tablets that records the Baal Epic (*CTA* 1–6 = *KTU* 1.1–6).[20] Some scholars have different opinions on the unity and continuity of the tablet series. This is not only because some pieces of the extant texts are highly fragmentary, but also because some accounts are not likely to be in the proper order.[21] However, since all six broken tablets in the series contain materials relating to the Baal Cycle, the major opinion among scholars maintains the sequence of tablets 1 to 6 and understands them as the Baal Epic.[22]

---

19. Ibid., 77.

20. With her system of enumerating the tablets, Mlle. Herdner produced an edition of the Ugaritic texts (*CTA*) that is generally considered standard. The edition of Dietrich, Loretz and Sanmartin is supplementary (*KTU*). In this examination, all quotations of the texts accept the transliteration and translation that John C. L. Gibson, adopting the *CTA* system, produces in his work, *Canaanite Myths and Legends*.

21. The fragmentary ruins of the beginning columns blur the original picture of tablet 1. For possible reconstructions, see Ginsberg, "Ugaritic Myths, Epics, and Legends," 129–55. Secondly, in his work, "Baal's Fight with Yam," 241–54, Meier argues that the narrative contained in tablet 2 does not belong with the storyline found in tablets 3–6, because it contains many anomalous characteristics that isolate it from the rest of the corpus, and because its epic singer is not likely to be the same person as the one dictating in the subsequent tablets. Furthermore, Margalit, in *A Matter of "Life" and "Death,"* 10–11, suggests that tablets 3 and 4 are variants of the same myth of the establishment of Baal's palace with no continuity between them. In agreement with this point, Clifford goes further to suggest that only tablets 5–6 are in proper sequence, in his "Cosmogonies in the Ugaritic Texts," 188–93. Concerning the position of tablet 2, Whitney makes a good point in arguing that the establishment of a temple or palace as a manifestation of a god's triumph and kingship is a part of the mythic pattern, as shown clearly in the *Enuma Elish* and in some biblical passages. With this conjecture, he suggests that tablet 2 is possibly an alloform of the Baal-Mot and the Baal-Anat-Leviathan myths (*Two Strange Beasts*, 5 n. 29).

22. For instance, Gibson, "Theology of the Ugaritic Baal Cycle," 202–19; Mosca, "Ugarit and Daniel 7," 503.

The Ugaritic Myth Known as the Baal Cycle

The myth centers on the divine combat between the Canaanite god Baal and several monstrous figures in a manner reminiscent of the *Chaoskampf* in the *Enuma Elish*. The combat scene most relevant to the present study is the conflict between Baal and Yam. Baal is the son of Dagon,[23] renowned under the title "the rider on the clouds,"[24] also, on one occasion, called "[the god] Haddu, lord of the Stormcloud" or "lord of the Nimbus."[25] Yam is the deified Sea, also known as prince Yam or judge Nahar.[26] Other related actors include El, who is the supreme god,[27] Anat, Baal's sister,[28] Mot, the ruler of the underworld,[29] and Kothar-and-Khasis, the craftsman of the gods.[30] Beginning with tablet 2, in the divine council held in the tent of El, two messengers sent by Yam came and demanded, on behalf of their master, that Baal be given over to him. Feeling intimidated, the gods sitting at the banquet lowered their heads onto their knees in fear. Being furious, Baal standing by El rebuked the gods (*CTA* 2.1.11–35). However, Baal's opposition was futile, as El announced the judgment:

> Baal is your slave, o Yam,
> Baal is your slave, o Nahar,
> the son of Dagon is your prisoner.
> Even he must bring you tribute like the gods,
> [even he] must bring you gifts like the sons of the Holy one.[31]

---

23. *CTA* 2.1.19. Although Baal's father is El on some occasions (*CTA* 3.5.43; 4.1.5; 4.4.47; etc.), the references are a fixed oral formula to describe the relationship between El and any of his sons, that is, any god (Cross, *Canaanite Myth and Hebrew Epic*, 15 n. 14). Hence, Dagon and El are not identical. As a matter of fact, Dagon is distinguished from El in the god-lists (Gibson, *Canaanite Myths and Legends*, 5 n. 2).

24. *CTA* 3.4.48.

25. *CTA* 10.2.33.

26. *CTA* 2.3.16. Gibson surmises that "ruler" may be a better translation than "judge," when in parallel with the title "prince" (*Canaanite Myths and Legends*, 3 n. 3).

27. In RS 24.252 (= *KTU* 1.108), El is called "the Hale One, eternal king," presiding at a courtly banquet. For details of the connotation of the Ugaritic name, see Cross, *Canaanite Myth and Hebrew Epic*, 20. In the Baal Epic, El is remote, but his supremacy is unquestionable (Gibson, *Canaanite Myths and Legends*, 5 n. 2).

28. *CTA* 3.5.34–52.

29. *CTA* 5.2.13–16.

30. *CTA* 3.6.21–23.

31. *CTA* 2.1.36–38.

Due to a lacuna between the end of this column and the next surviving column,[32] it is not certain how Baal challenged El's judgment, but we do have his immediate response in anger (*CTA* 2.1.38–43). However, it is certain that the judgment took effect, since according to the next extant piece, Baal, dying, lost his power and ability to speak and sank under the throne of Yam (*CTA* 2.4.1–7). In his despair, Kothar-and-Khasis suddenly appeared, exhorting the rider on the clouds that he smite his foes and take his everlasting kingdom:

> Truly I tell you, o prince Baal,
> I repeat (to you), o rider on the clouds.
> Now (you must smite) your foes, Baal,
> now you must smite your foes,
> now you must still your enemies.
> You shall take your everlasting kingdom,
> your dominion for ever and ever.[33]

Having said that, Kothar fashioned two maces for him, Yagrush and Ayyamur, which mean "Let him chase away!" and "Let him expel anyhow!," respectively (*CTA* 2.4.11–22).[34] With the two clubs, Baal killed Yam, and his victory was definitive:

---

32. There is an uncertain length of lacuna between columns 1 and 4 in tablet 2. In 1931, two pieces of fragmentary tablets were unearthed during the excavations. The first fragment contained the lower portion of a first column on one side and the upper portion of a final column on the reverse. The unusually long lines led Herdner to surmise that the tablet did not seem to have had the normal six columns. Therefore, Herdner assigned numbers 1 and 4 to these two columns. The second piece of fragment contained a critically damaged column leaving no writing on one side and a partially preserved column on the reverse. The long lines on the reverse led Herdner to associate this fragment with the first piece as part of the tablet, and to assign the badly damaged column number 2 and to allocate the partially preserved one number 3. But because the content of this column number 3 did not match the context of columns 1 and 4, some commentators understood this partially surviving column to be the upper part of column 1. Hence, it is uncertain how much text has been lost in the lacuna. But it is certain that the beginning of column 1 and the ending of column 4 are missing. See Gibson, *Canaanite Myths and Legends*, 2–3.

33. *CTA* 2.4.8–10.

34. Cross argues that like personal names and divine names, the two names are shortened from sentence length names, in *Canaanite Myth and Hebrew Epic*, 115 n. 11. The connotation of the name Yagrush, "Let him chase away!," echoes Isa 57:20 (Gibson, *Canaanite Myths and Legends*, 44 n. 1). The name Ayyamur means "Let him expel anyhow!" (Gibson, *Canaanite Myths and Legends*, 40 n.1), and its first syllable, *āy*, is cognate with Hebrew *hōy* or *ōy* (Cross, *Canaanite Myth and Hebrew Epic*, 115 n. 12).

> And the club danced from the hand of Baal,
> [like] and eagle from his fingers.
> It struck the crown of prince [Yam],
> between the eyes of judge Nahar.
> Yam collapsed (and) fell to the earth;
> his joints quivered
> and his form crumpled.
> Baal dragged out Yam and laid him down,
> he made an end of judge Nahar.[35]
> Yam is indeed dead! Baal shall be king![36]

The loser survived in the preceding tournament, but not this time. The triumphal shout in favour of Baal and the words of Kothar-and-Khasis to him make clear that what was at stake in the Baal Epic was a competition for kingship among the gods.[37] From Gunkel onwards, many scholars find in the Baal Cycle a number of striking parallels to biblical passages and imagery. The Baal-Yam conflict contains some examples. In *CTA* 2.1.38, the term "gifts" echoes the gifts of the kings of Sheba and Seba in Ps 72:10.[38] In *CTA* 2.4.8–10, the "rider on the clouds" is an epithet for the heavenly divinity of the thunderstorm and now a reference to Yahweh on many occasions (Ps 68:4; also, cf. Pss 18:9; 29:1ff.; 68:33; Isa 19:1; Deut 33:26);[39] the eulogy, "dominion for ever and ever," has parallels in Ps 145:13; Dan 3:33; 4:31;[40] and, in terms of both structure and content, the passage is paralleled neatly in Ps 92:10 and compares well to Pss 8:3; 143:12.[41] In *CTA* 2.4.32, the triumphal shout, "Yam is indeed dead! Baal shall be king!," is analogous to the victory cry in Exod 15:18.[42] Among these parallels, the most important one with respect to Dan 7 is the "rider on the clouds" because the imagery is germane to the context around the reference to the "one like a son of man" (7:13).

---

35. *CTA* 2.4.23–27.
36. *CTA* 2.4.32.
37. Smith, "Interpreting the Baal Cycle," 323.
38. Gibson, *Canaanite Myths and Legends*, 42 n. 3.
39. Baal has the attribute *rkb 'rpt*, which means "cloud rider." See Kraus, *Psalms 60–150*, 2:46, 51; also, Gibson, *Canaanite Myths and Legends*, 43 n. 5.
40. Gibson, *Canaanite Myths and Legends*, 43 n. 7.
41. Ibid., 43 n. 6; Cross, *Canaanite Myth and Hebrew Epic*, 114 n. 10.
42. Gibson, *Canaanite Myths and Legends*, 45 n. 1.

A Study of the Prominent Imagery in Daniel 7 as It Relates to Revelation 13

Another pertinent constituent is a figure with many heads found in several combat scenes in tablets 3–5. The figure occurs in an address to Baal by Mot:

> for all that you smote Leviathan the slippery serpent
> (and) made an end of the wriggling serpent,
> the tyrant with seven heads?
> The heavens will burn up (and) droop (helpless),
> for I myself will crush you in pieces,
> I will eat (you)..........................(and) forearms.[43]

The figure in question is called *ltn* in Ugaritic, which John C. L. Gibson translates into Leviathan.[44] The text describes the Ugaritic monster as "the slippery serpent" and "the wriggling serpent," the same attribute applied to Leviathan in Isa 27:1.[45] This monster with its seven heads and Leviathan in Ps 74:14 parallel each other.[46] Therefore, due to the fact that they resemble each other physically and due to the etymological kinship of their names, many scholars believe that the Ugaritic monster and the biblical Leviathan are identical.[47]

Leviathan appears with the title "dragon" in an address by Anat in tablet 3:

---

43. *CTA* 5.1.1–5. Cross, judging from the form *tkly* in the second line, argues that it was Baal who was being addressed in this passage (*Canaanite Myth and Hebrew Epic*, 119 n. 23).

44. There is an argument concerning the name of this figure. In his work, "New Light on Early Canaanite Language," 19 n. 18, Albright proposes *Lôtān* for the vocalization of the Ugaritic *ltn* and argues that *Lôtān* and *Liwyātān*, the Hebrew word for Leviathan, are based on two noun stems, *lawt* and *lawyat*, respectively, plus the adjectival suffix *ān*. From his argument, it appears that Albright understands the two noun stems as derivatives of the Ugaritic root *lwt* and the Hebrew root *lwy* correspondingly, although he remains uncertain as to which one is more original. But the two words are very unlikely to be from different roots, because of their lexical and morphological similarity. In his work, "Leviathan and *LTN*," 327–31, Emerton argues that the Hebrew *Liwyātān* represents the more original form of the two and that through several stages of development, the Hebrew form begets *Lītānu* as the vocalization of the Ugaritic *ltn*. The Hebrew root *lwy* means "to twine," and thus *Liwyātān*, "twisting one." Also see Day, "Leviathan," 4:295–96.

45. The reference in Isa 27:1 helps in understanding the development of the *Chaoskampf* because the passage manifests a transformation of the tradition from the creation context into the eschatological context.

46. In his work, *Psalms II 51–100*, 205, Dahood argues that the employment of the pronoun seven times in Ps 74:13–17 is a poetic reference to the seven-headed attribute of Leviathan.

47. Collins, *Combat Myth*, 77; Kaiser, *Isaiah 13–39*, 221 n. d.

> Did I not destroy Yam the darling of El,
> did I not make an end of Nahar the great god?
> Was not the dragon captured (and) vanquished?
> I did destroy the wriggling serpent,
> the tyrant with seven heads;[48]

The figure that Anat claimed to have slain is called *tnn* in Ugaritic. Etymologically, the term *tnn* is a close parallel to the Hebrew *tannin*, "dragon" (Isa 27:1; 51:9; Job 7:12; etc.),[49] and therefore, too, the dragon. Here since the dragon is described as "the wriggling serpent" with "seven heads," it has the same formulaic peculiarity as Leviathan in the Baal Epic (*CTA* 5.1.1–5). To sum up, etymologically, the Ugaritic *tnn* is closely related to the Hebrew *tannin*, and the Canaanite dragon and Leviathan have the same physical characteristics. For these reasons, it is highly likely that the Ugaritic dragon and Leviathan are identical and that they generate the biblical dragon and Leviathan correspondingly, which in turn are identical in the Jewish tradition too.

In addition to the tablet series, two fragmentary pieces from another group of texts (*UT* 1001–1003),[50] also record the dragon in battle with Baal and with Anat in the following two different contexts:

> Baal smote,
> he destroyed the Dragon
> and he rejoiced and poured out a libation
> [ ] to the earth . . .[51]

> In the land of *Mhnm* he stirred up the sea.
> (His) forked tongue licked the heavens.
> (His) twin tails stirred up the sea.
> She put the dragon in a muzzle.
> She bound him to the heights of Leba[non].[52]

---

48. *CTA* 3.3.35–39.

49. For the relationship of the two verbal forms, see Whitney, *Two Strange Beasts*, 10 n. 62.

50. The transliteration and translation of this quotation is cited from Gordon, *Ugaritic Textbook*.

51. *UT* 1001.1–2. Although the remainder of line 2 is obscure, line 3 likely describes the god *Rešep* as an archer firing arrows into the kidneys and heart of the monster (Whitney, *Two Strange Beasts*, 9 n. 55).

52. *UT* 1003.3–10.

Here the dragon is essentially related to the creation of the world. According to Johannes Cornelis de Moor, the Baal Cycle narrated in *CTA* 1–6 contains a seasonal element, in which the emergent threat caused by the sea monsters Arsh and the dragon signifies the end of the year and the approach of the New Year, as it occurs at the end of the cycle (*CTA* 6.6.50–52).[53] In line with this order, the actual combat between the gods and the sea monsters denotes the beginning of the New Year, which, supposedly, commences in the opening piece of the cycle that is now lost. This cyclic aspect of the epic seems to imply that the Canaanites regarded the creation of the world as having happened at the beginning of the very first New Year. Hence, the context of the two fighting scenes quoted above is the creation of the world, and the references to the "earth" and "Leba[non]" as being already present designate their primordial chaotic state (Gen 1:1–2; Ps 74:12).[54] This understanding of the Canaanite mythic cycle concurs with the correlation of creation and the divine conflict with the sea and the related monsters in the biblical tradition (Gen 1:1–2; Ps 74:12–14).

Another significant theme is the imagery of stirring up the sea in the battle between the dragon and Anat (*UT* 1003.3–10). The same imagery is also found in the *Enuma Elish* (4.42–48), in which Marduk summoned the four winds to stir up the inside of Tiamat, the goddess of watery chaos. Gunkel notes that the imagery in this Babylonian myth is reminiscent of the ferocious behaviour of the dragon that precipitates Yahweh's judgment in Ezek 32:3 and Job 41:23.[55] In Dan 7:2, it was the same act of stirring up the sea that instigated the emergence of the four great beasts.[56] Hence, the theme of stirring up the sea as an incitement to battle is common to the *Chaoskampf* of the Canaanite, Babylonian and biblical traditions.

To summarize, among the Ugaritic cuneiform tablets unearthed in Ras Shamra, these fragmentary texts of the Baal Epic are generally considered relevant to Dan 7 and the related biblical passages. The principal theme of these fragments and their larger contexts is divine combat with watery chaos, in which the divine is represented by either Baal or Anat and the antagonist is either, Yam, or the personification of the deified Sea variously called, Leviathan, the dragon or the wriggling serpent. The Canaanite cosmological combat is the counterpart of the Babylonian *Chaoskampf*

---

53. Day, *God's Conflict*, 17 n. 41.
54. Ibid., 17 n. 42.
55. Gunkel, *Creation and Chaos*, 55.
56. Collins, *Daniel*, 294.

between Marduk and Tiamat and of the Hebrew *Chaoskampf* between Yahweh and the biblical Leviathan, Rahab or the dragon depending on the context.[57] Notably, the deified Sea and related beings are the common enemies in all these combat myths.

Furthermore, due to the etymological kinship of the Ugaritic *ltn* and the Hebrew *Liwyatān* and their physical resemblance, the two figures are identical and so both are Leviathan. Likewise, since the Ugaritic *ltn* and *tnn* in the Baal Epic both share the physical attributes of having seven heads and wriggling, and due to them having the same corporeal characteristics and the etymological connection of the Ugaritic *tnn* to the Hebrew *tannin*, if *tnn* is identical to the biblical dragon, it is, in turn, identical to Leviathan. In addition, the end and the beginning of *CTA* 1–6 indicate the cyclic nature of the epic, in which the emergence of conflict ends a cycle and the actual battle begins a new cycle. Finally, stirring up the sea and the rider on the clouds are two images particularly important to Dan 7. Stirring up the sea agitates the emergence of the four beasts (7:2–3) as it rouses Tiamat in the *Enuma Elish* (4.42–48), and the rider on the clouds is germane to the context of the "one like a son of man" and the "Ancient of Days" (7:13).

The Imagery of Stirring up the Sea in Daniel 7

Daniel 7 is a piece of apocalyptic work. It was written in Israel in approximately 166–165 BCE.[58] There is consensus that the chapter occupies a pivotal position in the book, in the sense that, on the one hand, it belongs to the first half of the book since it is written in Aramaic and since it carries the motif of the four kingdoms found in chapter 2, and on the other, it fits into the second half since it commences, in its introduction, the vision genre prevalent in the subsequent chapters.[59] The chapter has a clear structure, in which, in between the introductory and concluding statements (7:1–2a, 28), are a vision of the appearance of and judgment on four ferocious beasts (vv. 2b–12), a vision of "one like a son of man" (vv.

---

57. The Ugaritic combat myth is also the counterpart of the Sumerian Asag, the Vedic Vitra and Kaliya, the Egyptian Apophis and Seth, the Hittite Hahhimas, the Hurrian Kumarbi and Ullikummi, the Greek Typhon, and many others (Gibson, *Canaanite Myths and Legends*, 7 n. 3).

58. Casey, *Son of Man*, 10–11.

59. Raabe, "Daniel 7," 271; Davies, *Daniel*, 58; Collins, *Daniel*, 277; Meadowcroft, *Aramaic Daniel*, 198 n. 2.

13-14), an interpretation of the four-beast vision (vv. 15-18) and a further explanation of the fourth beast (vv. 19-27).[60] The imagery most relevant to the Baal Epic includes stirring up the sea (v. 2), "one like a son of man" (v. 13) and the "Ancient of Days" (v. 13).

First and foremost, a few years after the discovery of the Ugaritic tablets, Otto Eissfeldt saw, in the fourth beast in Dan 7:7, an echo of the monstrous figure which opposed Baal in the myth; that is Leviathan (*CTA* 5.1.1-5).[61] As the previous section of this chapter demonstrates, it is highly likely that Leviathan is identical to the dragon, which is an opponent of Anat in the same epic (*CTA* 3.3.35-39), and that the two have their corresponding parallels in the biblical tradition, which, too, are identical. According to Gunkel, the original setting of the Hebrew *Chaoskampf* tradition was the creation context.[62] During its circulation in Israel, the tradition underwent various transformations relating to a historicisation process in which the antagonist in the *Chaoskampf*, Leviathan, or its alternative manifestations, Rahab or the dragon, was identified as the historical oppressor of Israel, for instance, Egypt (Isa 30:7; Ezek 29:3-6; 32:2-8) or Babylon (Jer 51:34-44).[63] Ultimately, in some variant traditions, the *Chaoskampf* referred to the eschatological battle in which God terminated all evil powers by defeating the oppressors (Isa 27:1). In all these variants, Leviathan, although representing different entities in the different contexts, occurs consistently as a fleeing serpent with seven heads.

However, the fourth beast in Dan 7:7 is described as neither a seven-headed dragon nor a fleeing serpent. And its name is neither Leviathan nor Rahab. The single point of analogy, insofar as both the beast in Daniel and Leviathan represent the chaotic power in the combat, is that they are both sea-related in nature,[64] in the sense that the beast came up from the sea (7:3) and Leviathan was a beast of watery origin. The emergence from the sea, however, is no more important than a secondary level concern with respect to this beast because this peculiarity is not an individual characteristic of

---

60. Some scholars assign vv. 15-18 and vv. 19-27 together as the interpretation of the vision (e.g., Montgomery, *Daniel*, 282). But there is a clear difference between the two units because vv. 15-18 explains the four beasts in brief, whereas vv. 19-27 goes further to delineate the fourth beast in detail in response to an additional request of the seer (v. 19).

61. Collins, *Daniel*, 287 n. 84.

62. Gunkel, *Creation and Chaos*, 55.

63. Ibid., 43-52.

64. Collins, *Daniel*, 288.

this beast but rather a common mythic background of all four beasts in the larger context (7:3), and more importantly, because the prime features of this beast are not its relationship to the sea but, apparently, its great iron teeth and ten horns, which symbolize the beast's destructive power and make it different from the previous three. Hence, if there is any value in using Leviathan to understand this beast, it is minor. On the other hand, some scholars argue in a broader context that in the Canaanite and Babylonian myths as well as the Hebrew Bible, the primary enemies of the cosmic conflict are the chaotic sea and the various related deities.[65] Although logical, the argument is too broad to produce a nuanced understanding with which to study the subject matter.

Nevertheless, there is one point of analogy relating to the sea between Dan 7 and the Canaanite myth, which is the imagery of stirring up the sea (7:2). In the Ugaritic fragment (*UT* 1003.3–10), the dragon stirred up the sea in the land of *Mhnm* in the battle with Anat. In the *Enuma Elish* (4.42–48), to stir up the inside of the watery deity, Tiamat, Marduk sent forth the south wind, the north wind, the west wind and the east wind, together with the other three winds he had created. The imagery of stirring up the sea is also found in many similar contexts in the Hebrew Bible (Ezek 32:2; Job 38:80). Of these passages, Dan 7:2, in particular, has a close link with the *Enuma Elish* (4.42–48), since it was the four winds of heaven that "stirred up" the great sea in Daniel, just as Marduk created the four winds to stir up the inward parts of Tiamat in the Babylonian myth. Therefore, it is likely that the background imagery in Dan 7:2 reflects a mixture of the Canaanite and the Babylonian *Chaoskampf* traditions, with stirring up the sea reflecting the Canaanite myth and the four winds the Babylonian.

One Like a Son of Man in Daniel 7

There is little doubt that of all the imagery used in Dan 7, כבר אנש, "one like a son of man" (7:13) stands out, at least in terms of its theological significance and the complications in understanding it. Though not from the Baal Epic, the figure is germane to the investigation. This is because it appears as a rider on the clouds and as a parallel to the Ancient of Days, which are, respectively, the epithet of the Canaanite god of thunderstorms and a possible allusion to El, and also because the figure is found in relation to the Leviathan-Behemoth motif in apocalyptic writings contemporaneous with

---

65. Gray, *Legacy of Canaan*, 90–91, 286–87; Collins, *Daniel*, 288 n. 88.

Revelation. This investigation aims to identify the man-like figure by examining how relevant expressions are employed in the biblical tradition and in the Second Temple apocalypse, paying attention to philological meanings and functions in the individual contexts.

THE USE OF THE EXPRESSION "SON OF MAN" IN THE HEBREW BIBLE

First and foremost, there is general consensus that the indefinite Aramaic expression, בר אנש, normally speaks of a human being. According to Geza Vermes, from the philological perspective, the phrase is neither a name nor a title but a circumlocution for the first person as it so functions in pieces of extant Aramaic texts in the Midrash Rabbah.[66] An alternative view, which is held by Maurice Casey,[67] Barnabas Lindars,[68] and Richard Bauckham,[69] who, with slight degrees of difference from one another, argues that the term functions not only as an idiomatic form of exclusive self-periphrasis but also as a frame of reference to a broader group of people. While nuanced, the two perspectives are in general agreement that the idiom is normally found as a reference to a human being. The term occurs for the first time in one of the treaty stipulations in the third Sefire inscription (Sf III 16–17), in which it denotes no more than "someone" or "anyone," that is, "a man," a member of the human race.[70] The term is also found in the literature from Qumran, in which it means "no one" in 1QapGen 21:13 and "a human being" in the generic sense in 11QtgJob 9:9; 26:2–3.[71] In the Hebrew Bible, the corresponding Hebrew singular phrase, בן אדם, "son of man," occurs ninety-three times in Ezekiel as a form of address to the prophet[72] and fourteen times elsewhere in poetic and solemn contexts.[73] In

66. Vermes, "Appendix E," 326–28; especially, 326 n. 2, for evidence.
67. Casey, Son of Man, ch. 9; also, Solution, 56–81, 314–15.
68. Lindars, Jesus Son of Man, 24.
69. Bauckham, "Son of Man," 29.
70. Fitzmyer, "New Testament Title," 147.
71. Ibid., 148; Collins and Collins, King and Messiah, 164 n. 57.
72. Di Lella, "One in Human Likeness," 1.
73. Num 23:19; Jer 49:18, 33; 50:40; 51:43; Isa 51:12; 56:2; Pss 8:5; 80:18; 146:3; Job 16:21; 25:6; 35:8; Dan 8:17. Another corresponding Hebrew phrase, בן אנוש, is found once in Ps 144:3. See Fitzmyer, "New Testament Title," 146; Bowman, "Background," 284 n. 1. Di Lella believes that the preferred reading in Dan 10:16 is ben ādām and therefore also counts this verse ("One in Human Likeness," 1 n. 2; 2 n. 6).

these passages, the phrase refers to a human being, either specifically or generically, just like the indefinite Aramaic expression.

For the present quest, Ezekiel is particularly important not only because "son of man" appears most in this prophetic work among the books in the Hebrew Bible, but also because Ezekiel is closely related to Daniel in many ways. The primary connection is their common historical setting.[74] Ezekiel, though full of vision imagery, is written for a specific historical situation, the Babylonian captivity in the sixth century BCE. This central theme is consonant with the structure of the book, in which the accounts from the besieged Jerusalem to the fall of the city (chs. 24–33) stand as the fulcrum between the first section of denunciation explaining why exile happens (chs. 1–24) and the last section of restoration forecasting the return to the land with the jubilee freedom (chs. 34–48).[75] Thus, the motif of divine absence and return runs through the book. Daniel specifically purports to have originated in the Babylonian exile.[76] Chapter 7 is clearly a reference to this milieu. Another piece of evidence for the link is the name Daniel, since in the Hebrew Bible only Ezekiel contains references to this prophet in 14:14 and 28:3, where Daniel appears as a legendary righteous and wise man like Noah and Job.[77]

In terms of imagery, Ezek 1 and Dan 7 have a lot in common, which has led many scholars to argue for an influence of the former chapter on the latter.[78] In Ezek 1, a stormy wind and a great cloud with brightness around make up the revelatory milieu (v. 4). In Dan 7, the four winds of heaven stirred up the sea (v. 2) and on the clouds of heaven came the man-like figure (v. 13). In Ezek 1:5 four living creatures appeared from the midst of the revelation, just as in Dan 7:3 four great beasts came up from the sea. Each creature in Ezekiel had four faces and four wings (1:6), whilst the third beast in Daniel had four heads and four wings (7:6). Each creature in Ezekiel had a wheel upon the earth (1:15), just as the throne of Ancient of Days in Daniel had (7:9). In Ezek 1:13 something like fire moved to and fro among the living creatures, while in Dan 7:9 the wheels were burning fire.

---

74. Slater, "One Like a Son of Man," 191.

75. Blenkinsopp, *Ezekiel*, 6.

76. In both the first part (chs. 1–6) and the second (chs. 7–12), the narrative chronology commences with the Babylonian kingdom (Collins, *Daniel*, 31).

77. Collins, *Apocalyptic Imagination*, 86–87.

78. Scott, "Behold," 129; Bowman, "Background," 285, 284 n. 2; Lacocque, *Daniel*, 167 n. 41; Slater, "One Like a Son of Man," 191.

In Ezek 1:26 there was the likeness of a throne, while in Dan 7:9 a throne was placed for the Ancient of Days. Above all is the similarity between the one upon the throne described "as it were of a human form" in Ezek 1:26 and "one like a son of man" in Dan 7:13. The parallel imagery and the common historical setting, in actuality for Ezekiel and in implication for Daniel, indicate that Daniel is dependent upon Ezekiel to a considerable degree. Hence, how the motif "son of man" functions in Ezekiel is particularly important for the present inquiry.

Many times in Ezekiel "son of man" is a formulaic expression God employs to address the exilic prophet (2:1; 5:1; 15:2; 22:24; 30:21; 37:3, 11; 38:2, 14; 39:1, 17; 40:4, etc.). It functions in the same way in some instances in Daniel (8:17; cf. 10:19).[79] As a matter of fact, the address to Daniel as "son of man" by a river (8:16–17) is derived from the calling experience of Ezekiel (1:28—2:1), in both of which the term underlines the divine caring for the fragile mortal.[80] Notably, in the Hebrew Bible, it is only in these two books that the phrase functions as a form of address to a prophet.[81] Since, in these occurrences, the expression is used as a means of address, it has nothing to do with anything celestial in nature here.

Another context in which "son of man" is frequently found as a generic reference to humanity is synonymous parallelism, which is a key stylistic element of Hebrew poetry. In this parallelism, the same sentiment is repeated with different but equivalent terms.[82] One of the many examples is Ps 8:4, which reads as follows:

> —what is man that you think of him,
> and the son of man, that you take care of him![83]

In this synonymous parallelism, the phrase, בן אדם, "son of man," functions as a parallel to אנוש, "man," in order to emphasize the sentiment. This rhetorical question forms the center of the hymn, both halves of which are amazed at God's providence towards frail human beings.[84] A more striking example is Ps 80:17, in which, in replicating the sentiment about

---

79. Towner, *Daniel*, 90–103.
80. Eichrodt, *Ezekiel*, 61; Bowman, "Background," 284 n. 2.
81. Di Lella, "One in Human Likeness," 2; Slater, "One Like a Son of Man," 191.
82. Petersen and Richards, *Interpreting Hebrew Poetry*, 24–25 nn. 11–15.
83. This quotation adapts the translation of Kraus, *Psalms 1–59*, 1:178.
84. Ibid., 1:179, 182.

the "man," the term works as a reference to a specific character rather than to humanity in general, as follows:

> Let your hand be over your man at your right hand,
> over the son of man, whom you have raised for yourself![85]

The Psalm is a pre-exilic work since the three tribes of the northern kingdom are still present (v. 2).[86] Here "son of man" is an honorable reference to the king who sits at the right hand of Yahweh. Josiah is likely to be the king meant here.[87] Though not used in a generic sense, the idiom is still a description of a human being. There are many more other instances where, either in the singular or the plural, "son of man" is found as a parallel to "man" in synonymous parallelism in the Hebrew Bible and the Pseudepigrapha as well.[88] In each of these examples, the phrase has nothing to do with a heavenly entity but rather refers to human beings mostly in a generic sense.[89] Such usage of the expression has a long tradition, since it also occurs in an ancient piece of Ugaritic incantation, in which *adm*, "son," and *bn adm*, "son of man," appear in parallelism too.[90]

A human likeness makes the term different, however. In both Ezekiel and Daniel, there are several instances that with the nuance of human likeness, the figure referred to is something other than an earthly being. In Ezek 1:26–28, for instance, at the end of the vision, the one sitting above the likeness of a throne is very likely to represent the Lord, for in similar heavenly portrayals and vocabulary, he is the one revealed "as it were of a human form" (v. 26), דמות כמראה אדם, and "as the appearance of the likeness of the glory of the Lord" (v. 28), מראה דמות כבוד־יהוה. In Ezek 8:2–4, "a form that had the appearance of a man" in a vision (v. 2) refers to either God or, more possibly, a heavenly messenger. In Ezek 9:2–11, "a man clothed in linen" (v. 2) with a writing case at his side is a messenger of God. In Ezek 40:3–4, "a man, whose appearance was like bronze" (v. 3) occurs

---

85. Kraus, *Psalms 60–150*, 2:138.

86. Ibid., 2:140.

87. Ibid., 2:143.

88. In the Hebrew Bible: Job 25:6; 35:8; Jer 49:18, 33; 50:40; 51:43; Num 23:19; Ps 146:3 (Collins, *Daniel*, 304 n. 243). In the extra-canonical writings: *Jub.* 4:18; 1 Esd 4:37; Tob 7:7; Jdt 8:12, 16; Wis 9:6; *T. Levi* 2:5; 3:10; 4:1; Sir 17:30; *1 En.* 60:10 (Slater, "One Like a Son of Man," 184 n. 4).

89. Slater, "One Like a Son of Man," 184 n. 4.

90. Moor, "An Incantation against Evil Spirits," 429–32; Smith, "'Son of Man' in Ugaritic," 59–60 n. 6.

as a heavenly guide to the prophet.[91] In these passages, in addition to the celestial depictions, a common feature of the divine beings is the likeness of human countenance. In each case, the sense of resemblance is signified by the preposition כ, "like." The prefix leads some to argue for an angelic interpretation for the man-like figure in Dan 7:13, as the phrase in the rider on the cloud sentence uses the same preposition.[92] On the other hand, the man clothed in linen (9:2) hints at the dependence of Ezekiel upon Daniel since the imagery is paralleled twice in Daniel (10:5; 12:6–7).

As early as the beginning of the twentieth century CE, Nathaniel Schmidt pointed out that angels in Daniel are uniformly described in a distinctive phrasal construction.[93] In 8:15, the angel Gabriel is introduced as "one having the appearance of a man," who, according to 5:16, has the voice of a man. In 10:16, Gabriel is described as "one in the likeness of the sons of men." In this typical expression, angels are sometimes described as men. Gabriel, again, for instance, is described as "the man Gabriel" in 9:21, and as "a man clothed in linen" in 10:5 and so again in 12:6–7.[94] In 3:25, of the four men walking in the midst of the fire, the appearance of the fourth is like "a son of the gods." Thus, the angels in Daniel are portrayed in the same fashion as the heavenly beings in Ezekiel, in which the central feature is the countenance of human likeness. Since the phrase, "one like a son of man," in Dan 7:13 contains the same attribute, in both connotation and the way it is expressed and is constructed with the preposition כ, its referent is likely to be an angelic being.

The archangel Michael is very likely to be the referent for the Danielic man-like figure. In Daniel, every nation has its angelic representative in heaven and, Michael, who is described as the "great prince" in charge of Israel (10:21; 12:1) is the only heavenly counterpart of Israel in this work. He is described as a princely angel in 1QM 17:6–8 and is identified with Melchizedek in 11QMelch 13–15, the warrior who defeats the dragon for Christ in Rev 12, the holder of the keys to the kingdom of the heavens in *3 Bar.* 11:2, and even Christ in *Herm. Vis.* 3.[95] The angelic identification cor-

---

91. Meadowcroft, *Aramaic Daniel*, 201–2; Slater, "One Like a Son of Man," 192.

92. Young, *Daniel's Vision*, 20.

93. Schmidt, "'Son of Man' in Daniel," 26.

94. Many scholars believe that the angel in Dan 8 and the one in Dan 10 are the same, namely, Gabriel. See Segal, *Two Powers in Heaven*, 201 n. 54.

95. Lacocque, *Daniel*, 133–34; Schmidt, "'Son of Man' in Daniel," 26–27; Collins, *Daniel*, 310 n. 290; also, "Son of Man and the Saints," 66.

responds to the "saints," who, too, are celestial beings granted the kingdom (7:18, 22),[96] and so are their people (7:27),[97] just as is the "one like a son of man" (7:14).

In consequence, there are a few concluding remarks concerning the "son of man" and related expressions, applicable to both their singular and plural forms. In terms of philological meaning, the phrase, בן אדם, "son of man," refers to a human being in the generic sense. Enough evidence proves that there is a high degree of consistency in Ezekiel and Daniel in referring "son of man" to a human being, either as a form of address or as an element of parallelism, and in employing varying expressions such as "a form that had the appearance of a man" (Ezek 8:2–4) or "one having the appearance of a man" (Dan 8:15) to describe a heavenly, angelic being. "One like a son of man" in Dan 7, therefore, very likely does the same as the latter two descriptions. Accordingly, it is evident that Ezekiel has influenced Daniel considerably with respect to this set of vocabulary.[98]

---

96. There is enough evidence for an angelic interpretation for the "saints." The closest Ugaritic equivalent *bn qdš* is found in *CTA* 2.1.21, 38; 17.1.4, in which the term represents Asherah (Miller, *Divine Warrior*, 14–15). The term occurs with reference to angelic beings a number of times in the Hebrew Bible and the Qumran literature. In the Hebrew Bible: Ps 89:6, 8; Job 5:1; 15:15; Zech 14:5 (Collins, *Daniel*, 314 n. 327). In Qumranic literature: 1QM 1:16; 10:11–12; 12:1, 4, 7; 15:14; 1QS 11:7–8; 1QH 3:21–22; 10:35; 1QDM 4:1; 1QSb 1:5; 1Q 36:1; 1QapGen 2:1; 11QMelch 1:9; *4Q181* 1:3–6 (Brekelmans, "Saints of the Most High," 319; Dequeker, "'Saints of the Most High' in Qumran," 134–37, 139, 161–62).

97. Only the Masoretic Text has the collective noun "people," עם. In the phrase, "the people of the saints of the covenant" found in 1QM 10:10, the genitive is possibly possessive, and the "saints" are angelic like those in Dan 7:18, 22, as the term unambiguously refers to angels in the context (1QM 10:11–12). Since the Qumran piece is a parallel to "the people of the saints of the Most High" in v. 27 of the OG reading, the genitive in the phrase is likely to be possessive, and therefore, the "people" are those who belong or pertain to the angels (Dequeker, "'Saints of the Most High' in Qumran," 156; Collins, *Daniel*, 318, 322). In addition, Brekelmans points out that עם is never found with reference to celestial beings in all the literature from Qumran or in the Hebrew Bible, in arguing that in v. 27 the context requires a human referent ("Saints of the Most High," 323; 319–26). Since עם normally takes a singular verb, the "people" is the referent of the ambiguous "him," לה, who receives an everlasting kingdom (Meadowcroft, *Aramaic Daniel*, 232 n. 84).

98. Employing the Syrian tradition, Casey produces a significant argument on the interpretation of "one like a son of man" and "the saints of the Most High." According to Ephraem, one of the authors from the Syrian tradition who preserved the original rendering of Dan 7, the four kings mentioned in Dan 7:17 were the Babylonians, the Medes, the Persians and the Greeks. Casey sees that this identification was obvious for the contemporary Jews, especially those who suffered under Antiochus Epiphanes and

A Study of the Prominent Imagery in Daniel 7 as It Relates to Revelation 13

The Expression "Son of Man" in the Second Temple Apocalypses

In order to have a thorough understanding of the differences between "son of man" and its variant expressions used to express a human likeness, this inquiry goes further to probe whether the Second Temple authors employed the two expressive modes in the same way as Ezekiel and Daniel. By identifying the heavenly being in human resemblance as the descriptive comparison and comparing it to "son of man" in a generic sense in *1 Enoch*, *4 Ezra*, *Apocalypse of Abraham*, and some canonical passages, Thomas Slater argues that the traditions of the two expressive modes had existed before the Common Era.[99] The following study aims to examine the relevant evidence found in these writings.

The *First Book of Enoch*, also known as the Ethiopic *Book of Enoch*, is a composite of five independent volumes in a larger Enochic tradition, each with an individual system of thought, authorship and date.[100] These volumes are the *Book of the Watchers* (chs. 1–36),[101] the *Similitudes of Enoch*

---

hoped for deliverance. Another Syrian author, Galipapa, commented on Dan 7:18 that the saints of the Most High who would receive eternal kingdom forever referred to the Hasmoneans. Ephraem made the same point at the end of his comment too. Therefore, Casey concludes that "one like a son of man" is a symbol for Israel, who in the present context is described in the interpretative section as "the saints of the Most High," "the saints," and "the people of the saints of the Most High." See Casey, *Solution*, 82–86. Casey's interpretation, though a remarkable contribution, is not unquestionable. Firstly, it does not appear to be dependent on an impartial treatment of the symbolic figure in the broader context of the Hebrew Bible but mostly on the Syrian tradition. Secondly, it seems to give excessive weight to the importance of the Syrian tradition.

99. I am greatly indebted to Professor Thomas Slater for his explanation for the term "descriptive comparison" in several pieces of private correspondence.

100. Charles, *Book of Enoch*, xliii–xlix.

101. The *Book of the Watchers* (chs. 1–36) is one of the oldest, pre-Maccabean Enochic compositions and provides the most explicit illustration of the life of Enoch (Collins, *Apocalyptic Imagination*, 47). Nickelsburg is convincing in dating the book to the period before 175 BCE (*Jewish Literature*, 48), because, firstly, the earliest Aramaic manuscript indicates that chapters 1–11 had been a literary unit in the first half of the second century BCE (Milik and Black, *Books of Enoch*, 6), and because, secondly, the book appears to be presupposed in the book of *Jubilees* from the mid second century BCE, which contains accounts inspired by the victories of Judas Maccabeus (37:1—38:14; also, possibly, 34:2–9) (VanderKam, "Enoch Traditions in Jubilees," 1:235; Collins, *Apocalyptic Imagination*, 83–84 n. 115), and therefore had been extant before the death of Judas Maccabeus in 160 BCE.

(chs. 37–71), the *Astronomical Book* (chs. 72–82),[102] the *Book of Dreams* (chs. 83–90)[103] and the *Epistle of Enoch* (chs. 91–108).[104] By September 1952, eleven Aramaic manuscripts of all these compositions, apart from the *Similitudes* (chs. 37–71), had been identified from the fragments of leather scrolls found in Cave 4 at Qumran.[105] Most of these fragments were written in Aramaic, but a few were in Hebrew. The entirety of *1 Enoch* is only extant in Ethiopic.[106]

To the present quest, the most relevant volume is the *Similitudes of Enoch*, also known as the *Parables of Enoch*, because the phrase "sons of men" occurs many times as a major theme in this composition (39:1, 5; 42:2; 64:2 [twice]; 69:6 [twice], 12, 14). Its absence from Qumran leads

---

102. The *Astronomical Book* (chs. 72–82) contains a lot of cosmic and astronomical speculation on the sun, moon and stars, based on Babylonian and Hellenistic knowledge (VanderKam, *Enoch and the Growth*, 91–104). Based on paleographical evidence, Milik dates the oldest manuscript of the book from Cave 4 to the late third or early second century BCE, and thus the earliest Enochic composition (*Books of Enoch*, 7–8).

103. The *Book of Dreams* (chs. 83–90) contains two dream visions about future events. The first dream vision (chs. 83–84) echoes the flood with stories about Noah in *1 En.* 65, 106–7. The second vision (chs. 85–90) speaks of human history in allegorical form, in which biblical figures, for instance, Adam, Moses and Noah, are represented by animals, and therefore is also called the *Animal Apocalypse*. Internal evidence suggests that the book was composed during the Maccabean revolt (Charles, *APOT*, 2:170–71; Milik and Black, *Books of Enoch*, 44).

104. The *Epistle of Enoch* (chs. 91–108) is addressed ostensibly to Enoch's children but in actuality to the author's contemporaries who "dwell upon the earth and for the last generations who will practice (14r, c15) uprightness and peace" (92:1; cf. 1:1–2; 37:2). Within this work, according to one fragment (En^g) from Qumran, the materials in 93:1–10, together with its conclusion in 91:11–17 that had been misplaced in the Ethiopic version, form a self-contained unit that is known as the *Apocalypse of Weeks*. For the original order of the *Apocalypse of Weeks* according to the Aramaic manuscript, see Milik and Black, *Books of Enoch*, 260–70. For different opinions on the independence of this piece, see Black, "The Apocalypse of Weeks," 464–69. On the other hand, because the book of *Jubilees* alludes to both the *Apocalypse of Weeks* and the *Epistle of Enoch* (*Jub.* 4:18), and because *Jubilees* was written in the late Hasmonean period, according to several copies at Qumran (VanderKam and Milik, "Jubilees," 1–185), the two Enochic documents were written no later than the late Hasmonean period. Charles dates the *Epistle of Enoch* to the Hasmonean period in the early first century BCE and the *Apocalypse of Weeks* before the Maccabean revolt because "there is in it no reference to the persecution of Antiochus" (*APOT*, 2:171). The *Epistle of Enoch* concludes with chapter 105. The account of Noah's birth (chs. 106–7) is an additional piece, and chapter 108 an epilogue to *1 Enoch*.

105. Milik and Black, *Books of Enoch*, 4–6.

106. For the text and translation, see Knibb, *Ethiopic Enoch*. The present quest adapts Knibb's translation in all quotations of the *Similitudes*.

some to date the work to a later time after the destruction of the community in 70 CE. Józef T. Milik, for example, dates the book to the late third century CE, since he finds in it many parallels with Christian sections of the *Sibylline Oracles* circulating in that period.[107] Based on this dating, Milik argues that the other four Enochic volumes, together with a pile of manuscripts of the *Book of Giants* found in the same cave, reflect a pre-Christian Enochic Pentateuch.[108] Many scholars have criticized this dating on many grounds.[109] Of these reasons, the most important is internal evidence, which includes the allusion to the invasion of Palestine by the Parthians in 40 BCE (56:5–7) and the reference to the hot springs as judgment of the kings (67:5–13), which indicate a date approximately mid first century CE, prior to the Jewish revolt of 66–70 CE.[110] Above all, it is highly unlikely that a Jewish apocalyptist would have employed "son of man" as a key motif after the expression had become a christological title in the Gospels (Matt 19:28; 25:31).[111]

There is general agreement that the book contains five major divisions. It begins with a brief introduction (37:1–4) and concludes with two epilogues (70:1–4; 71),[112] in between which are three large blocks of revelatory discourse fashioned as parables (chs. 38–44; chs. 45–57; chs. 58–69). An important piece of information is found in 46:1–3 as follows:

> And there I saw one who had a head of days, and his head (was) white like wool; (6r, a5) and with him (there was) another, whose face had the appearance of a man, and his face (was) full of grace, like one of the holy angels. And I asked one of the holy angels who went with me, and showed me all the secrets, about that Son of Man, who he was, and whence (6r, a10) he was, (and) why he went with the Head of Days. And he answered me and said to me: "This is the Son of Man who has righteousness . . . and through uprightness his lot has surpassed all before the Lord of Spirits for ever.

---

107. Milik and Black, *Books of Enoch*, 89–98.

108. Ibid., 4.

109. For example, some scholars argue that the addition in 61:1 is not in the Ethiopic version and therefore date the book to the first century CE. See Charlesworth, "SNTS Pseudepigrapha Seminars," 315–23; Knibb, "Date of the Parables of Enoch," 345–59.

110. Collins, *Apocalyptic Imagination*, 178.

111. Ibid.

112. The epilogue to the third parable is 70:1–4. It is generally agreed that 71:1–17 is an appendix to the *Similitudes* (Stone, "Apocalyptic Literature," 401 n. 97; 403 n. 106); Collins, *Apocalyptic Imagination*, 180.

Here, the description of the one "whose face had the appearance of a man" (v. 1) is very similar to those of the heavenly figures in Ezekiel and Daniel mentioned above (e.g., Ezek 1:26; Dan 7:13); they are all looked human. The last phrase in the same verse reveals the angelic nature of the figure. More importantly, this figure is the primary point of reference for the many subsequent references to "that Son of Man" or "this Son of Man" (46:2, 3, 4; 48:2; 62:7, 9, 14; 63:11; 69:26, 27; 70:1; 71:14, 17).[113] Although the expression carries different roles and attributes depending on each individual context, such as a universal ruler (62:6f.), a judge upon his glorious throne with his final verdict (69:26–29), and, on some other occasions, the righteous one and the chosen one (chs. 53–56; e.g., 53:6), it refers back to the primary referent (46:1) in all these instances.[114] Also, although this group of expressions contains no human-likeness reference, on each occasion it refers back to the one that does. By contrast, in another group of passages (39:1, 5; 42:2; 64:2 [twice]; 69:6 [twice], 12, 14),[115] "the sons of men," the phrase with no mention of looking human functions as a generic expression for humanity, since it represents earthly recipients to whom the angel comes down from heaven to deliver heavenly visions or messages. In these occurrences, the contrast between heavenly and human beings is explicit.[116]

---

113. Slater, "One Like a Son of Man," 195. In the Ethiopic *Similitudes*, there is no demonstrative adjective in the Ethiopic phrase in three instances (62:7; 69:27; 71:14). Since the demonstrative adjective corresponds to the Greek definite article and thus, in the present context, a hint for the figure "whose face had the appearance of a man" in 46:1 as the referent of the phrase, some scholars argue that in the three cases the referent is something other than that figure (Black et al., *Book of Enoch*, 206). While this is a pointed philological analysis, however, in each of the three instances the context hints at the heavenly nature of the referent, for instance, the preservation of the Son of Man by the Most High (62:7), the whole judgment and glorious throne of the Son of Man (69:27), and the link between the Son of Man and the Head of Days (71:14), which in turn still indicates the possibility of the figure in 46:1 as being the primary referent in the three cases. In addition to the concern about the demonstrative adjective, there are three Ethiopic expressions for "son of man" in these passages (Black et al., *Book of Enoch*, 206), which are possibly translation variants (Collins, "Son of Man in First-century Judaism," 452 n. 22). In any case, the three variants indicate that "son of man" was neither a technical term nor a title in the earlier document of which the Ethiopic version was a translation (Slater, "One Like a Son of Man," 192).

114. Caragounis, *Son of Man*, 115–19.

115. The list also includes 69:15, according to Charlesworth, *The Old Testament Pseudepigrapha*.

116. Slater, "One Like a Son of Man," 195.

On the other hand, the seer asked why "that Son of Man" went with the Head of Days (46:2). It is clear in 48:2 that "that Son of Man" is subordinate to the Head of Days, just as the man-like figure is subordinate to the Ancient of Days in Dan 7:13. Since the primary referent of "that Son of Man" manifests in human appearance (46:1) as does the Danielic man-like figure, and since with the same heavenly hierarchy, the present Enochic account is an allusion to Dan 7:13, "that Son of Man" is heavenly in nature. And this referent is Enoch. To sum up, the author of the *Similitudes* uses the son of man imagery to refer to both heavenly and human beings using two different expressions in the same way as Ezekiel and Daniel, with the former one having more explicit human likeness than the other.

Fourth Ezra is a Jewish apocalypse.[117] It was originally written in Hebrew, with some Aramaic influence,[118] in Palestine at approximately the end of the first century CE.[119] Evidence for this dating includes interpreting the vision of the eagle with twelve wings and three heads in chapters 11–12, with the twelve wings symbolizing the twelve Roman emperors from Caesar to Domitian and the three heads the three Flavian emperors, Vespasian, Titus and Domitian. Another piece of evidence is the report of the "thirtieth year after the destruction of our city" in 3:1, which purports to speak of the fall of Jerusalem in 586/587 BCE in the context, but is predominately interpreted as a fictional setting alluding to the destruction of the Jerusalem temple in 70 CE.[120]

---

117. The Jewish apocalypse is also preserved as chapters 3–14 of the Apocryphon commonly known as 2 Esdras. The relationship of the various pieces in the Ezra traditions to the Esdras composition is complex. Esdras is the Greek form of the Hebrew name Ezra. Since Jerome included 2 Esdras in his Vulgate, the book has come to be included in the Apocrypha. The Latin manuscripts generally distinguish the Jewish core of this work from its Christian additions, identifying 2 Esd 1–2 as *5 Ezra*, 2 Esd 3–14 as *4 Ezra*, and 2 Esd 15–16 as *6 Ezra*, in which *4 Ezra* is a Jewish apocalypse and *5* and *6 Ezra* are Christian additions. For details, see Collins, *Apocalyptic Imagination*, 195 n. 4; Nickelsburg, *Jewish Literature*, 305 n. 15.

118. Myers, *I and II Esdras*, 113–19, 129–31; Stone, *Fourth Ezra*, 10–11. The book is preserved in many ancient versions including the Latin, Syrian, Ethiopic, Georgian, Armenian and two independent Arabic versions, some fragments of Coptic and Greek translations. For a precise summary of the transmission history, see Stone, *Fourth Ezra*, 1–9.

119. Collins, *Apocalyptic Imagination*, 196; Stone, *Fourth Ezra*, 10; Nickelsburg, *Jewish Literature*, 287–88.

120. Myers, *I and II Esdras*, 299–302; Stone, *Fourth Ezra*, 9–10; Collins, *Apocalyptic Imagination*, 195–96; Nickelsburg, *Jewish Literature*, 287–88.

The Identities of the Beast from the Sea and the Beast from the Land in Revelation 13

The key passage for this inquiry is 13:1–3, in which a figure in human likeness emerged in the seer's dream as follows:

> After seven days I dreamed a dream in the night; and behold, a wind arose from the sea and stirred up all its waves. And I looked, and behold, this wind made something like the figure of a man come up out of the heart of the sea. And I looked, and behold, that man flew with the clouds of heaven . . .

With little doubt, the passage reflects the influence of Dan 7. The vision begins with the wind rousing and stirring up the sea like the vision in Dan 7:2, and over the chaos the figure flew with the clouds of heaven like the man-like figure in Dan 7:13. The figure is described as "something like the figure of a man." The nuance of human likeness is in essence the same as those of the heavenly, angelic beings in Ezekiel, *1 Enoch* as well as Daniel.

There is general agreement that *4 Ezra* consists of seven units: 3:1—5:19; 5:20—6:34; 6:35—9:25; 9:26—10:59; 10:60—12:51; 13:1–58; and 14:1–48.[121] The turning point of the entire work is the fourth unit (9:26—10:59), in which Ezra converts from being a skeptic into being a faithful mediator to others (10:29–59).[122] Following Ezra's transformation is a pair of dream visions (chs. 11–12; 13). In the first vision, the eagle coming up from the sea interprets the Danielic fourth beast (12:11–12) and reflects the traditional hope for a Davidic messiah.[123] In the second vision, the man flying with the clouds of heaven is reminiscent of the Danielic man-like figure, and his assault by the multitude, carving out of a great mountain for himself (13:5–7; cf. Ps 2; Dan 2), and slaying enemies with his flaming breath (13:8–11; cf. Isa 11:4) are theophanic symbols of the divine warrior, the last of which signifies the messianic identity of the figure.[124]

---

121. Nearly all scholars are in agreement with the sevenfold structure of *4 Ezra* since Gustav Volkmar argued for this configuration in his work, *Handbuch der Einleitung in die Apokryphen* (Willett, *Eschatology*, 54 n. 28); Collins, *Apocalyptic Imagination*, 197; Stone, *Fourth Ezra*, 50–51; Nickelsburg, *Jewish Literature*, 288.

122. Ezra's breakthrough took place at the moment he encouraged the woman to rely on the justice of God in 10:16 (Stone, *Fourth Ezra*, 319; Willet, *Eschatology*, 62 n. 50). Stone notes that "The woman whom Ezra saw symbolizes Zion, while the city he saw, her true nature, does not symbolize Zion, it is Zion" (*Fourth Ezra*, 334).

123. Collins, *Apocalyptic Imagination*, 208.

124. Ibid., 207. The passages in which the messianic figure is definitely referred to include 7:28–29; 11:37—12:1; 12:31–34; 13:3–13, 25–52; and 14:9 (Stone, *Fourth Ezra*, 208–9).

The *Apocalypse of Abraham* is essentially a Jewish composition.[125] It was originally written in Aramaic or Hebrew of Palestinian origin,[126] and was later translated into Greek whence it was incorporated into the corpus of Slavonic church literature.[127] The work is extant in a number of Slavonic recensions and a Romanian version.[128] Since the fall of Jerusalem plays a main role in it (chs. 27–31), the book is very likely to have been composed in the same period as *4 Ezra* and *2 Baruch*, approximately the end of the first century CE.[129] The apocalypse centers on Abraham's discovery of God, a tale widespread in various forms in Jewish Apocrypha and midrashim.[130] Its rich imagery is analogous with other apocalypses of eschatological interest and with mystical writings of cosmological interest.[131] For instance, like *4 Ezra* and *2 Baruch*, it raises a concern for theodicy with respect to the destruction of the temple (chs. 27–31). And the celestial song the angel instructed Abraham to sing (ch. 17) is similar to those recorded in the *merkabah* books.[132] But the mixture of the motif of the heavenly journey

---

125. Most scholars agree that a considerable part of chapter 29 is a Christian interpolation (Stone, "Apocalyptic Literature," 415–16). Box argues for an Ebionite origin, i.e., Jewish-Christian (Box and Landsman, *Apocalypse of Abraham*, xxi). Rubinkiewicz identifies 29:3–13 and some other passages (9:7; 10:6–12; 17:8b–19; 20:5, 7; 22:5; 23:4–10) as interpolations by a Bogomil editor from the Christian sect founded by Pope Bogomil in the tenth century CE (Rubinkiewicz and Lunt, "Apocalypse of Abraham," 1:684). In any case, the passage to be examined (10:1–5) shows no signs of Christian redaction and so is of Jewish origin.

126. Box and Landsman, *Apocalypse of Abraham*, xv-xvi; Rubinkiewicz and Lunt, "Apocalypse of Abraham," 1:682.

127. Ibid. In the "Apocalypse of Abraham," 1:686, Lunt notes that there can be no question that the Slavonic version was translated from the Greek; on the other hand, in 1:682–83, Rubinkiewicz doubts this traditional scholarly view and suggests a possibility of direct translation from Hebrew into Slavonic, by citing evidence that there were educated men who were able to produce the translation from Hebrew into Slavonic in Bulgaria around the eleventh century CE.

128. For details of the Slavonic transmission as known until the early twentieth century, see Landsman's analysis in Box, *Apocalypse of Abraham*, x-xv.

129. Box and Landsman, *Apocalypse of Abraham*, xv-xvi; Rubinkiewicz and Lunt, "Apocalypse of Abraham," 1:683; Collins, *Apocalyptic Imagination*, 225.

130. Josephus, *Ant.* 1.1.7; *Jub.* 11–12; Philo, *Abr.* 15; for a list of the sources, see Box and Landsman, *Apocalypse of Abraham*, 88–94.

131. Stone, "Apocalyptic Literature," 418.

132. Scholem, *Jewish Gnosticism*, 23.

and the review and periodisation of history makes the book unique among the Jewish apocalypses.[133]

Most scholars divide the apocalypse into two parts.[134] The first part (chs. 1–6, 8) is a haggadic account that describes how Abraham was gradually disenchanted with and abandoned idolatry and in consequence converted to faith in the patriarchal God.[135] The patriarchal legend is echoed in a different form in *Jub.* 11:14—12:14 and also found in some rabbinic writings.[136] The second part (chs. 9–32) is made up of four narrative units, each of which begins with a different locale. The first two units make up an expansion of Gen 15, in which the first unit (9:1—12:2) describes Abraham's journey from his father's house to Mount Horeb and the second (12:3—15:4) details the sacrifice the patriarch offered on the mountain. The third unit (15:5—29:22) begins with his ascent to the heavens and the fourth (30:1—32:6) his return to earth.[137] The following event takes place early on on his first journey in 10:1–5:

> And it came to pass when I heard the voice pronouncing such words to me that I looked this way and that. And behold there was no breath of man. And my spirit was amazed, and my soul fled from me. And I became like a stone, and fell face down upon the earth, for there was no longer strength in me to stand up on the earth. And while I was still face down on the ground, I heard the voice speaking, "Go, Iaoel of the same name, through the mediation of my ineffable name, consecrate this man for me and strengthen him against his trembling." The angel he sent to me in the likeness of a man came, and he took me by my right hand and stood me on my feet.[138]

---

133. Collins, *Apocalyptic Imagination*, 225.

134. Ibid.; Box and Landsman, *Apocalypse of Abraham*, vii; Rubinkiewicz and Lunt, "Apocalypse of Abraham," 1:681; Stone, "Apocalyptic Literature," 415; Nickelsburg, *Jewish Literature*, 294.

135. Rubinkiewicz and Lunt argue that 7:1—8:1 is the only part of the work that occurs in the early redaction of the Explanatory Palaia and hence appears to be a later insertion from the legend of Abraham found in the Palaia, "Apocalypse of Abraham," 1:684, 692 n. 7a.

136. *Midr. Gen. Rab.* 38:13.

137. Whitney, *Two Strange Beasts*, 60 n. 105.

138. The quotation adapts Rubinkiewicz's translation with Lunt's revision in "Apocalypse of Abraham," 1:693–94.

When Abraham heard the divine call, he fell down in affrighted spirit like a stone upon the earth and had no strength to stand. His response echoes the seers' when hearing the heavenly voice in the related apocalyptic writings (Ezek 1:28; Dan 8:17; 10:8–9; *1 En.* 14:14, 24; *4 Ezra* 10:29–30). The angelic guide Iaoel, or Jaoel,[139] possessed the power of the ineffable name as the name is delineated in a later statement (v. 16). Etymologically, Iaoel, Yahoel in Hebrew, incorporates the divine name Iao, Yaho in Hebrew, the abbreviation of the Tetragrammaton YHWH.[140] Iaoel appears to be the angel in Exod 23:21, who was substituted by Metatron in a later period after Metatron had absorbed Yahoel (*Sanh.* 38b).[141] The legendary figure is described as an angel coming "in the likeness of a man." The expression is based on Ezekiel and Daniel,[142] and therefore, is the same in nature as the heavenly, angelic figures in *1 Enoch* and *4 Ezra*.

In consequence, having studied the related passages in *1 Enoch*, *4 Ezra*, and the *Apocalypse of Abraham*, it is clear the Second Temple apocalyptists describe human and heavenly beings in the same way as Ezekiel and Daniel, using "son of man" as the generic reference for humanity and using expressions such as the one "whose face had the appearance of a man," "something like the figure of a man," and "the angel in the likeness of a man" as the descriptive comparisons in reference to heavenly or angelic entities. In *1 Enoch* and *4 Ezra* the referent is very likely the messianic figure, while in the *Apocalypse of Abraham*, it is the legendary angel, Iaoel. Therefore, it is highly likely that the two expressive modes represent two traditions that had existed before the New Testament period, as Slater argues.

The Son of Man Expression in Revelation

The expression "son of man" occurs twice in Revelation (1:13; 14:14). The first reference to it can be found in 1:13 near the beginning of the first series (1:9—3:22),[143] as follows:

> Then I turned to see the voice that was speaking to me, and on turning I saw seven golden lampstands, and in the midst of the

---

139. Box and Landsman note that the name is spelt differently in various texts, *Apocalypse of Abraham*, 46 n. 5.
140. Schäfer, *Jesus in the Talmud*, 58.
141. Ibid., 58 n. 46.
142. Rowland, "Vision of the Risen Christ," 1–11.
143. For a brief review of the structure of Revelation, see ch. 4 of this thesis.

lampstands one like a son of man, clothed with a long robe and with a golden girdle round his breast . . .

First and foremost, it is the ὅμοιον υἱὸν ἀνθρώπου, "one like a son of man," that dictated to John the seven letters to "the seven churches that are in Asia" (1:11; cf. 1:4). The preeminence of this man-like figure is certain. In terms of attributes, the being has much in common with Gabriel in Dan 10 and with the angelic creatures in Ezekiel as well.[144] The figure is described as "clothed with a long robe" (v. 13), ἐνδεδυμένον ποδήρη. The description is similar to the Old Greek (OG) reading in Dan 10:5, ἐνδεδυμένος βύσσινα, and equivalent to the same textual rendering in Ezek 9:2, ἐνδεδυκὼς ποδήρη. Also, he was "clothed with a golden girdle round his breast" (v. 13), περιεζωσμένον πρὸς τοῖς μαστοῖς ζώνην χρυσᾶν, which is similar to the Theodotion depiction of Gabriel's loins in Dan 10:5, περιεζωσμένη ἐν χρυσίῳ Ωφαζ. The figure's eyes were like "a flame of fire" (v. 14), φλὸξ πυρός, a metaphor analogous to Gabriel's, λαμπάδες πυρός, according to both the OG and Theodotion translations of Dan 10:6.

The description of his feet, "burnished bronze" (v. 15), χαλκολιβάνῳ, and of his face, "the sun shining in full strength" (v. 16), ὁ ἥλιος φαίνει ἐν τῇ δυνάμει αὐτοῦ, are correspondingly comparable to the description of Gabriel's arms and legs, χαλκὸς ἐξαστράπτων, and of his face, ὅρασις ἀστραπῆς, in the OG and Theodotion renderings of Dan 10:6. The figure's voice was like "the sound of many waters" (v. 15), φωνὴ ὑδάτων πολλῶν, which, in terms of number, is in agreement with the depiction of the sound of Gabriel's words in Dan 10:6, φωνὴ θορύβου in the OG, φωνὴ ὄχλου in Theodotion, but, in image, closer to that the sound of the wings of the four living creatures in Ezek 1:24, φωνὴν ὕδατος πολλοῦ, according to the OG rendering.

In terms of role and function, the figure is a mixture of priest and judge. The term ποδήρης occurs twelve times in the Septuagint, where each time it designates priestly clothing.[145] Together with the golden lampstands and the angels coming out of the heavenly temple in the larger context (15:5-8), the term signifies the priestly role of the figure. On the other hand, the close allusions of the being to the Ancient of Days reflect his judicial attribute. The metaphor used about his eyes, φλὸξ πυρός, "a flame of fire" (1:14; also, 2:18; 19:12), just as the "flaming torches" in the case of Ga-

---

144. Most commentators agree with the dependence of the account on the related passages in Daniel and Ezekiel. See Charles, *Revelation*, 1:27-29; Collins, *Cosmology and Eschatology*, 173-75; Beale, *Revelation*, 208-10.

145. Beale, *Revelation*, 209.

briel (Dan 10:6), marks the judicial authority of the being, since the same fiery imagery represents the throne of the Ancient of Days in the divine judgment (Dan 7:9–12). The more important allusion is the description of his head and his hair, λευκαὶ ὡς ἔριον λευκὸν ὡς χιών, "white as white wool, white as snow" (1:14), since it denotes the supreme divine status of the being, just as the raiment of the Ancient of Days is "white as snow" and the hair of his head like "pure wool" (Dan 7:9). With allusions to these divine qualities in an early Christian context, the figure clearly refers to the risen Christ as his resurrection is reported in 1:18.

Another "son of man" reference is found in the sixth vision of the vision cycle (12:1—15:4) that stands in between the seven trumpets (8:2—11:19) and the seven bowls (15:5—16:21).[146] In the fifth vision (14:6–13) of the series, three angels emerged one by one to announce the upcoming judgment of the worshippers on the beast and its image (vv. 6–11). In the sixth vision (14:14–20), "one like a son of man" appeared with three other angels to carry out a harvest and to bring in the grapes that ended up in the great wine press of the wrath of God. The figure is found at the beginning of the vision (v. 14) as follows:

> Then I looked, and lo, a white cloud, and seated on the cloud one like a son of man, with a golden crown on his head, and a sharp sickle in his hand.

There is general agreement that the central imagery of the vision for the most part is dependent on the oracle in Joel 3:13 (MT 4:13),[147] in which the harvest and gathering in of the grapes represent the judgment upon the nations on the Day of the Lord in both national and eschatological terms (cf. 3:12, 14).[148] In the present passage, the judgment theme becomes explicit as the harvest vision shifts into battle imagery at the end (v. 20).

In the larger context (vv. 6–20), there are seven heavenly beings. Of them, the figure in question, is the only one that is described as ὅμοιον υἱὸν ἀνθρώπου, "one like a son of man," which is the same expression as the ones in Rev 1:13 and Dan 7:13.[149] Also, he appeared on a white νεφέλη, "cloud,"

---

146. Collins, *Combat Myth*, 18–19.

147. Charles, *Revelation*, 2:21–24; Collins, *Cosmology and Eschatology*, 189; Aune, *Revelation*, 2:843.

148. Wolff, *Joel and Amos*, 84–85.

149. The Greek term ὅμοιον is not found in the OG or Theodotion renderings of Dan 7:13. It is likely that the author of Revelation employed ὅμοιον as a translation of כ in the MT in alluding to the Danielic man-like figure in the passage. Evidence for this

like the beings in Dan 7:13.[150] On his head was a στέφανον χρυσοῦν, "golden crown," which represents his kingship as well as his authority, as the people who rule with him also wear "golden crowns" (4:4, 10; 6:2; 9:7; cf. 2:10; 3:11; 12:1).[151] In his hand was a δρέπανον ὀξύ, "sharp sickle," an instrument for the grape harvest (v. 17), which, together with the harvests in context, symbolizes the final judgment.[152] The reference to the being is consistent with the ones in Rev 1:13 and Dan 7:13, since it is described in human likeness. Carrying the attributes of a king and a judge with a human likeness, the figure is a heavenly being and it is very likely that it refers to the risen Christ as in 1:13.

To summarize, because of the commonalities in vocabulary, the "one like a son of man" in Rev 1:13 is dependent on the heavenly, angelic figures in Daniel and Ezekiel, which, too, are in principal described as beings in human likeness. With allusions to the supreme qualities of the Ancient of Days in an early Christian context, the figure clearly refers to the risen Christ as his resurrection is reported in 1:18. With exactly the same human appearance, "one like a son of man" in Rev 14:14 designates the same messianic figure. In the first case, the description and context highlight his priestly and judicial attributes, while the second promotes his judicial quality and kingship.

Four Beasts Coming up out of the Sea

In Dan 7:2–7, Daniel saw in a vision four great beasts, each different from the others, come up out of the sea. The first beast was like a lion and had eagles' wings. The second beast was like a bear and it had three ribs in its mouth between its teeth. The third beast was like a leopard with four

---

view is the use of ὅμοιον synonymously with ὡς both in meaning and construction in the apocalypse (Charles, *Revelation*, 1:36–37).

150. The singular νεφέλη, "cloud" (cf. 10:1; 11:12), leads Arthur Vos to suggest that here the picture does not allude to Dan 7:13, where the plural "clouds" is employed, but to Luke 21:27, which is the only occasion elsewhere in the New Testament the singular "cloud" is found (*Synoptic Traditions*, 146–47 n. 173). This rationale does not appear to be convincing, however. Probably, the author took up the singular form in order to produce a more vivid picture (Collins, *Cosmology and Eschatology*, 192), or to match the figure's gesture, since the imagery would be clumsy if the figure were sitting on a plurality of "clouds" (Aune, *Revelation*, 2:840).

151. Beale, *Revelation*, 770; Aune, *Revelation*, 2:842.

152. Aune, *Revelation*, 2:842–44, 849.

wings of a bird on its back and four heads. The fourth beast had great iron teeth and ten horns and was different from all the beasts that were before it. There is general consensus that the four beasts represent four different kingdoms, which are Babylon, Media, Persia and Greece.[153] And the ten horns of the fourth beast represent the ten rulers of the Seleucid dynasty.[154] The characteristics of these beasts have parallels in Rev 13. In Rev 13:1a, the apocalyptist saw a ἐκ τῆς θαλάσσης θηρίον ἀναβαῖνον, "beast rising out of the sea." The phrase is an allusion to LXX Dan 7:3, in which τέσσαρα θηρία ἀνέβαινον ἐκ τῆς θαλάσσης, "four beasts came up out of the sea." In depicting the sea beast, John combined some characteristics of the four beasts in Daniel[155] and described those features in reverse order:[156] the beast had κέρατα δέκα, "ten horns"; it was like a παρδάλει, "leopard"; its feet were like a πόδες ἄρκου, "bear's"; and its mouth was like a στόμα λέοντος, "lion's mouth."[157] On the other hand, John's beast has some exclusive distinctions: it had κεφαλὰς ἑπτά, "seven heads," with ὀνόμα[τα] βλασφημίας, "blasphemous names," upon its heads (13:1). Hence, the ultimate mythological background of the two passages is the *Chaoskampf* tradition, as in both cases the beasts came up out of the sea. The beast from the sea in Rev 13:1 carries some features of the four beasts in Dan 7. The principal characteristic of John's beast, however, is derived from the biblical Leviathan, since it has seven heads just as Leviathan does.

153. Collins, *Daniel*, 295; Caird, *Revelation*, 162; Mounce, *Revelation*, 245 n. 8.

154. Ibid.

155. Mounce notes that it is undeniable that John echoes Daniel's vision of the four beasts coming up from the sea (Dan 7:3) (*Revelation*, 244). Krodel points out that the four beasts text in Dan 7:3 is one of the sources, together with the mythological account of the combat between a god and a sea monster and the Nero legend, for the beast in Rev 13:1–2 (*Revelation*, 247–48). Charles notes that Dan 7:2–7 is clearly the basis for the description of John's first beast in Rev 13:1–2abc (*Revelation*, 1:345). Schüssler Fiorenza describes the beast as a combination of the four beasts of Dan 7 in "a surrealistic fashion" (*Revelation*, 83). For Caird, also, John's first beast (13:1) contains some of the characteristics of all four beasts in Dan 7, with an artistic freedom in their rendition (*Revelation*, 162). Duff notes that the beast's transparent allusions to Dan 7 and its reference to the head with the deathblow indicate its identity (*Who Rides the Beast?*, 67 n. 30).

156. Caird, *Revelation*, 162; Montgomery, *Daniel*, 290.

157. Three beasts, πάρδαλις, "leopard," λέων, "lion," and ἄρκος, "bear," are also found as God's opposition in LXX Hos 13:7–8.

Symbolic Descriptions of the Little Horn

In addition to the "one like a son of man," the "little horn" of the fourth beast (vv. 7, 20) is a prominent figure in Dan 7. The "little horn" is particularly relevant to the present study, because the symbolism related to it, "a mouth speaking great things" (vv. 8, 20), "made war with the saints" (v. 21), and the apocalyptic period for the war, "a time, two times, and half a time" (v. 25), has parallels in the vision of the beast from the sea in Rev 13 (vv. 5, 7). Daniel 7:8 describes a situation when, before this "little horn" appears, three of the former horns were plucked up by the roots. Later in 7:24, it is said that the "little horn" is different from the former horns. As early as the third century CE, Porphyry, a neoplatonist philosopher and a major witness of the Syrian tradition, identified this little horn as Antiochus IV.[158] The king usurped Seleucid power in 175 BCE by overthrowing several other claimants to the throne. Most modern scholars are in agreement with the identification of this "little horn."[159] The identification of the "little horn" corresponds to its difference from the former ten horns reported in 7:24, since Antiochus Epiphanes' legitimacy as king is denied in 11:21.[160]

A Mouth Speaking Great Things

It is believed that Antiochus IV wanted to indicate that he was divine when he gave himself the name Epiphanes. Antiochus' arrogance is most evident in the fact that he was the first Seleucid king who had his full title minted on coins. His title became gradually more sophisticated, as it was first minted as ΒΑΣΙΛΕΩΣ ΑΝΤΙΟΧΟΥ in the years 175–173/172 BCE and culminated as ΒΑΣΙΛΕΩΣ ΑΝΤΙΟΧΟΥ ΘΕΟΥ ΕΠΙΦΑΝΟΥΣ ΝΙΚΗΦΟΡΟΥ in the years 169–164 BCE.[161] Antiochus imposed the cult of Zeus Olympius in the Jerusalem temple and called the temple on Mount Gerizim the temple of Zeus the friend of strangers (2 Macc 6:2).

The phrase, στόμα λαλοῦν μεγάλα, "a mouth speaking great things," in LXX Theodotion Dan 7:8, 20, expresses the arrogance of Antiochus Epiphanes. The expression here and in 11:36, 40, 41, 45 appears to reflect

---

158. Porphyry's works were destroyed by Christians, and his identification of the little horn is recovered from Jerome's commentary on Dan 7:7–8.

159. Collins, *Daniel*, 299; Lacocque, *Daniel*, 141.

160. Collins, *Daniel*, 299.

161. Hengel, *Judaism and Hellenism*, 1:285.

the oldest reference in apocalyptic writings to an Antichrist.¹⁶² The motif of arrogant speech is described in more detail later in 11:36, where Antiochus' behavior during the persecution is recapitulated. The motif has parallels in the vision of the beast from the sea in Rev 13. In Rev 13:5a, the beast was given στόμα λαλοῦν μεγάλα καὶ βλασφημίας, "a mouth uttering haughty and blasphemous words"; also, in 13:6a, ἤνοιξεν τὸ στόμα αὐτοῦ εἰς βλασφημίας πρὸς τὸν θεόν, "it opened its mouth to utter blasphemies against God." The first phrase of the former piece, στόμα λαλοῦν μεγάλα, is a clear parallel to Dan 7:8, 20. The motif of blasphemy is based in part on Dan 7:25. The combination of the motifs of arrogant speech and blasphemy against God is also found in Dan 11:36. In Dan 7:8, 20, the ascription of a mouth to the little horn is a way of indicating that the horn represents a person and a way of allowing it to speak.¹⁶³ In Rev 13:5a, however, the beast is presumed to have had a mouth, and διδόναι στόμα, "give mouth," is a Semitic idiom meaning "to give someone something to say" (e.g. Luke 21:15).¹⁶⁴ The motif of arrogant speech, based on the descriptions of Antiochus Epiphanes in Daniel, is also employed to describe the king of Babylon in some Second Temple writings (*2 Bar.* 67:7; *4 Ezra* 11:43). Hence, the allusion to the motif of arrogant speech in Rev 13:5a indicates that the beast from the sea represents a powerful person on earth who is against God just as Antiochus Epiphanes is.

Make War with the Saints

In Theodotion Dan 7:21, it is reported that ἐποίει πόλεμον μετὰ τῶν ἁγίων καὶ ἴσχυσεν πρὸς αὐτούς, "the little horn made war against the saints and conquered them." A similar phrase has been added to LXX Dan 7:8, which says καὶ ἐποίει πόλεμον πρὸς τοὺς ἁγίους, "and he made war against the saints."¹⁶⁵ The expression is paralleled in Rev 13:7a, where the beast was allowed ποιῆσαι πόλεμον μετὰ τῶν ἁγίων καὶ νικῆσαι αὐτούς, "to make war on the saints and to conquer them." In Rev 11:7, in the same way, that beast made war on the two witnesses and conquered them and killed them.

The account in Dan 7:21–22 makes it difficult to argue for literary and logical unity in Dan 7, since this additional vision interrupts the context

---

162. Russell, *Method and Message*, 277.
163. Aune, *Revelation*, 2:742.
164. Ibid.
165. Ibid., 2:746.

in which Daniel asked one of those standing by for an interpretation of his vision (vv. 16–20, 23–28). Many scholars see this short report as secondary. Elias Bickerman argues that vv. 20–22 constitute an additional piece, produced in December 167 BCE, and added to a text written between Autumn 169 BCE and the end of 167 BCE, following the persecution of Antiochus Epiphanes.[166] Harold Louis Ginsberg comments that all accounts of an eleventh horn including vv. 20–22 are secondary, and that these additions to chapters 7 and 8, as well as all of chapter 9, were produced between the end of 167 BCE and the winter of 164 BCE, during the time of the royal amnesty.[167] According to Luc Dequeker, vv. 21–22 is a gloss the redactor added to the main body of Dan 7, which was originally a pre-Maccabean text, when he reworked the text in the Maccabean period.[168] In the same vein, some other commentators see the brief piece as secondary too, with nuanced perspectives in each case.[169] In the Hebrew Bible, the term ἁγίους, "saints," normally denotes heavenly beings.[170] Being a redactional piece responding to the persecution of Antiochus Epiphanes, however, "saints," on this particular occasion, is more likely to be a reference to Israel than to supernatural beings.[171] For these reasons, it is likely that just as the little horn and the saints in Dan 7:21 refer to Antiochus Epiphanes and the elected Israel respectively, the beast from the sea and the saints in Rev 13:7a represent an evil and powerful king, who is against God, and the people of God suffering from the threat of that king.

A Time, Two Times, and Half a Time

There is general consensus that the expression, "a time, two times, and half a time" (Dan 7:25), refers to the period during which the Jews suffered under the persecution of Antiochus Epiphanes in approximately 167–164 BCE.[172] With the term καιρός, "time," meaning one year, the expression is generally understood as three and a half years.[173] The length of this period

166. Lacocque, *Daniel*, 152 n. 135.
167. Ibid.
168. Dequeker, "Daniel 7," 353–92.
169. Lacocque, *Daniel*, 126–29.
170. Collins, *Daniel*, 313.
171. Noth, "Holy Ones," 226.
172. Collins, *Daniel*, 321–22; Lacocque, *Daniel*, 153–54.
173. Aune, *Revelation*, 2:743; Collins, *Daniel*, 322; Lacocque, *Daniel*, 154.

corresponds to "half of the week" mentioned in 9:27 and 12:7.[174] On three other occasions, the period is variously referred to as "two thousand and three hundred evenings and mornings" (8:14), "a thousand two hundred and ninety days" (12:11), and "the thousand three hundred and thirty-five days" (12:12). While the methods by which the numbers in these three cases were calculated are open to question, it is generally agreed that these figures bear a close relationship to the schematic three and a half years represented by "a time, two times, and half a time" (7:25; 12:7), or "half of the week" (9:27).[175]

In 8:14, 2300 evenings and mornings, equivalent to 1150 days, are slightly less than the schematic three and a half years (7:25). A possible reason for the variance is that chapter 8 was written somewhat later and some of the predetermined time was assumed to have elapsed.[176] In 12:11, 1290 days equal three and a half years plus one month. It may be that this extra month represents the period of the composition of the great vision in Dan 10–12.[177] In 12:12, the period of 1335 days is the preceding figure adding another month and a half. The extra time may represent the delay before the final completion of the whole book of Daniel.[178] It is likely that the three numbers indicate the revised calculations of the predictions that failed to be fulfilled.[179] According to 1 Macc 1:54; 4:52–54, the desolation of the temple lasted exactly three years.

In early Christianity, the period of three and a half years was widely held as a time for the rule of the eschatological antagonist.[180] The schematic duration has parallels in Revelation. In Rev 13:5b, it is said that the beast from the sea was allowed to exercise authority for μῆνας τεσσεράκοντα [καὶ] δύο, "forty-two months." The period is an allusion to Dan 7:25, and also to 12:7 and 9:27. The "forty-two months" is found again in Rev 11:2 as a period of time in which the nations will trample over the holy city. Then, two witnesses are granted power to prophesy for ἡμέρας χιλίας διακοσίας ἑξήκοντα, "one thousand two hundred and sixty days," that is, forty-two months of 30 days each (11:3). In Rev 12:6, it is reported that the woman

---

174. Collins, *Daniel*, 357; Lacocque, *Daniel*, 154.
175. Collins, *Daniel*, 400 n. 274.
176. Ibid., 336 n. 77.
177. Lacocque, *Daniel*, 250.
178. Ibid.
179. Collins, *Daniel*, 401 n. 278.
180. Irenaeus, *Haer.* 5.25.3; 5.30.4; Justin, *Dial.* 32.3–4.

was to be nourished in the wilderness for "one thousand two hundred and sixty days," which is referred to in 12:14 as καιρὸν καὶ καιροὺς καὶ ἥμισυ καιροῦ, "a time, two times, and half a time." Thus, in all these passages, the period is a clear allusion to Dan 7:25. It is clear that the apocalyptist intended to demonstrate that the period during which the sea beast was allowed to exercise authority coincides with the period during which the nations will trample over the holy city and the period during which the two witnesses prophesy.[181]

CONCLUSION

Having examined the pertinent materials, this chapter closes with several concluding comments. Firstly, of the various pieces of imagery found in the Baal myth, stirring up the sea provides a remote and broad context for the cosmological background to Dan 7, as it brings about the emergence of the four beasts. The most important imagery is the rider on the clouds, since it is employed to describe "one like a son of man" (7:13). Apart from these two elements, there seem to be few concrete allusions in Dan 7. On the other hand, there are many differences between the two pieces in terms of setting. In Dan 7, four beasts come out of the sea, one by one, each with its own characteristics. The order in which the four beasts emerge from the sea and their individual features have no parallels in the Baal cycle. More importantly, the seven-headed body, the most obvious characteristic of Leviathan, is not found in any of the four Danielic beasts, nor is the name "Leviathan" used. Therefore, any allusion to the Baal epic in Dan 7 is cursory.

Furthermore, apocalyptic literature from around the first century CE, both canonical and extra-canonical, consistently designates heavenly, angelic beings by using expressions like, "one like a son of man," or similar. In Dan 7:13, the phrase most likely refers to the archangel Michael. In Rev 1:13 and 14:14, the same idiom is used to mean the risen Christ. In Dan 7 the larger context in which the man-like figure appears is the Canaanite cosmological myth. In Rev 13, although, ultimately, the beast coming up out of the sea has the same mythological background as the four beasts in Dan 7, the man-like figure is not found in the chapter. The two contexts in which "one like a son of man" is found in the Apocalypse (1:13; 14:14) are not contextually related to chapter 13. Thus, the Danielic relevance of "one

---

181. Aune, *Revelation*, 2:743.

like a son of man" to the mythic background of Canaanite cosmology has nothing to do with the account of Leviathan and Behemoth in Rev 13.

Finally, there are allusions to the characteristics of Daniel's four beasts in the beast from the sea in Rev 13:1. The sea beast in Rev 13 shares characteristics with those of the four beasts in Dan 7, such as a lion's mouth, bear's feet and looking like a leopard. The sea beast in Rev 13 has ten horns like the fourth beast in Dan 7. The allusion to the "little horn" of the fourth beast in Dan 7 is particularly explicit. In Rev 13:5a, the sea beast is described as having "a mouth uttering haughty and blasphemous words" which is a clear allusion to the motif of arrogant speech in Dan 7:8, 20. In Rev 13:7a, it is reported that the sea beast "made war with the saints," just as the little horn in Dan 7:21 did. In Rev 13:5b, the duration of the war is reported as lasting for "forty-two months," which is clearly a reference derived from Dan 7:25.

3

The Leviathan-Behemoth Motif in the Second Temple Apocalypses

IN REV 13, THE principal characters are the pair of monsters, the beast from the sea and the beast from the land (vv. 1, 11). In studying the chapter, most commentators including prominent scholars such as Charles, Collins, Aune and so forth,[1] note that the two beasts reflect the Jewish myth of Leviathan, the female monster from the sea, and Behemoth, the male monster from the land. The two monsters are also familiar characters in the Second Temple apocalypses, in which the pair occur together in *4 Ezra* 6:49–52, *2 Bar.* 29:4, and *1 En.* 60:7–10, 24ab, and Leviathan appears alone in the *Apoc. Ab.* 10:10; 21:4 and the *Lad. Jac.* 6:13. All of these writings are roughly contemporaneous with Revelation. In all these passages, Leviathan and Behemoth have the same attributes and are placed in an eschatological context.

By examining these accounts, this chapter aims to investigate how Leviathan and Behemoth function in each text in order to discover the formulaic pattern with which the Second Temple apocalyptist employs the pair. These accounts are not sources that can be used to probe the origin or the development of the two beasts since there is a time interval of over a thousand years between the Canaanite myth and the Second Temple writings. However, they are reliable materials from which to interpret how Second Temple Judaism understood the Leviathan-Behemoth motif. This investigation contributes to the present thesis in that it demonstrates the

1. Charles, *Revelation*, 1:358; Collins, *Combat Myth*, 165; Aune, *Revelation*, 2:728–29.

differences between Revelation and the Second Temple apocalypses with respect to their employment of the tradition.

4 EZRA 6:49-52

Internal evidence (3:1; 11–12) indicates that *4 Ezra* was written after the destruction of the temple in 70 CE, at approximately the end of the first century CE.[2] Exegetes generally divide the book into seven units: 3:1—5:19; 5:20—6:34; 6:35—9:25; 9:26—10:59; 10:60—12:51; 13:1–58; and 14:1–48.[3] The transitional piece in this apocalypse is the fourth unit (9:26—10:59), in which, having learned the vision that would precipitate the forthcoming restoration of Zion, Ezra transformed from being a skeptic into a faithful mediator to others (10:29–59).[4] Prior to this turning point, the third unit (6:35—9:25) contains a long address to God by Ezra, in which God's ultimate power over human history, in the first part of the address (6:38–54), stands in stark contrast to God's inertia over the destruction of Jerusalem, in the second part (6:55–59). The entire address culminates with a theodicy related question: "If the world was indeed created for us, why do we not possess our world as an inheritance?" (v. 59).[5] Leviathan and Behemoth appear in the later first part (6:49–52) as follows:

> Then thou didst keep in existence two living creatures; the name of one thou didst call Behemoth and the name of the other Leviathan. And thou didst separate one from the other, for the seventh part where the water had been gathered together could not hold them both. And thou didst give Behemoth one of the parts which had been dried up on the third day, to live in it, where there are a thousand mountains; but to Leviathan thou didst give the seventh part, the watery part; and thou hast kept them to be eaten by whom thou wilt, and when thou wilt.

The wider context in which this account is found contains a creation story also known as *Hexaemeron* (vv. 38–54). Michael Stone discerns that in this *Hexaemeron*, there is a series of purpose statements basically parallel

---

2. See ch. 2, p. 43, nn. 117–120.
3. See ch. 2, p. 44, n. 121.
4. See ch. 2, p. 44, n. 122.
5. It is generally agreed that this verse is the climax of the larger context (Nickelsburg, *Jewish Literature*, 289; Collins, *Apocalyptic Imagination*, 203; Stone, *Fourth Ezra*, 181, 184).

to Gen 1 and following the biblical order.⁶ In 6:40, God commanded that a ray of light be brought forth "so that" his works might then appear (cf. Gen 1:3–5). In 6:42, God commanded that six parts of the earth be dried up and kept "so that" some of them might be planted and cultivated and be of service to God (cf. Gen 1:9–13). In 6:45–46, God commanded that the luminaries, the sun and the moon, come into being "to serve" humankind (cf. Gen 1:14–19). In 6:48, God commanded that living creatures be produced in the dumb and lifeless water "so that therefore" the nations might declare his wondrous works (cf. Gen 1:20–23). Following this verse is the Leviathan-Behemoth account (vv. 49–52), the ending of which also constitutes the last purpose statement. In 6:52, God has preserved Leviathan and Behemoth "to be eaten" by whom he wishes and when he wishes. This idea is clearly not dependent on Gen 1, but on the apocalyptic tradition and, therefore, has an eschatological implication. Then, the *Hexaemeron* closes with the role of Adam (v. 54) which forms the bridge between the universalistic theme of creation and the national theme of the election of Israel in the next part (vv. 55–59).⁷ It is in this context that Leviathan and Behemoth occur in order to substantiate the creative purpose theme through its emphasis on God's sovereign power over the pair.

The account in its present context contains three themes. The preservation of Leviathan and Behemoth has a striking role in the formation of the account. The two references to "keep" (vv. 49, 52) constitute an *inclusio* that begins and concludes the account, sandwiching the separation and the return of the two beasts. The proto-logical and eschatological themes are typical to all three Leviathan-Behemoth accounts in the present inquiry. However, such literary emphasis on the preservation of the pair is exclusive to the account in *4 Ezra*. Its larger context supports the notion that the preservation of the two figures has been part of the divine purpose of creation since the beginning.⁸ The uniqueness of the emphasis on their preservation indicates that the account in question is a preexisting tradition that is not only independent from the Gen 1 materials available to the final editor then, but that also varies slightly from the accounts in *2 Baruch* and *1 Enoch*.⁹ The

---

6. Stone, *Fourth Ezra*, 182.

7. The idea that lies behind the transition (vv. 54–55) is that, since the chosen people came from Adam, it was for the sake of Israel that God created the world. This view is also found in *T. Mos.* 1:12 and *2 Bar.* 14:18–19. The context of the latter account emphasizes more the righteous of Israel as the reason for its superior role in creation.

8. Whitney, *Two Strange Beasts*, 36.

9. Stone argues that because its length is out of all proportion to the extent to which

The Leviathan-Behemoth Motif in the Second Temple Apocalypses

inference of the incorporation of this account into the passage is that, by the time the final editor was working, the two mythic figures had not yet returned and the messianic banquet had not yet taken place. It is likely that the final editor schematized the core Leviathan-Behemoth materials within the two preservation references in order to encourage the people to endure the severe social conditions at the time with the hope of consuming the two mythic figures as an eschatological reward.

The second theme is the separation of Leviathan and Behemoth with the seventh part of the watery realm allocated to Leviathan and one of the parts of the dry land to Behemoth (vv. 50–52a). The idea is an expansion of the biblical reference to God's creation of the great sea monsters on the fifth day (Gen 1:21), since the *Hexaemeron* places the origin of the pair on this day (v. 47). Unlike Gen 1, however, the account here contains little sense of the creation of either of the beasts.[10] On the other hand, whilst its larger context places the creation of the two figures on the fifth day of creation, the account shows a considerable level of influence from the tradition of the creative act on the third day (Gen 1:9). This is not only because separation is an important theme on the third day of creation in Gen 1 and the present account, but also because both Leviathan and Behemoth and the watery realm and the dry land assigned to them in the account have the same essence as the objects of separation on the third day, that is to say, the waters under the heavens and the dry land (Gen 1:9). Thus, although it is an expansion of Gen 1:21, the account shows a preeminent interest in the creative act of separation in Gen 1:9. For this reason, the pertinent starting point for the present Leviathan-Behemoth motif is their separation rather than their creation. Being parallel to the division of the two spheres in creation, the separation of Leviathan and Behemoth and the allocation

---

each created item is described in the *Hexaemeron*, and because it is not found in the descriptions of eschatological events and rewards elsewhere in the book, the Leviathan-Behemoth account is a preexisting tradition that is also found in 2 Baruch and 1 Enoch (*Fourth Ezra*, 183). Whitney adds that since the abruptness of the opening reference to the preservation of the pair (v. 49), and the contexts in which the account occurs in the other two apocalypses are not of creation, the account is independent of its present context (*Two Strange Beasts*, 34, 36). In agreement with their views, the present thesis sees that the schematic arrangement of the double references to the preservation, too, is evidence for this argument.

10. In his translation, Stone preserves the phrase "which you created" at the end of the first sentence in v. 49. But the Latin text omits the phrase, and the Georgian text reads *ex illis creaturis* (*Fourth Ezra*, 179). RSV leaves it out.

of their realms represent symbiotically a proto-logical act symbolizing the divine ordering of chaos.[11]

The third theme is how Leviathan and Behemoth function on their final return (v. 52b). There had been a biblical tradition that the Lord would prepare a messianic banquet for the righteous at the time of the end (Isa 25:6). In both apocalyptic and rabbinic writings, the banquet includes Leviathan and Behemoth who will return and become food for the righteous in the new age.[12] The immediate source of the idea of consuming one's enemy is Ps 74:13–15, in which God crushed the heads of Leviathan and offered the beast as food to the people of the wilderness.[13] The *Sitz im Leben* of the psalm is the Feast of Tabernacles.[14] The passage forms part of a lament for the destruction of the temple in 586 BCE, in which the defeat of Leviathan and dragons by Yahweh in creation was appealed to as a basis for confidence in him delivering his chosen people from the national disaster of that time.[15] Given the date and social setting of *4 Ezra*, it is very likely that the reappearance of the two beasts denotes the same sense of petition to Yahweh to set free his elected people from the national crisis as does Ps 74. Being the antithesis of their separation, the return of the pair is an eschatological event that signifies the emergence of chaos from order.[16]

Between the separation and the return of the two monsters, there are several peculiarities in the account. The first is the "seventh part" of the world that makes up the watery realm (v. 50). The idea of a partitioned universe is not found in Genesis, but is in a number of works of various genres from the Second Temple onward.[17] In some of these writings, even the place where the souls of the dead assembled and waited for the day of judgment is divided, for instance, the "four hollow places" in a mountain

---

11. In his work, *Revelation*, 2:728, Aune describes the separation of the sea from the land as a "proto-logical act." Here, the term denotes the separation of and the assignment to the pair as a whole event.

12. Apocalyptic writings include *2 Bar.* 29:1–4 and *1 En.* 60:7–10, 24ab. For rabbinic references, see Ginzberg, *Legends of the Jews*, 1:27–28; 5:41–46.

13. Forsyth, *Old Enemy*, 217–18 n. 12. But the idea of consuming an enemy has its origin possibly in the Canaanite myth in which Mot swallowed up Baal once he has been defeated (*CTA* 23.61–62).

14. Day, *God's Conflict*, 19.

15. Ibid., 22.

16. Aune, *Revelation*, 2:728.

17. For example, *2 Enoch*, *3 Baruch*, *Apocalypse of Zephaniah*, *Testament of Levi*, *Life of Adam and Eve* [Greek recension], *Joseph and Aseneth*, and *Mart. Ascen. Isa.* 1–5.

(1 En. 22:2). In *4 Ezra*, the watery sphere is not the only element characterized by the number "seven." In chapter 7, eschatological events are mostly distinguished by "seven"; there will be a primeval silence for "seven days" in the world (vv. 30-31); the day of judgment will last for about "a week of years" (v. 43); the souls of the wicked will wander about in torment in "seven ways" (vv. 79-87); the souls of the righteous will rest in "seven orders" (vv. 88-99). The number is so fascinating to apocalyptists and frequently found in apocalyptic writings.[18] On the other hand, according to a number of sources, the world is partitioned into seven strata with a star or an angel presiding over each level.[19] However, none of these sources describe the watery realm as a limited domain within one of the seven parts of the world.[20] Thus the idea of this distinctive sevenfold structure reflects a mélange of various worldviews in Second Temple apocalyptic literature, which, for the final editor, is more important and influential than the Gen 1 tradition.

The second peculiarity relates to the power and size of the two mythic figures. The reason God separated Leviathan and Behemoth was that "the seventh part where the water had been gathered together could not hold them both" (v. 50). The portrayal of the power and size of the pair does not occur elsewhere in the three Second Temple apocalypses but does feature in Job 40–41. Though different in time and genre, Job and *4 Ezra* have the same tradition that both Leviathan and Behemoth are of watery origin (Job 40:21-23; *4 Ezra* 6:50).[21] In Job 40:6-14, God challenges Job to govern the

18. Russell, *Method and Message*, 127.
19. Stone, *Fourth Ezra*, 185 n. 32.
20. Ibid., 185.
21. There is a debate concerning the origin of Behemoth. According to *4 Ezra* 6:53, the creatures made on the sixth day of creation included the "beasts," $b^ehēmā$. Since $b^ehēmā$ and $b^ehēmōt$ come from the same Hebrew root, one may argue that Behemoth was a creation of the sixth day along with the "creeping things" and thus a land dweller of earthly origin. The reference to 6:47, however, clearly places the creation of both Leviathan and Behemoth on the fifth day. This idea accords with the reference in 6:50, a central piece of the present block. *Second Baruch* 29:4, too, reports the same information. In addition, in a passage introducing Behemoth (Job 40:15-24), the term *nāhār* found in v. 23 to describe the beast's quality is equivalent to Judge River in the Baal Epic, which is a title for Yam. On the other hand, in Job 12:7-8, the term $b^ehēmōt$ refers primarily to land creatures as a category alongside "fish," "birds" and the earth as in Gen 1:26 (Habel, *Job*, 565). The passages lead to an idea that the creation of Behemoth took place on the sixth day. It is likely that *4 Ezra* 6:53 belongs to this tradition. Also, there is another tradition that puts the creation of the marine and earthly creatures together on the fifth day and leaves the sixth for the creation of humanity alone (e.g., *2 En.* 30:7). This is clearly not the case here, however. Most scholars agree with the watery origin of Behemoth in the

universe with an arm as powerful and mighty as El's. Next, Behemoth is introduced as a key character with many distinctive qualities to illustrate the might of El as he subjugates the beast (40:15–24). The strong bestial loins, muscular belly, stiff tail, knitted thigh sinews, bronze bones and iron-like limbs make Behemoth unrivaled among other creatures on the earth (vv. 16–18). The supremacy of Behemoth is not limited to physical prowess. Unlike any other creatures, Behemoth is the only one that God made along with Job (v. 15), and therefore, the figure is not like the eagle or the wild ox, that Job can command and control, but is the same as Job in a sense and shares the same origin and destiny as the legendary sage in some way.[22] Due to this status, Behemoth is the first of the ways of El (v. 19). In a similar context, in Prov 8:22, the term "first" denotes wisdom as the governing principle or model that Yahweh utilizes in his work of creation.[23] The term has the same connotation in the present passage since the emphasis on primordiality is found a number of times elsewhere in Job (cf. 8:8; 15:7; 20:4; 28:24–27; 38:4, 21). Thus, Behemoth is the first of the created ways that El actually makes, just as wisdom is the first eternal principle.[24]

No-one can face or silence Leviathan, except Yahweh (41:9–12). The symbol of primordial chaos was well-known to the Palestinian Jews of the first century CE, since Leviathan is described as the "fleeing serpent" or "dragon" in the Hebrew Bible plenty of times (e.g., Isa 27:1; Ps 74:12–14; Job 26:13). The beast's invincibility is described using a series of mythic features (41:13–32), including sneezes that flash forth light, the flaming torches coming from his mouth, the smoke from his nostrils (41:18–20) and so forth. Above all, Leviathan is king over all creatures (41:33–34). There are plenty of rabbinic sources that contain an elaboration and exposition of the power and size of the pair (*B. Bat.* 75a; *Midr. Lev. Rab.* 22.10; *Pesiq. Rab Kah.* Suppl. 2.4). The level of agreement between the biblical and extra-biblical materials makes it evident that the apocalyptic reader had no doubt about the power of the two figures.

The third peculiarity is the naming of the pair by God (v. 49). In Gen 1, God only named the day and the night on the first day (v. 5); heaven on the second (v. 8); the earth and the seas on the third (v. 10). It was Adam

---

present account. For example, Box, *Ezra-Apocalypse*, 89 n. *n*. Both Gunkel and Box agree to the watery origin of both of them (Stone, *Fourth Ezra*, 187).

22. Habel, *Job*, 558.
23. Vawter, "Prov 8:22," 214–15.
24. Habel, *Job*, 566.

who gave names to all the living creatures (2:19–20). The divine act of naming creatures appears neither in biblical nor in extra-biblical writings; it is only found in the present passage. This uniqueness is evidence for the independence of the account. In Gen 1, "to name" can be paralleled to "to create," as in the opening lines of the *Enuma Elish* and in many other ancient texts.[25] Since, in cosmogony, the creator is lord over all he has created,[26] the naming of the two figures indicates God's dominion over the pair. Apart from those in Gen 1, the only two references to God naming creatures are found in Ps 147:4 and Isa 40:26. In the first reference, God gives names to the astral bodies directly; in the second, analogically. The two references presume that God gives names to individual angels since there has been a long tradition of identifying heavenly bodies as supernatural beings. With this identification, calling the astral bodies by name is similar to numbering off in a military sphere.[27] Thus, on the one hand, Leviathan and Behemoth are superior to any other creatures as they are the only two to which God directly gives names. On the other, being called by God, the two figures are God's servants who are entirely subservient to divine dominance.

In summary, by taking up the themes of the separation, return and preservation of Leviathan and Behemoth, the final editor intended to emphasize divine sovereignty throughout human history. Both the divine naming of the two figures and the description of their sizes highlight their incomparable statuses with respect to all God's other creations. God's greatness is both unutterable and unfathomable since from the beginning of history, God has been able to master the pair. The reference to the "seventh part" of the world reflects the worldview of Second Temple apocalyptic writings. In its larger context, the Leviathan-Behemoth account in *4 Ezra* contrasts with the ensuing address (6:55–59) that complains of God's inertia during the destruction of Jerusalem. The contrast raises a question of theodicy challenging why the one who has full control over human history is powerless over the fall of Jerusalem.

2 BARUCH 29:4

The relationship between *2 Baruch* and *4 Ezra* is so close that some form of interdependence must have taken place between them. The entire

25. Westermann, *Genesis 1–11*, 114.
26. Ibid.
27. Stone, "List of Revealed Things," 427.

manuscript of *2 Baruch* is extant in one Syriac manuscript that was translated from the Greek, which itself was very likely derived from a Semitic original.[28] Like *4 Ezra*, *2 Baruch* appears to have been written in the period between the two Jewish revolts,[29] and its account of the imminent destruction of Jerusalem in 586/587 BCE is likely to be an allegory for the fall of the city in 70 CE.[30] This apocalypse also consists of seven units: 1:1—9:2; 10:1—12:5; 13:1—21:1; 21:2—34:1; 35:1—47:2; 48:1—77:26; 78:1 to the end.[31] Unlike *4 Ezra*, however, *2 Baruch* contains neither skeptical questions of covenantal dilemmas nor any dramatic conversions of the prophet,[32] but a linear movement from the distress in the early chapters to the consolation provided by the visions in the later chapters.[33]

The Leviathan-Behemoth account is positioned in the latter part of the fourth unit (29:4). The unit departs from the previous ones in structure, as in this unit it is Baruch that initiates the contact with God and sets the

---

28. Charles, *APOT*, 2:472-74; Klijn, "2 (Syriac Apocalypse of) Baruch," 1:615-16. Another view is held by Bogaert, who argues that the book was originally written in Greek for circulation in the dispersion, in his work, *Apocalypse de Baruch*, 1:378-80.

29. The "twenty-fifth year" of Jehoiakin in the opening verse (1:1-2a) makes no historical sense because the king was taken into exile at the age of eighteen in the first year of his reign in 597. Bogaert considers the length of time to represent that period of time following the fall in 70 CE and thus dates the book to about 95 CE (*Apocalypse de Baruch*, 1:294-95). In any case, the book is roughly contemporary with *4 Ezra* (Collins, *Apocalyptic Imagination*, 213).

30. Collins, *Apocalyptic Imagination*, 212; Nickelsburg, *Jewish Literature*, 281.

31. Collins proposes this sevenfold division, by taking the four seven-day fasts (9:1-2; 12:5; 21:1; 47:1-2) as the endings of the first, second, third, and fifth units, by taking two of the three addresses by Baruch to the congregation (31:1—34:1; 77:1-26) as the endings of the fourth, sixth units and the other address (44:1—46:7) as a concluding remark reinforced by the fast ending the fifth unit (47:1-2), and by leaving 78:1 to the end as an epilogue (*Apocalyptic Imagination*, 213). Klijn, too, agrees that the seven-day fast and the consolation by Baruch are two indicators to mark the end of a unit, in his work, "The Sources and the Redaction," 68. There is far less consensus about the precise demarcation (Murphy, *Structure and Meaning*, 11-29). The different proposed structures, however, basically follow the same approach. For example, Bogaert suggests his sevenfold structure as follows: 1:1—12:5; 13:1—20:6; 21:1—34:1; 35:1—47:1; 47:2—52:8; 53:1—77:17; 77:18—87:1 (*Apocalypse de Baruch*, 1:62). Sayler suggests her own as follows: 1:1—5:7; 6:1—20:6; 21:1—30:5; 31:1—43:3; 44:1—52:8; 53:1—76:5; 77:1—77:26 (*Have the Promises Failed?*).

32. Collins, *Apocalyptic Imagination*, 213.

33. Sayler, *Have the Promises Failed?*, 38. The terminology "distress-consolation" originates from an article by Breech, "These Fragments," 267-74.

agenda for the ensuing dialogue.³⁴ This unit contains the first extensive eschatological revelation of the apocalypse.³⁵ Hence, the unit is a transitional piece of the composition. It begins with a short introduction (21:2–3), then a prayer by Baruch (21:4–25) leading to a dialogue with God in which the theme of the unit is found (21:26—30:5). The dialogue first centers on how God would complete the work he had begun in creation (21:26—25:4), then on what would happen in the final days (26:1—30:5). Following the dialogue is an interpretative address by Baruch to the people (31:1—32:7), ending with a conversation (32:8—34:1).³⁶ The two monsters are found in the second part of the dialogue (29:4) as follows:

> And Behemoth will reveal itself from its place, and Leviathan will come from the sea, the two great monsters which I created on the fifth day of creation and which I shall have kept until that time. And they will be nourishment for all who are left.³⁷

Since it is of eschatological focus, the passage in which the two beasts occur recounts a great number of signs related to the end-time. The most obvious is the final tribulation that consists of twelve woes (26:1—28:2). They are mostly natural disasters and typical signs of doom in the Hebrew Bible and the *Sibylline Oracles*, for instance, wars, famine and pestilence.³⁸ Subsequently, there is a dialogue concerning theodicy leading to an eschatological scenario in which the Messiah will be revealed and the reign of God will come on earth (28:3—30:5). A prominent feature of the scenario is the sustenance theme running from 29:4 through to 29:8, which describes a sumptuous banquet for the inhabitants after the tribulations at the end of time. It is in this independent body of tradition that Leviathan and Behemoth appear first and foremost as nourishment for those who are left, prior to the production of many other delicacies at the feast. The role of the two monsters emphasizes the sustenance theme at the messianic banquet. On the other hand, contextually, the sustenance theme functions as a response to the challenges to theodicy raised by the prophet (28:3—29:3).

---

34. Willett, *Eschatology*, 101.

35. Collins, *Apocalyptic Imagination*, 218. Rowland agrees, too, that the unit is the first extended eschatological passage found in the book. But in his structure, the unit runs from chapter 24 through to chapter 30 (*Open Heaven*, 171).

36. Willett, *Eschatology*, 90.

37. The quotation adapts the translation of Klijn, "2 (Syriac Apocalypse of) Baruch," 1:615–52.

38. Collins, *Apocalyptic Imagination*, 218.

Thus, in the present context, the solution to theodicy is eschatology,[39] which Leviathan and Behemoth are there to articulate.

The account is much briefer than that in *4 Ezra*. It contains no account of the pair's separation or their abode, except the marine origin of Leviathan. Like *4 Ezra* 6:49-52, however, it emphasizes the preservation of the pair for the present against their eventual role in the messianic banquet. Also, it recounts the creation of the pair on the fifth day, which is, though not explicitly stated in the account in *4 Ezra*, assumed in its larger context as the *Hexaemeron* places the origin of the pair on the fifth day (6:47). Whilst the present account omits these details about the pair, it shares common principal themes with *4 Ezra*. It is likely that the two accounts represent two forms of a single tradition drawn on by both authors.[40] In *4 Ezra*, the Leviathan-Behemoth account highlights the enormity of the beasts, since the final editor employed it to illustrate divine greatness, in order to contrast the inertia of God in the fall of Jerusalem. In *2 Baruch*, the account includes fewer details about the pair but rather emphasizes the eschatological theme, since the final editor took up the account to illustrate the scenario of the messianic banquet.

To summarize, the Leviathan-Behemoth accounts in *4 Ezra* and in *2 Baruch* represent two facades of the same tradition, since both carry the same principal themes. In *4 Ezra*, the account is found in a strategic position in the creation context as a piece of evidence for the greatness of the pair, which in turn reveals the superiority of God who has mastered the pair from the beginning. In *2 Baruch*, the account occurs as the first element of the sustenance theme that makes up the messianic banquet scenario, which in turn constitutes the larger eschatological context. In *4 Ezra*, the account functions as a critical element of creation that contextually stresses the flow that culminates in the theodicy related question (6:59). In *2 Baruch*, the account accentuates the end-time with its eschatological theme, which in the present context is a solution to theodicy (28:3—29:3).

1 ENOCH 60:7-10, 24AB

The *Similitudes of Enoch*, also known as the *Parables of Enoch*, is the second volume (chs. 37-71) of the larger Enochic tradition.[41] The references to the

---

39. Willett, *Eschatology*, 120.
40. Charles, *Apocalypse of Baruch*, 53 n. 4; Bogaert, *Apocalypse de Baruch*, 2:63.
41. See ch. 2, pp. 39-40, nn. 100-106.

Parthian invasion of Palestine in 40 BCE (56:5-7) and to the symbolic hot springs as judgment of the kings (67:5-13) indicate that the book was written in about the mid first century, prior to the Jewish revolt of 66-70 CE.[42] The numerous "son of man" references (e.g., 39:1, 5; 42:2) also support this date since a Jewish apocalyptist would be very unlikely to take up the expression as a key motif after it had become a recognized christological title for the evangelists (Matt 19:28; 25:31).[43]

The apocalypse contains three large blocks of revelatory discourse (chs. 38-44; chs. 45-57; chs. 58-69). The account of Leviathan and Behemoth is found in the early part of the last discourse (60:7-10, 24ab) and reads as follows:[44]

> And on that day two monsters will be separated from one another: a female monster, whose name (is) Leviathan, to dwell in the depths of the sea above the springs of the waters; and the name of the male (is) Behemoth, who occupies with his breast an immense desert, named Dendayn, on the east of the garden where the chosen and righteous dwell, where my great-grandfather was received, who was the seventh from Adam, the first man whom the Lord of Spirits made. And I asked that other angel to show me the power of those monsters, how they were separated on one day and thrown, one into the depths of the sea, and the other on to the dry ground of the desert. And he said to me: "Son of Man, you here wish to know what is secret ... And the angel of peace who was with me said to me: "These two monsters are prepared for the great day of the Lord (when) they shall turn into food.[45]

42. Collins, *Apocalyptic Imagination*, 178.

43. Ibid.

44. There are two striking displacements in the context from chapters 59 to 60 that are related to the present account. Nickelsburg notes that there is a gap between the question posed at the end of the first piece of the Leviathan-Behemoth material (60:7-10) and the response to that question (60:24ab), and that 60:1-10 separates two blocks of astronomical lore in 59:1-3 and 60:11-23. He proposes that by relocating 60:11-23 immediately after 59:1-3, and thus by reuniting 60:7-10 and 60:24ab, one can recover the original picture in which the two blocks of cosmological lore (59:1-3 and 60:11-23) work together coherently and so do the two references to Leviathan and Behemoth (60:7-10 and 60:24ab) in presenting the overall message in a logical sequence. Until any new discovery, this proposal is the best way to restore the original picture of the two chapters. See Nickelsburg, *Jewish Literature*, 219.

45. The quotation adapts Knibb's translation (*Ethiopic Enoch*, 2:143-48). The only exception is v. 24ab, which adapts the translation of E. Isaac who follows the reading of manuscript Tana 9, "1 (Ethiopic Apocalypse of) Enoch," 1:42. The text of v. 24c and v. 25 is out of order in the majority of the manuscripts because of the accidental omission

The introduction to the third revelatory discourse (58:1–6) defines the primary theme of the whole unit as dealing with the fate of the righteous and the chosen. Following the introduction is an episodic account of cosmology, in which the seer saw the secrets of the lights and of the flashes of lightning (59:1–3) and later learned from "the other angel" a great deal of speculation about heavenly secrets (60:11–23). Then, there are three eschatological visions. The first is a scene of the heavenly throne upon which sitting the Head of Days (60:1–6). The second is the emergence of Leviathan and Behemoth "on that day" (60:7–10, 24ab) concluding with a judgment reference (61:24c–25). The third includes the angels measuring the righteous in preparation for the final judgment (61:1–5) leading to the elevation of "the Chosen One" together with the praises of the heavenly host (61:6–13). The ensuing passage centers on the son of man figure and the judgment (62:7, 9, 14; 63:11; 69:26, 27; 70:1; 71:14, 17).[46]

The account contains the same core themes as those in *4 Ezra* 6:49–52. It begins with the separation of Leviathan and Behemoth from one another (v. 7) and concludes with their function in the messianic banquet (v. 24b), which is, in reality, another facet of the theme of their eschatological reappearance. Since these materials relate to Noah and the flood, the Leviathan-Behemoth account (60:7–10, 24ab) and some other passages (65:1–12; 67:1—68:5) are generally considered to be fragments of the lost book of Noah.[47] The transmission of the ancient mythic figures in this context reflects the likelihood that there had been an understanding of a cyclic bond between the creation and the eschatological motifs in the Leviathan-Behemoth tradition.

The most obvious element from which to gain an insight into the context of the account is the phrase with which the unit opens. "On that day" is a common biblical expression usually referring to the "Day of the Lord" in the Hebrew Bible (e.g., Isa 2:20; Amos 8:9–14; 5:18–27) and to

---

of some words in v. 24 and their subsequent insertion in v. 25 (Knibb, *Ethiopic Enoch*, 2:148).

46. In these occurrences, "that Son of Man" or "this Son of Man" refers back to the figure in human likeness in 46:1. See ch. 2, p. 42, n. 113.

47. Stone notes that in the *Similitudes*, at the very least, these three passages belong to the lost book of Noah ("Apocalyptic Literature," 402 n. 103). Chapter 69 is also considered part of this non-extant piece of work (Collins, *Apocalyptic Imagination*, 180 n. 11). Apart from the *Similitudes*, chapters 6–11 and 106–107 in *1 Enoch* are considered the major Noachic materials (Stone, "Noah, Books of," 12:1198). For more discussions about this work, see Charles, *Book of Enoch*, 24–26; Nickelsburg, *Jewish Literature*, 219–21.

the "day of judgment" in apocalyptic literature in the post-exilic period.[48] The eschatological idea reverberates at the end of the account. In v. 24, the majority of the Ethiopic manuscripts have the two monsters prepared in accordance with "the greatness of the Lord."[49] The only exception is Tana 9,[50] which reads "for the great day of the Lord." This text is characterized by many errors by way of misspellings, negligence in the use of case endings and the omission or addition of anomalous words and phrases.[51] On this occasion, however, the text does not seem to have been susceptible to such errors but rather represents a full reading and is thus reliable.[52] Hence, the eschatological focus of the account is evident in "On that day" at the beginning and "the great day of the Lord" at the end. The larger context in which the account is found supports this focus too, since both the vision of the heavenly throne (60:1–6) and that of the heavenly judgment upon the righteous (61:1–13) are set in an eschatological framework.

The verbal tenses employed in the account reflect tension within the tradition between an eschatological reading and a primordial reading. Manuscript BM 491 leads some to argue that "On that day" refers to the day of the creation of the world, since in this text the opening verb occurs in the imperfect, and therefore, Leviathan and Behemoth "were separated."[53] However, a primordial reference to "that day" is hardly ever found in apocalyptic literature, and BM 491 is unlikely to contain the original Ethiopic reading.[54] It is more likely that "On that day" refers to the end-time, as the phrase usually does in an eschatological context, and, accordingly, that would mean the pair "will be separated," as translated in the Ethiopic version.[55] Then, a tension exists between this separation at the end-time and the separation in v. 9, in which the two monsters "were separated" and "thrown" into their territories "on one day." Both of these verbs are in the

---

48. Russell, *Method and Message*, 94–95.

49. One of the examples is Rylands Ethiopic MS 23, which is the base-text from which Knibb produces his edition and translation (*Ethiopic Enoch*, 2:32, 47, 148).

50. The text is one of the four earliest extant manuscripts dated to the sixteenth century or earlier, representing the text-type that Charles designates as Eth 1. The other three are BM 485, Berl and Abb 55. See Knibb, *Ethiopic Enoch*, 2:27.

51. Knibb, *Ethiopic Enoch*, 2:32.

52. Whitney, *Two Strange Beasts*, 49.

53. Charles, *APOT*, 2:224.

54. Knibb, *Ethiopic Enoch*, 2:143.

55. Black et al., *Book of Enoch*, 56, 227; Knibb, *Ethiopic Enoch*, 2:143.

perfect tense in the Ethiopic text and are thus, apparently, references to a primordial event.

In both the *Enuma Elish* and the Baal Cycle, the fight between the mythic figures is a primordial battle through which the creation of the world happens. In Isa 27:1, taking up the tradition, the prophet shifted the primordial combat at the time of creation into an eschatological battle at the end-time, the latter of which, in particular, spreads widely in rabbinic writings (e.g., *Midr. Lev. Rab.* 13.3; *Midr. Ps.* 18.23). According to Gunkel, this shift indicates that the ancient myth had undergone a transformation in which the importance of the battle between the pair shifted from the creation context into an eschatological one,[56] which in turn reflects the temporal fluidity of the *Chaoskampf* applicable to primordial myths, contemporary events and eschatological concerns in biblical tradition.[57] Here in the account, however, the separation theme is symbiotic in nature; it is both eschatological and primeval. This mélange indicates that the account appears not to fall under the influence of the temporal shift but to remain in the original cyclic nature of the Baal Epic, in which endings and new beginnings are set in continuous rotations and correspondingly are emergences of chaotic forces and their defeats in new creations. Of the related Second Temple writings, only this passage has this uniqueness. Therefore, it is likely that the present Leviathan-Behemoth account adapts a tradition that is rawer than that of the other two passages. Since the focus is on the end-time in the larger context, "On that day" the two monsters will participate in an eschatological expectation.

The second theme is how Leviathan and Behemoth function in their final return (v. 24ab). In v. 9, the seer asked the angel to show him the power of the beasts and how they were separated on one day and allocated to their realms. Based on their recovery of this Noahic chapter,[58] some scholars comment that the answer to the seer's question is not found in the ensuing lines until v. 24ab, in which the angel of peace said, "These two monsters are prepared for the great day of the Lord (when) they shall turn into food."[59] Whilst this comment is correct, this verse is also a further explanation of

---

56. Gunkel, *Creation and Chaos*, 360, 362, 367.
57. Ibid., 113–14.
58. See ch. 3, p. 69, n. 44.
59. This is the answer to the seer's question in v. 9 (Knibb, *Ethiopic Enoch*, 2:148; Charles, *Book of Enoch*, 118; Black et al., *Book of Enoch*, 228). It appears that originally v. 24 entails a certain portion of information concerning the eschatological meal with reference to the seer's question, which is now lost (Knibb, *Ethiopic Enoch*, 2:148).

the immediate response found in v. 10, right after the question, in which the angel said, "Son of Man, you here wish to know what is secret." The twofold answer raises two relevant points. Firstly, since it is a secret, the separation of the pair together with the allotment of their territories belongs to the category of cosmological matter juxtaposed with a series of heavenly secrets found in the previous passages (59:1–3; 60:11–23). Secondly, having said that that was secret, the angel did not go further to explain why but shifted the topic to how the pair would be prepared for the great day of the Lord. Hence, what is emphasized here is the role of Leviathan and Behemoth at the end-time as opposed to their origin. This represents a shift of concern from creation to eschatology.

In between the two themes, there are details concerning the two monsters found exclusively in the account in *1 Enoch*. Firstly, out of the biblical, pseudepigraphical and rabbinic writings only the present passage states explicitly that Leviathan is female and Behemoth is male, which together appear to represent a matched couple of two monstrous species. A possible reflection of this monstrous pair is found in the *Apoc. Ab.* 10:10, in which the angel Iaoel is appointed to hold the "Leviathans." The relationship between number and gender comes clear in a rabbinic debate preserved in *Gen. Rab.* 7:4, redacted in approximately 425 CE. There, citing R. 'Aha, R. Pinhas notes that the plural *tanninim* in Gen 1:21 refers to Behemoth and Leviathan, who have no mates. A retort from R. Šim 'ôn b. Laqîš follows immediately, arguing that Behemoth has a mate but no desire, since "the sinews of his thighs are knit together" (Job 40:17). A more coherent interpretation of the monster's number and gender is found in an important rabbinic piece redacted about a century later. In *B. Bat.* 74b, the opening statement tells us that all creatures were created in both genders. On this basis, the passage goes further to refer to "Leviathan the fleeing serpent" and "Leviathan the twisting serpent" in Isa 27:1 as a pair, male and female respectively, where the Holy One castrated the male and slew the female and preserved her body in salt for the righteous in the world to come, since the beasts would have destroyed the whole world should they have coupled together.[60]

---

60. From the modern scholarly point of view, the two occurrences of Leviathan in Isa 27:1 do not represent two figures but the same beast for the purpose of emphasis, since they are in parallel. Under the influence of *B. Bat.* 74b, however, later Jewish commentators commonly referred to them as a pair of Leviathans, male and female (Whitney, *Two Strange Beasts*, 117 n. 64).

From these writings, it appears that from the Second Temple period to the first few centuries CE, there had been a general idea in Jewish tradition that Leviathan and Behemoth were created as two species with each having both genders. Since the plural *tanninim* in Gen 1:21, the plural "Leviathans" in the *Apoc. Ab.* 10:10 and the double occurrences of "Leviathan" in the parallel phrases in Isa 27:1, there appears to have been a tradition of referring to one monstrous species in the plural as a couple, male and female. On the other hand, there had been tensions in describing the gender of the two beasts. In the present account, both Leviathan and Behemoth are grammatically feminine. In *2 Baruch*, both figures have third masculine singular pronouns.[61] It is only in the passage in *1 Enoch* that Leviathan and Behemoth are explicitly stated as being female and male, despite the fact both are grammatically feminine. For this reason, the account of Leviathan as female and Behemoth as male is one but not the only one of the traditional variants concerning the two beasts renowned particularly in the Second Temple period. After considering all the evidence, it is very likely that this expression originates from the present account.

Secondly, the place occupied by Behemoth's breast is "an immense desert, named Dendayn, on the east of the garden where the chosen and righteous dwell" (60:8). Where Dendayn was is contentious. One important perspective is provided by Milik, who suggests that in the Ethiopic text, "Dendayn" corresponds to "Dudael" in 10:4, a place of desert where the rebellious angel Azazel was incarcerated. Then, he argues that the reading of this prison in the Greek Codex Panopolitanus, "Dadouel" is superior to "Dudael" in the Ethiopic text and supported by the Greek fragments of *1 Enoch* found in Syncellus. Comparing "Dadouel" to the Aramaic *Dadduʾel*, "the twin breasts of El," Milik notes that "Dendayn" is a variant form of *deddain*, "twin breasts."[62] There is not enough evidence for the connection between "Dendayn" and "Dudael," however.[63] More importantly, it is highly unlikely that a place once used for incarcerating the rebellious angel would become a dwelling place for the chosen and righteous and the ancestors of Enoch.

While Dendayn is complicated etymologically, the account has a great deal of information concerning its locality; it is "on the east of the garden where the chosen and righteous dwell, where my great-grandfather was

---

61. Whitney, *Two Strange Beasts*, 51 n. 72.
62. Milik, *Books of Enoch*, 29–30 nn. 1–2.
63. Knibb, *Ethiopic Enoch*, 2:144; Black et al., *Book of Enoch*, 134, 227.

received, who was the seventh from Adam, the first man whom the Lord of Spirits made." Emil G. Hirsch argues that the name "Dendayn" is a corruption of the word "Nod" and therefore reads the "land of Nod."[64] According to Gen 4:16, Cain was assigned the "land of Nod," which is on the east of the garden, too, to inhabit.[65] At the east of the garden of Eden, God placed "the cherubim, and a flaming sword which turned every way, to guard the way to the tree of life" (Gen 3:24). Thus, from the beginning, the east of the garden is a place with God's protection and blessing and the home for many ancient Jewish fathers.[66] Until any new discovery, the "land of Nod" is the best candidate for "Dendayn" because a venue with divine protection fits the criteria for a dwelling place for the chosen, the righteous and great Jewish figures. On the other hand, it is clear from the context that the whole block of data culminates with Enoch because only he can be the seventh from Adam. For this reason, the Leviathan and Behemoth motif had long been an important piece of material, since in this Noahic fragment, it functions as an element to illustrate the superior status of Enoch, who dwelt in the same place as Behemoth.

To sum up, like the Leviathan-Behemoth account in *4 Ezra*, the account in *1 Enoch* contains the core elements of the myth that highlight the power of God throughout human history, which are: the separation of the two beasts and their role in the messianic banquet. The beginning phrase, "On that day," the angelic response and the eschatological focus of the larger context indicate that the account points towards the end-time. The blend of the verbal future and perfect in the separation theme appears to be a surviving vestige of the cyclic nature of the Baal Epic. Of the three Leviathan-Behemoth accounts, only the account in *1 Enoch* describes Leviathan as female and Behemoth as male. The connection between Enoch and Behemoth shows the incorporation of the myth into the Noahic fragment, which in turn indicates the widespread promulgation of the Leviathan-Behemoth tradition at that time.

---

64. Charles, *Book of Enoch*, 115 n. 8; *APOT*, 2:224; Isaac, "1 (Ethiopic Apocalypse of) Enoch," 1:40.
65. Charles, *APOT*, 2:224.
66. Ibid.

APOCALYPSE OF ABRAHAM 10:10; 21:4

The *Apocalypse of Abraham* is similar to *4 Ezra* and *2 Baruch* in many ways. It was originally written in Aramaic or Hebrew and later translated into Greek and is now extant mainly in Slavonic recensions.[67] It is very likely that it was composed at about the end of the first century CE, since it contains a great deal of discussion concerning the fall of Jerusalem leading to questions of theodicy (chs. 27–31) as in the other two apocalypses.[68] The two references to Leviathan occur in the first and third units of the second part of the book (chs. 9–32). The first unit (9:1—12:2) and the second (12:3—15:4) together constitute an expansion of Gen 15 describing how Abraham followed the instruction to offer a sacrifice on the mountain.[69] In the first unit, during Abraham's journey to Mount Horeb, the angel Iaoel appeared to him and delivered a fourfold monologue (10:5—11:6) each ending with an exhortation to boldness (10:7, 15a, 17; 11:6). Leviathans (10:10) occur in the second monologue as follows (10:8–15a):

> I am Iaoel and I was called so by him who causes those with me on the seventh expanse, on the firmament, to shake, a power through the medium of his ineffable name in me. I am the one who has been charged according to his commandment, to restrain the threats of the living creatures of the cherubim against one another, and I teach those who carry the song through the medium of man's night of the seventh hour. I am appointed to hold the Leviathans, because through me is subjugated the attack and menace of every reptile. I am ordered to loosen Hades and to destroy those who wondered at the dead. I am the one who ordered your father's house to be burned with him, for he honored the dead. I am sent to you now to bless you and the land which he whom you have called the Eternal One has prepared for you. For your sake I have indicated the way of the land. Stand up, Abraham, go boldly, be very joyful and rejoice.[70]

Prior to this exhortation to Abraham (v. 15a), the passage contains a self-description by Iaoel that lists his angelic commissions and powers

---

67. See ch. 2, p. 45, nn. 125–28.

68. See ch. 2, p. 45, n. 129.

69. See ch. 2, p. 45, nn. 130–31.

70. The quotation adapts the translation of Rubinkiewicz and Lunt, "Apocalypse of Abraham," 1:694.

across the realms of the universe.⁷¹ Iaoel's commissions to loosen Hades and to destroy the cult of the dead reflect his infernal and earthly powers respectively, the latter of which finds an example in the case of Abraham's father (vv. 11–12).⁷² His power in heaven is more descriptive; he is commissioned to restrain the threats of the living creatures of the cherubim against one another,⁷³ to teach them to sing the song of peace⁷⁴ and to hold the Leviathans as he is to subjugate the attack and menace of every reptile. The most intriguing piece of imagery here is the living creatures menacing one another. This idea is found nowhere else in Jewish literature but exclusively in the present account and in 18:8–10 as follows:

> And when they finished singing, they would look at one another and threaten one another. And it came to pass when the angel who was with me saw that they were threatening each other, he left me and went running to them. And he turned the face of each living creature from the face which was opposite it so that they could not see each other's faces threatening each other.

For the most part, *Apoc. Ab.* 18 is an interpretive reading of Ezek 1 with additional features drawn from Isa 6.⁷⁵ The four fiery living creatures (v. 3), the chariot with fiery wheels full of eyes round about (v. 12) and the fiery throne and the collective sanctification like the voice of a single man

---

71. For information concerning Iaoel, see ch. 2, p. 47, nn. 139–41.

72. The Slavonic verb *diviti sja* means "wonder" or "be astonished at" and is often used to render *thaumazein* in Greek (Rubinkiewicz and Lunt, "Apocalypse of Abraham," 1:694 n. j). Since the Greek verb can mean "honor" or "venerate," here the Slavonic term is very likely to refer to the cult of the dead.

73. The "cherubim" is an apposition explaining "living creatures" (Rubinkiewicz and Lunt, "Apocalypse of Abraham," 1:694 n. f).

74. In their translation (vv. 6–7), Box and Landsman omit "medium" and invert the phrase to read "and teach those (living creatures) who carry Him (the throne of glory) the song of the seventh hour of the night of man," citing a number of rabbinic and biblical texts as evidence (*Apocalypse of Abraham*, 47 nn. 6–7). Rubinkiewicz and Lunt note that this treatment requires justification ("The Apocalypse of Abraham," 1:694 n. h). Until any new discoveries, however, it appears to be the best way to make sense out of this cryptic reference, since there are enough parallels to the idea of angelic praise and prayer at specific hours (Stone, *Armenian Apocrypha*, 56–57). The more important parallel is the only other reference to the living creatures threatening each other found in the same apocalypse (18:8–11), which, though without a note of "the seventh hour," basically carries the same idea (v. 11). The closet parallel to "the seventh hour" in the present context is the reference to the heavenly praise at the seventh hour of the day preserved in the Armenian text (Stone, *Armenian Apocrypha*, 65).

75. Halperin, *Faces of the Chariot*, 108–9.

(vv. 13–14) have close parallels in Ezek 1 (vv. 5–12, 15–25, 26–28). Like the author of the apocalypse in question, Ezekiel identified the living creatures as cherubim (10:15–22). Although Ezekiel did not recount the creatures threatening each other, the exilic prophet left a remote clue of this obscure motif. In Ezek 1:12, the living creatures mobilized in the following distinctive way:

> And each (creature) went straightforward; wherever the spirit would go, they went, without turning as they went.

The wheels beside the living creatures moved in a similar manner (1:17) as follows:

> Whey they (wheels) went, they went in any of their four directions without turning as they went.

The same description of the wheels occurs again in 10:11. Also, at the end of the chapter (10:22), there is the following precise depiction of the living creatures:

> They (the living creatures) went every one straightforward.

Certainly, the living creatures are too enigmatic to delineate in this brief investigation. However, the Ezekiel passages do reveal an underlying feature of the living creatures, namely, being, or moving, straight forward without turning. There seems to have been a tradition that the living creatures either function appropriately when they go/look straight forward or cause tension going/looking otherwise. This observation could, possibly, explain why in the *Apoc. Ab.* 18, the angel turned the face of each living creature from the face which was opposite it in order to avoid calamities (v. 10), and why the creatures had no problems singing when, presumably, they were not looking at one another and were going/looking straight forward (v. 8).[76] In the appropriate position, their primary function is to sing (10:9; 18:8), which, is the duty of the cherubim in Rev 4:6b–8, too, which in turn shows influence from the cherubim in Ezekiel (10:15–22). Whilst bound to the divine praise, the living creatures appear to have some sort of

---

76. A major solution as to why the living creatures threaten each other is provided by Box, who notes that "the underlying idea of this strange representation seems to be that of emulation and rivalry (in service)," by citing the *Midr. Tanh.* on Gen 2:4 and Job 25:2 as pieces of evidence (*Apocalypse of Abraham*, 62–63 n. 13). But this argument cannot be substantiated.

fundamentally savage and chaotic nature that needs vigilant monitoring.[77] This conjecture is consistent with the representation in the larger context in which Iaoel described himself by emphasizing his control over a series of sinister forces including the following Leviathans and Hades.

It is highly likely that the plural Leviathans represent a couple, a female and a male.[78] His angelic power to "hold the Leviathans" comes through his authority over reptiles. Leviathan is the archetypal reptile. Of the biblical and pseudepigraphical writings, it is only in this account that Leviathan is explicitly described in relation to reptiles. According to the *Book of Raziel* (fol. 4a), the name of the archangel Michael is a powerful charm against reptiles (cf. Lueken, p. 28), and, as the prince of snow, the archangel belongs to the element of water (*Deut. Rab.* 5.12), to whom all reptiles and Leviathan, the sea monster par excellence, are subject.[79] In the cosmological battle in Rev 12, Michael cast down from heaven the dragon, which, as shown later in Rev 13:1, was a seven-headed beast and thus identical to Leviathan. Michael's defeat of the dragon in Rev 12 and his name as a powerful charm against reptiles in the kabbalistic sources in principal carry the same motif, which in turn reflects a tradition of the archangelic defeat of Leviathan. The plural Leviathans, their implied identification as the prototypal reptiles and their close connection to the angel Iaoel in the current passage are all unique from most accounts of the monsters in the related passages. For this reason, the present account appears to originate from a variant tradition about the mythic pair. The final editor said little about the details of the Leviathans but inserted the reference to the dreadful couple, as the last celestial species, through the control of which Iaoel addressed his authority in heaven. It is in this contextual culmination that the Leviathans demonstrate their significant roles in the cosmological context.

It is not clear why Iaoel had to hold the Leviathans until the second occurrence of the beast in 21:4, which reads as follows:

> And I saw there the sea and its islands, and its cattle and its fish, and Leviathan and his realm and his bed and his lairs, and the world which lay upon him, and his motions and the destruction he caused the world.

---

77. Halperin, *Faces of the Chariot*, 113.
78. With respect to the beast's number and gender, see pp. 73–74.
79. Box and Landsman, *Apocalypse of Abraham*, 47–48 n. 8.

Following the expansion of Gen 15, the third unit (15:5—29:22) combines Abraham's heavenly journey (15:5—21:7) and a historical revelation (22:1—29:22). The Leviathan account comes at the end of the heavenly journey. The celestial journey comes to its pinnacle in chapter 19, since from there onwards Abraham stood on the seventh firmament upon which he gazed down through the successive veils of the different firmaments to discover the substances of both the heaven and the earth below. In chapter 21, remaining at the same vantage point, the patriarchal father saw various elements of "the terrestrial world beneath the sky" divided into smaller units, each of which begins with an introductory phrase, "I saw there" (vv. 3, 4, 5, 6, 7). These units are related to life, creatures and sources on earth apart from the cosmological concern in v. 4.

In a sense, this passage is closer to the Leviathan-Behemoth accounts in *4 Ezra*, *2 Baruch* and *1 Enoch* than it is to 10:10 in the same apocalypse, because it shows an interest in the dwelling place of Leviathan as do those three. The most striking similarity is found in *1 En.* 60:7, in which Leviathan is assigned "to dwell in the depths of the sea above the springs of the waters." Here, the oceanic nature of the beast is evident in the parallel of Leviathan and his realm, his bed and his lairs to the sea and its islands, its cattle and its fish. Upon the sea monster lay the "world," which, literally, is the "inhabited world." The inhabited world founded upon Leviathan is not an uncommon concept and is found in the later rabbinic literature. *Pirqe Rabbi Eliezer* 9, a Jewish text dated to approximately the eighth century CE, reports that Leviathan dwells in the lower waters and between his two fins stands the middle bolt of the earth.[80] In his commentary on Gen 1:1, Ibn Ezra (1089–1164 CE) notes that the idea of the world being created upon Leviathan exists in a midrash, which bases its reading on Job 40:19, in which it refers to "the first of the works of God" as being Leviathan.[81] Hence, there had been a tradition that Leviathan resided over the deep waters and provided the foundation upon which the world was created. Being the underpinning of the world, his movements would naturally cause the destruction of the world. This is the reason that holding Leviathan is a significant task that requires massive power, which in turn shows the pre-eminence of Iaoel as he is the one appointed to do this and has, presumably, been endowed with the power to execute this task.

---

80. Herr, "Pirkei de-Rabbi Eliezer," 13:558–59.
81. Whitney, *Two Strange Beasts*, 115 n. 57.

To summarize, with respect to the power of the monsters, the two Leviathan passages in the *Apocalypse of Abraham* agree with each other and with the Leviathan-Behemoth accounts in *4 Ezra*, *2 Baruch* and *1 Enoch*. The second passage (21:4), though without Behemoth, comes from the same tradition as the three accounts of the pair since it parallels those three in describing the watery nature of Leviathan. The first passage (10:10) is likely to have originated from a variant tradition, since 'Leviathans' is a plural, their being the archetypal reptile and how they relate to Iaoel are unique in the related Second Temple Apocrypha. However, these two passages share in common the notion that Leviathan is the quintessence of enormity and power.

LADDER OF JACOB 6:13

The fragmentary pseudepigraphon called the *Ladder of Jacob* is complicated in most aspects. Known only from the medieval Slavonic *Tolkovaja Paleja*, or Explanatory Palaia, the text is preserved in a number of versions. The Explanatory Palaia is a retelling of the Hebrew Bible stories, in which the Slavic editors made considerable changes in the order of the sentences and paragraphs and, most importantly, inserted anti-Jewish commentaries on the narratives.[82] In the history of the Palaia text, the work developed in two recensions. Recension A is attested in three manuscripts, and since it lacks the materials normally assigned to chapters 6 to 7, it is the shorter recension. Recension B is attested in thirteen manuscripts. It contains the materials allotted to chapters 6 and 7 as well as some others not found in the shorter version, and thus, is the longer recension.[83] The date and provenance of the work are uncertain.[84]

---

82. Lunt, "Ladder of Jacob," 2:401.

83. Ibid., 2:402–3.

84. There are two major pieces of speculation on the topic. Lunt proposes that the work stemmed from "a Jewish story composed in Jewish-Gk. for a Palestinian audience," which was transmitted through Byzantine circles where it was then translated into a Greek copy for a Slavonic church by about 900 CE and eventually found its way into the Palaia in the thirteenth to fifteenth centuries CE ("Ladder of Jacob," 2:404 n. 3). In studying the textual transmission of the work, Pennington suggests that since the Greek Palaia is normally dated to the eighth or ninth century, "a Greek Ladder must be pushed back into the 7th or 8th cent. at the latest, and it may well be very much earlier" (Pennington, "Ladder of Jacob," 453). Furthermore, in a recent study, by pointing out the connection between the pseudepigraphon and rabbinic exegetical traditions and by noting the Hebrew words surviving in transcription in the text, Kugel argues that the work is more

The *Ladder of Jacob* is an elaboration of Jacob's dream at Bethel (Gen 28:11–22). The first two chapters retell the vision/dream and Jacob's prayer in response to it. The third and fourth chapters introduce the archangel Sariel, who provides an interpretation of the dream in the fifth to the sixth chapters. The seventh chapter purports to be a continuation of the interpretation but is a Christian addition, at least in part, inserted into the apocryphon when it was incorporated into the Palaia.[85] The section on Leviathan occurs near the end of the angelic interpretation in 6:13 as follows:

> And the Lord will pour out his wrath against Leviathan the sea-dragon; he will kill the lawless Falkon with the sword, because he will raise the wrath of the God of gods by his pride.[86]

Leviathan is called "the lawless Falkon." Taking up the descriptions of Leviathan in Isa 27:1, the "fleeing," or "twisting," serpent, Horace Lunt argues that the Hebrew epithet, *nāḥāš ăqallātôn*, had been taken as a proper name and transcribed into Greek as *kalthōn*, with the omission of the initial *ayin*, which, through a mechanical transposition of letters, turned into *Thalkōn*, which, due to the east Slavic confusion of the letters *theta* and *phi*, in turn became Falkon.[87] Then, Lunt notes that the pagan god Falkon in the apocryphal *Life of St. Pancratius*, the first bishop of Taormina, possibly had an influence on the enigmatic name.[88] Until any new discoveries, this argument best explains the origin of the name Falkon.

This conjecture concerning the connection between the two passages finds support in their common expressions. Both the barrenness of the storehouses, earthquakes in the present context (6:10–12) and the beginning phrase, "In that day," in Isa 27 are marks of the eschatological context. Both passages describe the figure using parallel phrases. In Isa 27:1, Leviathan is depicted as "the fleeing serpent," "the twisting serpent" and "the dragon that is in the sea." Here, the figure is described as "the sea-dragon" and "the lawless Falkon." On both occasions, the Lord will kill Leviathan with the "sword." For this reason, in usage, the present passage reflects the same transformation of the combat tradition from the creation context to the eschatological milieu as does Isa 27:1. On the other hand, while the

---

likely to be of a Semitic origin than of a Greek (*Ladder of Jacob*, 24 n. 21).

85. Lunt, "Ladder of Jacob," 2:404–5.

86. The quotation, also the citations elsewhere, adapt the enumeration system of eclectic translation provided by Lunt, "Ladder of Jacob," 2:410.

87. Lunt, "Ladder of Jacob," 2:404.

88. Ibid.

passage reflects the influence of Isa 27:1 in its mode of expression, it also shows an affinity to the *Apoc. Ab.* 10:10 in tradition. Here, the contextual relationship of the reptile swarm (6:11) to God's defeat of Leviathan echoes Iaoel's appointment to hold the Leviathans through his power to subjugate "the attack and menace of every reptile" in the latter passage. This propinquity shows that the two passages are closely related in terms of tradition.

Moreover, the structure of Sariel's interpretation of the dream demonstrates how the Leviathan passage works in the apocalypse. In the first unit of the interpretation (5:1–11), in congruence with the representations of the ladder and of the human faces standing there (vv. 1–4),[89] the "four ascents" (vv. 7, 9) and the "four busts" (vv. 10–11) reflect an adaptation of the four-kingdom motif found in Dan 2, 7 and the *Sib. Or.* 4:49–101,[90] and thus represent Babylon, Medea-Persia, Greece and Edom. This representation foretells the end of Edomite rule since the related haggadic texts so interpret with reference to Obad 1:4.[91] The second unit (5:12–17) makes clear that what is at stake is the eschatological assurance of the end of the current political power, namely, the Roman Empire, since Esau symbolized Rome then (*4 Ezra* 6:8–10).[92] The unit concludes, in vv. 16–17, quoting Gen 15:13–14, which, in forecasting the exile of Jacob's descendants, assures a judgment on Edom consistent with the haggadic texts on the one hand, and, on the other, alludes to the enslavement of the Jews under Roman

---

89. In v. 7, "this place will be made desolate by the four ascents . . ." It is not clear whether "this place" is singular or plural due to the corruption of the text (Lunt, "Ladder of Jacob," 2:409 n. 5b). In the text, however, there appears to be an identification of the site of the dream/vision with that of the temple. This is not only because the site is described as the "House of God" in the narrative of Jacob's dream (2:4) as Bethel is so identified in Gen 28:17–19, but because, more importantly, as the argument carries on, it is clear that the venue of the dream is closely associated to the Jerusalem temple, with the desolations of "this place" by the "four ascents" alluding to the destructions of the temple. The identification is also found in rabbinic literature (*b. Sanh.* 95b and *Pirqe R. El.* 35).

90. The reading of the term in v. 7 is debatable. In his translation, Lunt takes up the Slavonic instrumental plural *vŭsxody*, which means "ascents" ("Ladder of Jacob," 2:409 n. 5d). Pennington adapts the major reading *sxody*, and so translates as "descents" ("Ladder of Jacob," 459f.). It is not certain whether "busts" or "faces" in v. 11 is the original reading, since the text is corrupt (Lunt, "Ladder of Jacob," 2:409 n. 5h). Whitney, citing a group of rabbinic haggadic interpretations of the dream as evidence (*Pesiq. Rab. Kah.* 23:2; *Midr. Exod. Rab.* 32:7; *Midr. Lev. Rab.* 29:2; especially *Pirqe R. El.* 35), is convincing in arguing that the angelic figures upon the ladder represent a series of earthly kingdoms rising and falling one by one (*Two Strange Beasts*, 81).

91. *Midr. Lev. Rab.* 29:2; also *Pesiq. Rab Kah.* 23:16; *Pirqe R. El.* 35.

92. Stone, *Fourth Ezra*, 161 n. 127.

control, which in turn suggests a date for the apocryphon after the destruction of the temple in 70 CE.[93]

The passage in question occurs near the end of the third unit (6:1–15). The material in vv. 5–15 is from an independent block found only in the long recension and is the original ending of the apocalypse. Beginning with the assurance of the mercy of the Most High (vv. 5–8), it recounts a list of eschatological woes that will befall the earth at the end-time, which are the barrenness of storehouses, the plague of reptiles and earthquakes (vv. 10–12). The eschatological theme concludes with the defeat of Leviathan by God (v. 13). In terms of contextual arrangement, the passage is similar to *2 Bar.* 26:1—30:5, in which, after a series of final tribulations comprising twelve woes (26:1—28:2), Leviathan and Behemoth occur as food for the righteous near the end of the eschatological context (29:4). A similar arrangement also takes place in *4 Ezra* 6, in which a list of eschatological woes (6:18–28) precedes the *Hexaemeron* (6:38–54) and has the Leviathan-Behemoth account inserted near the end (6:49–52) to contrast with the ensuing challenge to theodicy (6:59). Cataloguing the signs of the end-time is one of the features of apocalyptic literature. The barrenness of storehouses is found in *4 Ezra* 6:22; earthquake is more familiar (e.g., *Apoc. Ab.* 30; *2 Bar.* 27). Hence, from the allusion to the end of Edom to the assurance of the collapse of Rome, and to the signs of the end-time such as the infertile storehouses and earthquakes, there is a development of the eschatological theme in the angelic interpretation of the dream through the three units. The defeat of Leviathan stands as the final struggle of the eschatological order and thus takes the role of the contextual climax. The position of Leviathan matches the thematic shift at the end of the chapter (6:14–15) as follows:

> And then your justice will be revealed, Jacob, and that of your children who are to be after you (and) who will walk in your justice. And then your seed will sound the horn and all the kingdom of Edom will perish together with all the peoples of Moab.

The chapter concludes with the forecast of the vindication of Jacob's descendants and the promise of the judgment upon their enemies. The shift from the final struggle to the eschatological denouement points to the importance of Leviathan because the defeat of Leviathan marks the end of time.

---

93. Whitney, *Two Strange Beasts*, 82–83.

To summarize, *Lad. Jac.* 6:13 describes Leviathan in a manner similar to that in Isa 27:1, and its mysterious name "Falkon" is likely to derive from the Hebrew "fleeing" or "twisting" serpent found in the latter passage. Therefore, Isa 27:1 has an influence on the current passage. The relationship of Leviathan to reptiles echoes Iaoel's power over the same species in the *Apoc. Ab.* 10:10, which in turn shows a common tradition for both passages. Finally, Leviathan is important because its defeat is the last act in the eschatological order.

CONCLUSION

This chapter aims to examine how Leviathan and Behemoth function in the apocalyptic writings of Second Temple Judaism. In *4 Ezra* 6:49–52, *2 Bar.* 29:4, and *1 En.* 60:7–10, 24ab, the two beasts appear together and their descriptions are relatively comprehensive. In *Apoc. Ab.* 10:10; 21:4 and *Lad. Jac.* 6:13, Leviathan is found alone and its portrayal is terse. The two groups of passages reflect two variants of the same tradition. Having studied them, this chapter concludes with the following points.

Firstly, the enormity of the beasts is common to all passages, but the emphases differ in each case. The first three accounts of the pair are in agreement in the principal themes of the two beasts that their separation signifies the beginning of the world, their return the end-time and they are preserved to become food for the righteous at the messianic banquet. *Fourth Ezra* and *1 Enoch* are, in particular, informative in their accounts of the abodes and origins of the two figures with Leviathan of watery origin and Behemoth of earthly origin. In *4 Ezra*, the limitation of "the seventh part" indicates the massiveness of the pair and the divine naming signifies their preeminent status. In *1 Enoch*, the common dwelling place of Behemoth and Enoch describes the superior status of the land monster. The aquatic essence of Leviathan appears to be particularly well-known as it is reflected in all the apocalypses under examination. In the *Apocalypse of Abraham*, Leviathan is the groundwork upon which the universe is created, and therefore, the beast's motion can cause the destruction of the world.

Secondly, everywhere it occurs the portrayal of the immensity of the beasts is a means by which the Second Temple apocalyptist highlights the ultimate power of God. In the first three accounts of the pair, God's ultimate authority is evident in his dominion over the universe from the beginning to the end of history, the separation and the return of Leviathan and

Behemoth. It is clear in *1 Enoch* that knowledge concerning details about the pair is a heavenly secret, not accessible to earthly beings. The same use of the monstrous power is found in the variant tradition in the *Apoc. Ab.* 10:10, in which the prominence of Iaoel is indicated by his power to hold the Leviathans, which in turn reflects the ultimate power of the one who grants the angel power.

Finally, it is through context that the Leviathan-Behemoth motif exhibits it nuances in each case. In *4 Ezra*, the two beasts are incorporated in the *Hexaemeron* with a comprehensive description of their greatness and power to show the supremacy of God, who takes charge of them, in order to contrast God's inertia at the fall of Jerusalem reported at the contextual climax (6:59). In *2 Baruch*, being the first element of the nourishment theme, the pair prompts the messianic banquet scenario with its function as food for the righteous at the end-time. In *1 Enoch*, being the second of the three eschatological visions, the emergence of the pair enhances the end-time theme with its distinctive cycle of separation. Due to their enigmatic nature, the two monsters belong to a class of heavenly secrets. In the *Apoc. Ab.* 10:10, Leviathans are found along with the cherubim as the last celestial species at the pinnacle of the cosmological context. In 21:4 of the same work, Leviathan is found as the foundation of the universe at the end of the heavenly journey of Abraham. In the *Ladder of Jacob*, the defeat of Leviathan as the final woe of the end-time brings to a head the eschatological theme. As a result, from the lens of Second Temple apocalyptic writings, Leviathan and Behemoth are above all creatures through his control of which God exhibits his ultimate sovereignty. In each occurrence, the two monsters, or Leviathan alone, stand in a strategic position in the eschatological context in order to enhance a specific theme.

4

An Examination of the Tripartite Ideology in Revelation 12 and 13

HAVING STUDIED THE RELATED accounts from the Second Temple period in chapter 3, it is clear that there was a formulaic pattern in which the apocalyptist then employed the Leviathan-Behemoth tradition, or that of Leviathan alone, with general agreement on the implications of the particulars and themes of the two mythic figures. These usages are not found in the Apocalypse of John, however. Scrutiny of Rev 13 indicates that in employing the Leviathan-Behemoth tradition, John dispensed with many of the characteristics of the motif and merely retained the primary framework, which he incorporated into an underlying principle interwoven into chapters 12 and 13, in which the beast from the land was subordinate to the beast from the sea, which in turn was subordinate to the dragon, with each figure playing a distinctive role corresponding to its unique context. This hierarchical structure did not belong to the Leviathan-Behemoth motif but to an Indo-European ideology, which had long existed from the Capitoline period and was still present in the imperial period of the Greco-Roman world, namely, the tripartite ideology.

This chapter aims to argue that the tripartite ideology is the underlying principle according to which John stratifies the dragon and the two beasts in Rev 12–13. There are two major parts in this chapter. The first part explores three different issues concerning the relationship of the dragon to the two beasts in three sections. The second part outlines the basic argument for the tripartite ideology and examines the evidence for it in five sections. Then, the chapter closes with several concluding remarks.

REVELATION 12 AND 13

In this part, the first section briefly reviews recent scholarship concerning the structure of Revelation, with an outline of its relevance to the present topic. The second section investigates the connection between Rev 12 and 13, through a source and literary analysis. The third section analyses the two vision narratives presented in chapter 13, in order to demonstrate their literal and underlying subject matters and the hierarchical relationship of the dragon and the two beasts.

A Brief Review of the Structure of the Book of Revelation

Despite much erudite endeavor, biblical scholars have reached little agreement on the structure of Revelation. The primary debate on the subject is whether the vision narratives in the book, in particular the events that constitute the core chapters, that is chapters 6–19, are reported in chronological order leading to the end-time or as a number of repetitions of the same sequence, perhaps with some variation. There is a variety of methods as well as theories for studying the topic. This section of the thesis is not a thorough examination of the scholarship on the structure of the Apocalypse, which is a considerable issue more suitable for an independent research topic, but rather a very brief review of three major perspectives on the subject matter. It aims to demonstrate that, however one structures the book, the position of chapters 12–13 is central, and to show that it is appropriate to study the dragon and the two beasts in the two chapters independently.

Recapitulation theory has had considerable influence in the history of interpretation. As early as the third century CE, Victorinus of Pettau proposed that the seven bowl cycle (15:1—16:21) does not follow the seven trumpet cycle (8:6—11:15) chronologically as part of a continuous series but in actuality is an account of the same event, recapitulating the prediction of the eschatological punishment of the unbelievers in another form.[1] In the early twentieth century, reviving this idea, Günther Bornkamm argued that the seven trumpet series and the seven bowl series each begins

---

1. Collins, *Combat Myth*, 8 nn. 24–25.

An Examination of the Tripartite Ideology in Revelation 12 and 13

with a large section (8:2—14:20; 15:1—19:21), the structures and contents of which parallel each other and make up the main body of the book.[2] For many scholars, the sets of cycles of seven are seen as major heptads that provide the structure of the book. For example, Austin Farrer divided the book into six sections, each of which is based on the number seven.[3] In his scheme, there is a sequence of topics in the book, including the trial of the saints, the reign of the antichrist and the triumph of God. These topics do not adhere to an historical timeline, however.[4]

In her landmark work, *The Combat Myth in the Book of Revelation*, Collins revises Farrer's scheme and goes further to structure the book into a sevenfold series of visions as follows: prologue (1:1–8); the seven messages (1:9—3:22); the seven seals (4:1—8:5); the seven trumpets (8:2—11:19); seven unnumbered visions (12:1—15:4); the seven bowls (15:1—16:20), with the Babylon appendix (17:1—19:10); seven unnumbered visions (19:11—21:8), with the Jerusalem appendix (21:9—22:5); and epilogue (22:6–21).[5] Then, in the seven seals, the seven trumpets, the seven bowls, and the two seven unnumbered visions, she discerns three motifs recurring most regularly as follows: persecution, the punishment of the nations and the triumph of God, the Lamb and/or the faithful.[6] With the recapitulation of these motifs, she argues that the Apocalypse is organized in two great cycles of visions, namely, 1:9—11:19 and 12:1—22:5. The first great cycle consists of the seven messages, seals and trumpets. The second cycle consists of the seven unnumbered visions, the seven bowls and the second series of seven unnumbered visions.[7] Thus the midpoint of the book is chapter 12.[8]

Another approach basically follows the chiastic structure. Schüssler Fiorenza comments that the central apocalyptic section of Revelation (4:1—22:5) creates difficulties for the interpretation of a linear-temporal sequence of visions because it mixes together past, present and future elements of time. For this reason, the book contains neither a linear-logical

---

2. Bornkamm, "Die Komposition der apokalyptischen Visionen," 132-49. See Collins, *Combat Myth*, 11 nn. 46–47.
3. Farrer, *A Rebirth of Images*, 45.
4. Ibid., 7, 23.
5. Collins, *Combat Myth*, 19.
6. Ibid., 32.
7. Ibid., 31–32.
8. Ibid., 20.

or linear-temporal development nor any systematic claim to be a history of salvation.[9] Then, she argues that the Apocalypse is arranged in an end-orientated spiral structure with the interpolation of symbols, visions of salvation through which the interrelationship between the eschatological future and the present struggle emerges.[10] The main concern of the book is not the history of salvation, but eschatology, that is, the breaking-in of God's kingdom and the destruction of hostile godless powers.[11]

In her schematization, the book is structured in a concentric A-B-C-D-C'-B'-A' pattern in which the center of the book is the prophetic interpretation of the political and religious situation of the community. Here is the pattern:[12]

A—Prologue and Epistolary Greeting (1:1–8);

B—Rhetorical Situation of the Cities of Asia Minor (1:9—3:22);

C—Opening the Sealed Scroll: Exodus Plagues (4:1—9:21; 11:15-19);

D—The Bitter-Sweet Scroll: "War" against the Community (10:1—15:4);

C'—Exodus from the Oppression of Babylon/Rome (15:5—19:10);

B'—Liberation from Evil and God's World-City (19:11—22:9);

A'—Epilogue and Epistolary Framework (22:10-21).

In agreeing with the eschatological theme being the fundamental theological conception in the Apocalypse, Pablo Richard argues for a similar chiastic structure with variant underlying concepts.[13] In Schüssler Fiorenza's schema, the center is 10:1—15:4, whilst in Richard's it is, 12:1—15:4. In either case, chapters 12–13 belong to the central unit from this chiastic perspective.

According to Bauckham, it is important to recognize that the Apocalypse was written in the first place for "hearers" (1:3), and thus for oral performance.[14] In his schematization, the main body of the composition between the prologue (1:1–8) and the epilogue (22:6-21) is a single

---

9. Schüssler Fiorenza, *Revelation*, 33–34.

10. Ibid.

11. Schüssler Fiorenza, *Justice and Judgment*, 46 n. 82; "The Eschatology," 553 n. 82.

12. Schüssler Fiorenza, *Revelation*, 34–37; *Justice and Judgment*, 175–76.

13. Richard, *Apocalypse*, 33–34. In addition, there are some other scholars who hold the chiastic view. For example, Snyder, "Combat Myth," 84. For a review of her argument, see Beale, *Revelation*, 141–44.

14. Bauckham, *Climax*, 2–3.

visionary experience John received on Patmos on the Day of the Lord (1:9).[15] The entire visionary journey begins with the technical phrase, ἐγενόμην ἐν πνεύματι, "in the spirit" (1:10), which, as a linguistic marker, recurs in slight variants three more times (4:2; 17:3; 21:10), each time indicating a major transition within the whole vision.[16] The whole visionary journey by and large develops in a progressively linear mode that climaxes with the two final parallel visions in 17:1—19:10 and 21:9—22:9, the former of which details the destruction of Babylon and the latter its replacement by the new Jerusalem.[17] The parallelism between them is evident in their corresponding openings and conclusions.[18]

For the present investigation, the most relevant point is how the three approaches interpret the three seven cycles in relation to chapters 12 and 13. According to Collins, the technique of interlocking is one of the key literary devices that link the different portions of the book together.[19] She discerns this technique in the following places. Firstly, the seven messages (1:9—3:22) have a dual literary function in that on the one hand, in terms of content they fulfill the epistolary expectation (1:4-8), and on the other, they are part of the initial vision and audition beginning with 1:9-10.[20] The series of seven seals (4:1—8:5) interlocks that of seven messages by repeating the motifs of the trumpet-like sound and of the seer's being in the spirit (1:10) at the beginning (4:1).[21] The opening of the seventh seal (8:1-5) entails three effects: the silence in heaven for about half an hour (8:1), the introduction to the seven angels with the seven trumpets (8:2) and the vision of the angel with a golden censer (8:3-5).[22] Thus, the opening of the seventh seal results in the entire series of seven trumpets.[23] Another point of interlocking is evident in the transitional vision in 8:3-5, since the imagery of the altar and the prayers of the saints (8:3) allude back to those following

15. Ibid., 3.
16. Ibid.
17. Ibid., 3–5.
18. Ibid., 4.
19. Collins, *Combat Myth*, 16–19.
20. Ibid., 16–17.
21. Ibid., 17.
22. Ibid.
23. Ibid.

the fifth seal (6:9–11), and since its motif of casting fire upon the earth (8:5) foreshadows the catastrophes of the first four trumpets (8:6–12).[24]

Chapter 12 is the starting point of certain open-ended elements that continue in the ensuing series.[25] The first series of seven unnumbered visions (12:1—15:4) interlocks the seven bowls, which actually begin in 15:5, by introducing it at 15:1 before the seventh vision in 15:2–4, which thus, too, interlocks that series to that of the seven bowls.[26] The rebellion of Satan, which is described first in 12:8–9, 12 then in 13:1, 2, 4; 16:13–14; and 20:7–10, links the two series of seven unnumbered visions and the seven bowls.[27] The beast from the sea, which is first introduced in 11:7, described fully as a key figure in chapter 13, and then interpreted in chapter 17, interlocks the seven trumpets (8:2—11:19), seven unnumbered visions (12:1—15:4) and the Babylon appendix (17:1—19:10).[28] The messianic office of the child announced in 12:5 links the first and second series of seven unnumbered visions, since it is fulfilled in 19:11–21 and 20:4–6. The relationship between the announcement and fulfillment functions as a kind of literary bracket, qualifying the material in between as the eschatological period between the heavenly installation and earthly manifestation of the messiah.[29] On the other hand, the way in which the parallel between the first and second commissions of the seer (1:9—3:22; 10:8–11) and that between the scroll with the seven seals (ch. 5) and the open scroll given to the seer (ch. 10) are integrated into the structure of the work, points to 12:1 as the midpoint of the Apocalypse.[30] Hence, both the various points of interlocking and the partition of the two great cycles of visions (1:9—11:19; 12:1—22:5) indicate that chapters 12–13, in which the dragon and the two beasts are key figures, are the center of Revelation.

According to Schüssler Fiorenza, the pivotal point of the structure of Revelation is the literary technique of intercalation. She elaborates this technique in this way: the author narrates two episodes or employs two symbols or images that essentially belong together. Between these two sections or symbols (A and A'), he then intercalates another unit different in

24. Ibid.
25. Ibid., 28.
26. Ibid., 18–19.
27. Ibid., 29–31.
28. Ibid., 18.
29. Ibid., 28, 31.
30. Ibid., 20.

form and content from the other two (B). In so doing, the author compels the reader to see the whole text as an indivisible whole.[31] An example of this technique is found in 8:2–6 as follows:[32]

A: "Then I saw the seven angels who stand before God . . . " (8:2);

B: "And another angel came and stood at the altar with a golden censer . . . " (8:3–5);

A': "Now the seven angels who had the seven trumpets made ready to blow them . . . " (8:6ff.).

According to Schüssler Fiorenza here, the author sandwiches the heavenly liturgy in 8:3–5 (B) between the appearance of the seven angels with seven trumpets in 8:2 (A) and their execution of the plagues in 8:6—9:21 (A').[33] By way of a double intercalation, she argues, the author then inserts between the execution of the plagues in 8:6—9:21 (a) and the blast of the seventh trumpet in 11:15-19 (a') an interlude, in 10:1—11:14 (b), which in turn connects with chapters 12-14 by referring to the same time period and the same kind of persecution by the beast as do the two chapters.[34] Being in the center of the chiastic structure, chapters 12-14 and 15:2-4 are the innermost heart of the matter, as it is in this central piece that knowledge and perception of such tensions as civil disorder and class conflict are symbolized and explored with urgency. Schüssler Fiorenza concludes that, structurally, the central part represents this prophetic "witness of witness" of the symbolic drama of Revelation.[35]

Bauckham argues that the seven seals (6:1—8:1; 8:3-5), the seven trumpets (8:2; 8:6—11:19) and the seven bowls (15:1; 15:5—16:21) basically describe one reality in progressively more intense ways since all three series conclude with a final judgment expanding, alternatively, the theophanic elements in 4:5, the core of which is basically an allusion to the Sinai theophany (Exod 19:16).[36] The formulaic judgment is found in the judgment at the opening of the seventh seal (8:5), which brings the seven seals to an end and encompasses the whole course of the seven trumpets, and simi-

---

31. Schüssler Fiorenza, *Revelation*, 33–34.
32. Ibid., 34, 69–70.
33. Ibid., 69–70.
34. Ibid., 34, 70, 74.
35. Ibid., 37.
36. Bauckham, *Climax*, 7–10.

larly, at the judgment of the seventh trumpet (11:19b), which concludes the seven trumpets and encompasses the whole series of the seven bowls, and finally climaxes in its fullest elaboration in 16:18–21.[37] The seven seals are linked to the seven trumpets by the technique of overlapping or interweaving found in 8:2, at which the seer introduced the seven angels with their trumpets for the first time to fill the heavenly silence for about half an hour (8:1), a moment during which God received the prayers of the saints and then responded to them (8:3–5).[38] The seven trumpets are connected to the seven bowls by interweaving the first and second parts of 11:19 in 15:5–6 and 16:17–21 respectively, which together frame the seven bowls. With this overlapping, therefore, the whole sequence of bowls occurs as a development of the seventh trumpet.[39] Between the seven trumpets and the seven bowls is the combat myth in chapters 12–14. The triumph of the people of God over the beast in heaven (15:2–4) is sandwiched between the emergence of the seven angels with seven plagues (15:1) and their preparation for the pouring out of the bowls on the earth (15:5–8).[40] The seven angels are introduced by a variation of the formula that introduced the woman and the dragon at the beginning of the combat myth (12:1–3).[41] The two points of interweaving make the seven bowls a continuation of the combat myth.[42] On the other hand, the introductory formula of the combat myth (12:1, 3) is a fresh expression, unlike any others the apocalyptist has used before.[43] As a result of the use of this formula, chapter 12 is not a continuation of the account of the seventh trumpet (11:15–19) because the imagery in 11:19b describes the final judgment and concludes the account of the seventh seal (8:1–5).[44] Since the conflict of the dragon and the woman reflects the primordial enmity between the woman and the serpent (Gen 3:15), the myth is a fresh start in the larger context of the three seven series and chronologically earlier than any previous part of the seer's visionary narrative.[45] Being a fresh start, the combat myth in chapters 12–13 is unique from other parts

37. Ibid., 8.
38. Ibid., 8–9.
39. Ibid., 9.
40. Ibid., 16.
41. Ibid.
42. Ibid.
43. Ibid., 15.
44. Ibid.
45. Ibid.

of the book, in terms of its position, and goes beyond other series, in terms of the logic underlying the series.

Having briefly reviewed the three approaches, it is clear that Revelation contains features in its structure upon which many different theological perspectives agree. All three approaches see the overlapping of a motif or imagery frequently found as a technique that interlocks different sections of the book together, although they are nuanced in detailing this technique. For this thesis, two findings are most relevant. Firstly, there is general agreement on the unique position of chapters 12 and 13, which are central to the book, from the chiastic perspective, and beyond the sequential order in both eschatological and historical terms, from the lens of the other two approaches. Secondly, since the book does not display a linear-temporal development, the different sections of it narrate the same reality, either in a progressively more intense way, or a recapitulated way, or an end-orientated spiral way. With this arrangement, the seven-headed beast from the sea in the Apocalypse (11:7; 13:1–18; 17:3–17; 19:17–21; 20:7–10), with slight variant articulations in different contexts, refers to the same figure.

The Link Between Revelation 12 and 13

The best point of departure for the present study is the connection between Rev 12 and Rev 13. The first and foremost sign that they are linked is the transitional phrase in 12:18, which reads as follows:

καὶ ἐστάθη ἐπὶ τὴν ἄμμον τῆς θαλάσσης.
And he stood on the sand of the sea.

This brief expression suggests there were originally two variants; the first-person singular ἐστάθην, "I stood,"[46] and the third-person singular ἐστάθη, "he stood."[47] If the first reading were the case, ἐστάθην and εἶδον (13:1) would share the same subject, and, accordingly, it would have been John that stood on the sand of the sea and saw a beast coming up from the sea. The second reading receives the support of the most authoritative

---

46. For a list of manuscripts that support the first-person singular ἐστάθην, "I stood," see Aune, *Revelation*, 2:716 n. 18.a.

47. For a list of manuscripts that support the third-person singular ἐστάθη, "he stood," including Nestle-Aland27 and UBSGNT4, see ibid.

manuscripts, however.⁴⁸ In addition, since the two verbs, ὠργίσθη, "was angry," and ἀπῆλθεν, "left," in 12:17, are third-person singular as is ἐστάθη, and since the subject of both the preceding verbs is clearly the δράκων, "dragon," in chapter 12, it is highly likely that it was the same dragon that stood still on the sea, having been thrown down to the earth by the archangel Michael.⁴⁹ The transitional piece is episodic in connecting the larger portrayal across chapters 12 and 13, since it is not clear whether the dragon standing on the shore was waiting for, or even summoning, the beast from the sea to fight again as some scholars argue,⁵⁰ or to carry on the war on the rest of the woman's offspring. Likewise, it is also not quite certain whether the link is the ending of chapter 12 or the opening of chapter 13.⁵¹ As early as the beginning of the twentieth century, this distinctive transition led Weiss to argue that 12:18 is a redactional verse with which the final editor connected the two chapters.⁵²

In agreement with Weiss' view, Aune surmises that, since 12:18 was a redactional link, the accounts of the dragon in 13:2b, 3a, 4a and 11 were also not originally parts of either of the two visions in 13:1–10 and 13:11–18 but rather examples of redactional glosses that the author introduced to unite these two visions more closely with chapter 12.⁵³ Aune then discerns in this collection two instances of contextual tension as evidence for his argument. Firstly, the datum in 13:2b, καὶ ἔδωκεν αὐτῷ ὁ δράκων τὴν δύναμιν αὐτοῦ καὶ τὸν θρόνον αὐτοῦ καὶ ἐξουσίαν μεγάλην, "And to it the dragon gave his power and his throne and great authority," is revealed as knowledge concerning the relationship between the dragon and the beast from the sea that the omniscient seer possessed, not as part of the seer's vision.⁵⁴

Secondly, in 13:4a, καὶ προσεκύνησαν τῷ δράκοντι ὅτι ἔδωκεν τὴν ἐξουσίαν τῷ θηρίῳ, "And they worshiped the dragon because he gave the authority to the beast." This sentence is extraneous, not only because taking

---

48. Commentators who take the reading ἐστάθη include Charles, *Revelation*, 1:344; Aune, *Revelation*, 2:731–32; Caird, *Revelation*, 158, 160; Mounce, *Revelation*, 243 n. 1; Witherington, *Revelation*, 172; Roloff, *Revelation*, 152; Beale, *Revelation*, 681; Harrington, *Revelation*, 135 n. 18; Beasley-Murray, *Revelation*, 208.

49. Aune, *Revelation*, 2:731–32.

50. Ibid., 2:732; Charles, *Revelation*, 1:344; Beale, *Revelation*, 681; Harrington, *Revelation*, 136.

51. Aune, *Revelation*, 2:731–32.

52. Weiss, *Offenbarung*, 85.

53. Ibid., 84–85; Aune, *Revelation*, 2:725–26.

54. Aune, *Revelation*, 2:735.

it out does not interrupt the sense of the passage as Aune argues,[55] but also because, if it is left out, the verse recovers its primary interest in the ensuing rhetorical question, "Who is like the beast, and who can fight against it?" (v. 4bc) The praise to the beast parodies such hymns from the Hebrew Bible as Exod 15:11 (cf. Pss 35:10; 89:6, 8; 113:5; Isa 40:25; 46:5; 44:7; Mic 7:18).[56] The phrase, καὶ προσεκύνησαν τῷ θηρίῳ λέγοντες, "and they worshiped the beast chanting" (v. 4b), introduces the parody. However, the similar phrase that begins the entire verse, καὶ προσεκύνησαν τῷ δράκοντι, "and they worshiped the dragon" (v. 4a), appears to be out of context since it is not clear why the transfer of authority to the beast by the dragon made men worship the dragon. It is likely that the author inserted this initial phrase in v. 4a in order to substantiate the supreme status of the dragon in the hierarchy, since it does not make sense that the supreme one would receive no worship while his agent did. Hence, the primary idea of the whole verse is the dragon's transfer of authority to the beast, which basically repeats what is said in v. 2b.

Unique from the other glosses, these two fragments (vv. 2b, 4a) reflect an original treatment of the biblical Leviathan tradition, assigning the seven-headed attribute to two figures simultaneously, the dragon and the beast from the sea, and having them in a hierarchical structure, with the former figure being superior to the latter. This original treatment makes the two fragments distinct from the other glosses of the same redactional group. As the investigation carries on, it will become clear that these two fragmentary texts are essential in structuring the two chapters since they introduce the hierarchical relationship of the dragon and the beast from the sea.

In addition to these two verses, there is one more instance of tension between the dragon cluster (13:2b, 3a, 4a, 11; also, 12:18) and its larger context. In v. 3a, it is reported that καὶ μίαν ἐκ τῶν κεφαλῶν αὐτοῦ ὡς ἐσφαγμένην εἰς θάνατον, καὶ ἡ πληγὴ τοῦ θανάτου αὐτοῦ ἐθεραπεύθη, "And one of its heads seemed to have a mortal wound, but its mortal wound was healed." This fragment is out of context in any case.[57] Excluding it from the redactional glosses, there is a clear flow from vv. 2b to 4a that describes

---

55. Ibid., 2:740–41.

56. Charles, *Revelation*, 1:351; Aune, *Revelation*, 2:741; Witherington, *Revelation*, 182; Mounce, *Revelation*, 249; Roloff, *Revelation*, 157; Beale, *Revelation*, 694; Harrington, *Revelation*, 138; Beasley-Murray, *Revelation*, 211.

57. Charles, *Revelation*, 1:341.

the superior status of the dragon to that of the beast as the reason men worshiped the dragon as follows:

> καὶ ἔδωκεν αὐτῷ ὁ δράκων τὴν δύναμιν αὐτοῦ καὶ τὸν θρόνον αὐτοῦ καὶ ἐξουσίαν μεγάλην.
> καὶ προσεκύνησαν τῷ δράκοντι ὅτι ἔδωκεν τὴν ἐξουσίαν τῷ θηρίῳ.
>
> And to it the dragon gave his power and his throne and great authority.
> And they worshiped the dragon because he gave the authority to the beast.

If this fragment connecting vv. 2b and 4a does not break the flow, it is extraneous. Also, when it and the other two redactional phrases (vv. 2b, 4a) are left out, there is a clear flow from vv. 2a to 3b, describing how the beast, with its outlandish appearance, astonished the whole earth as follows:

> καὶ τὸ θηρίον ὃ εἶδον ἦν ὅμοιον παρδάλει, καὶ οἱ πόδες αὐτοῦ ὡς ἄρκου, καὶ τὸ στόμα αὐτοῦ ὡς στόμα λέοντος.
> καὶ ἐθαυμάσθη ὅλη ἡ γῆ ὀπίσω τοῦ θηρίου.
>
> And the beast that I saw was like a leopard, its feet were like a bear's, and its mouth was like a lion's mouth.
> And the whole earth followed the beast with wonder.

In linking vv. 2a and 3b, the fragment is not only extraneous but breaks the flow, since, supposedly, it was not the beast's fatal wound but his horrific looks that astonished the whole earth. Since it is out of place in its context, the fragment in v. 3a must have been separate from the redactional cluster containing vv. 2b and 4a and from the present passage leaving out that cluster.

The data in v. 3a is more germane to the information in vv. 12c, οὗ ἐθεραπεύθη ἡ πληγὴ τοῦ θανάτου αὐτοῦ, "whose mortal wound was healed," and 14c, ὃς ἔχει τὴν πληγὴν τῆς μαχαίρης καὶ ἔζησεν, "which was wounded by the sword and yet lived," than to its present context. In v. 3a, μίαν ἐκ τῶν κεφαλῶν αὐτοῦ, "one of the heads of the beast" seemed to have a mortal wound, but it was the same beast that recovered from the wound on its head,[58] since the second pronoun αὐτοῦ would normally be αὐτῆς, if it referred to μίαν ἐκ τῶν κεφαλῶν.[59] The beast in vv. 12c and 14c was the same beast that suffered from the mortal wound in v. 3a. The reference to the

---

58. Aune, *Revelation*, 2:736; Mounce, *Revelation*, 248; Beale, *Revelation*, 690.
59. Mounce, *Revelation*, 248 n. 26.

same wound reveals that the three fragments belong to the same source. However, it appears that there are two source variants here, with one describing the beast's head and the other the beast.

On the other hand, in the second vision in 13:11–18, the expressions in v. 12ab, τὴν ἐξουσίαν τοῦ πρώτου θηρίου πᾶσαν, "all the authority of the first beast," ἐνώπιον αὐτοῦ, "in its presence," and τὸ θηρίον τὸ πρῶτον, "the first beast," are clear enough to identify that it was the first beast in 13:1 from which the second beast was granted full authority. Likewise, the phrase in v. 14a, ἐνώπιον τοῦ θηρίου, "in the presence of the beast," is clear enough to indicate that it was by the authority of the first beast that the second beast deceived the inhabitants of the earth through miracles. The data in vv. 12c and 14c are by and large repetitive of those in v. 3a, and therefore, add nothing in referring back to the beast from the sea. The only new datum is the way the beast was hurt which is reported in v. 14c, that is, τῆς μαχαίρης, "by the sword."[60] Since the beast's mortal wound is the focus of all three fragments, and since the beast refers to the one with seven heads that came up from the sea (13:1), it is very likely that the accounts in vv. 3a, 12c and 14c did not originally belong to either of the vision narratives, but rather to the same cluster of texts describing in particular the legend of Nero's return,[61] which in turn were elements of the glosses telling of the seven-headed monster. During the final editorial work, vv. 12c and 14c became two fragments of interpolation,[62] which the final editor inserted into positions accentuating the hierarchy in which the beast from the sea is superior to the beast from the land (vv. 12–15).

Furthermore, with the transitional link between chapters 12 and 13, there is an interconnection between the reports of the dragon (12:3bc, 4b, 7b [occurring twice], 9a, 13, 16b, 17a; 13:2b, 4a, 11b) and those of the beast from the sea (13:1, 2a, 3b, 4ab [occurring thrice]). The dragon and the beast carry the same distinctiveness with only a slight nuance. They both have κεφαλὰς ἑπτά, "seven heads," and κέρατα δέκα, "ten horns," but the dragon has ἐπὶ τὰς κεφαλὰς αὐτοῦ ἑπτὰ διαδήματα, "seven diadems upon his heads," while the beast has ἐπὶ τῶν κεράτων αὐτοῦ δέκα διαδήματα, "ten diadems upon its horns" (12:3c; 13:1c). The "diadems," though worn on different parts of the two figures' anatomies, function consistently to

---

60. This is a hint about the identification of the wounded head. According to Suetonius, Nero killed himself with a dagger (*Nero* 49; *Lives of the Caesars*, 195–227.).

61. For details of the legend, see ch. 5.

62. Weiss, *Offenbarung*, 33–34.

reinforce the image of imperial power in both cases, just as the many diadems signify the royal authority of Christ in 19:12.[63] In antiquity, bearing several crowns symbolized sovereignty over as many kingdoms.[64] When Ptolemy VI Philometer entered Antioch in approximately 169 BCE, he wore two diadems, with one representing his kingship over Egypt and the other that over Asia (1 Macc 11:13; Josephus, *J.W.* 13.113).[65] In apocalyptic tradition, the heads of multi-headed creatures normally symbolize rulers. In *4 Ezra* 12:22–25, the three heads of the eagle are interpreted as representing three kings, which are the three Flavian emperors, Vespasian, Titus and Domitian.[66] In Dan 7:6, the four-headed leopard represents Persia and its four heads the four Persian kings (11:2).[67] The explanation of the "seven heads" and "ten horns" is not found in chapters 12 or 13 but in chapter 17.

To summarize, due to the common attribute of having seven heads, both the dragon and the beast from the sea in chapters 12 and 13 derive from the same traditional source of the seven-headed monster. Of this group of materials, the accounts in vv. 3a, 12c and 14c, in particular, belong to a cluster describing the legend of Nero's return. The reports in vv. 2b and 4a are the most distinctive, since they reflect an original treatment of the biblical Leviathan tradition, assigning the seven-headed attribute to two mythic figures in accordance with a hierarchical relationship, with the dragon being superior to the beast from the sea. The two figures and the two chapters are connected by the transitional link in 12:18.

The Hierarchical Relationship of the Three Figures in Revelation 12 and 13

This section will demonstrate that in producing chapters 12 and 13, the author separated the biblical Leviathan materials into two portions, assigning some pieces to create the dragon in chapter 12 and the others to the beast from the sea in 13:1–10, then went further to arrange the beast from the sea

---

63. Caird, *Revelation*, 163; Mounce, *Revelation*, 245; Beale, *Revelation*, 684; Beasley-Murray, *Revelation*, 209.

64. Aune, *Revelation*, 2:733.

65. Another example is found in Dio Chrysostom, *Or.* 1.78–82, in which an allegorical female figure called Τυραννίς, "Tyrant," is described as wearing many diadems, each of which symbolizes a tyrant.

66. Stone, *Fourth Ezra*, 365.

67. Collins, *Daniel*, 298 n. 190; 377; Lacocque, *Daniel*, 140.

and the beast from the land in 13:11–18, according to the relationship between Leviathan and Behemoth. Unlike the Leviathan-Behemoth account in the Second Temple apocalypses, however, chapter 13 speaks little of the mythic implications apart from with respect to the reappearance of the pair. By contrast and different from all the apocalyptic accounts, what lies behind Rev 12 and 13 is a fundamental principal that interweaves the dragon and the two beasts together, that is, a tripartite hierarchical structure. In this structure, the beast from the land is subordinate to the beast from the sea which, in turn, is subordinate to the dragon, with each figure having a specific function corresponding to its context.

The departure point for the examination of the two beasts will be a brief review of the dragon. Collins argues that the combat myth in Rev 12 reflects a mélange of the combat traditions from the Near East (12:7–9) and Hellenism (12:4b–6, 13–17). In examining the overall pattern of Rev 12, she identifies nine themes arranged in sequence that correspond to the thematic pattern that Joseph Fontenrose finds in many combat myths.[68] Then, Collins discerns that there are thematic similarities between the dragon's pursuit of the pregnant woman in Rev 12, the attack of Seth-Typhon on Isis in the Egyptian myth of Seth-Isis-Horus and the Python's threat to kill Leto in the Greek myth of Python-Leto-Apollo, since, in each case, the intention behind the attack is to prevent the hero's son, correspondingly, Horus and Apollo, from taking over universal kingship.[69] Using the complete version of the Python-Leto-Apollo myth found in Hyginus,[70] she finds that the Greek parallel is closer to Rev 12 than the Egyptian one since there are striking similarities between their themes. Both describe an attack by a serpentine monster on a woman heavy with child. The flight of the woman from the serpent with the two wings of the great eagle (Rev 12:14) is analogous to that of Leto from Python with the help of the north wind. The aid of the personified earth (Rev 12:16) is similar to that of Poseidon, god of the sea, and, in the same way, the ultimate source of aid from God, that from Zeus.[71] Having compared them in this way, she concludes that Rev 12 is, at least in part, an adaptation of the myth of the birth of Apollo.[72]

---

68. Collins, *Combat Myth*, 59–61; 59 n. 10; Fontenrose, *Python*, 6–11.
69. Collins, *Combat Myth*, 61–65.
70. Ibid., 65 n. 51.
71. Ibid., 67.
72. Ibid.

In studying Rev 12, Aune raises some questions concerning the parallels between the chapter and the Greek myth that Collins suggests.[73] He comments that it is noteworthy to pay attention to the version of the Egyptian myth, preserved in Herodotus, an Osiris hymn and the Metternich Stele that impressed Bousset in his treatment of the topic,[74] since the three sources consistently record the impregnation of Isis by Osiris and the secret birth of Horus.[75] In addition, Aune notes that Isis is depicted as having two wings just as the woman in Rev 12:14 is, but Leto is not.[76] Hence, from Aune's perspective, the Seth-Isis-Horus myth is not necessarily more distant than the Python-Leto-Apollo myth as a parallel for Rev 12. While there is room for debate as to which model is the closest parallel to the combat myth in Rev 12, there is a thematic consistency behind all three myths in that the central motif is a battle for ultimate sovereignty in a mythological context. Therefore, similarly, the center of Rev 12 is a combat myth in which the war between the antagonist, who is the dragon, and the protagonists, the woman, the male child, and the archangel Michael, in the cosmological sphere is for ultimate kingship over the universe. The subject matter is entirely supernatural.

There are many places in 13:1–10 that demonstrate that the beast from the sea is subordinate to the dragon (vv. 2b, 4a, 5ab, 7ab). In v. 2b, the dragon ἔδωκεν, "gave," the beast τὴν δύναμιν αὐτοῦ, "his power," τὸν θρόνον αὐτοῦ, "his throne," and ἐξουσίαν μεγάλην, "great authority."[77] Again, in v. 4a, the dragon ἔδωκεν, "gave," the beast τὴν ἐξουσίαν, "the authority." Unique from their related glosses,[78] the two fragments exhibit an original idea that being derived from the same biblical Leviathan motif, the dragon and the beast emerged in a hierarchical relationship, in which, as presented in the vision narrative, the beast functioned as an earthly agent or plenipotentiary of the dragon.[79] Although the dragon lost the heavenly war and his legal right of accusation (12:7–12), he still had a throne and power to confer on the

---

73. Aune, *Revelation*, 2:671–72.

74. Bousset, *Offenbarung*, 353–55; Herodotus, *Hist.* 2.156.

75. Aune, *Revelation*, 2:672–74.

76. Ibid., 2:674.

77. Beale notes that the three items are synonyms (*Revelation*, 687).

78. The dragon (12:3bc, 4b, 7b [occurring twice], 9a, 13, 16b, 17a; 13:2b, 4a, 11b); the beast from the sea (13:1, 2a, 3b, 4ab [occurring thrice]; 13:3a, 12c, 14c particularly relating to the legend of Nero's return).

79. Aune, *Revelation*, 2:735.

earthly beast.[80] Hence, the picture reveals both the hierarchical relationship of the two figures and the different levels of their corresponding realms, since the loss of rights in the heavenly sphere did not affect that power and authority on earth. The direct transferal of the dragon's authority is emphasized by the use of the pronoun αὐτοῦ, "his," with the first two items endowed in v. 2b.[81] The throne of the dragon recalls the reference to the throne of Satan in Pergamum in 2:13; in both cases a metaphysical being sits upon the throne. The throne of the beast is found again in 16:10, where the beast is clearly the head of a kingdom on earth.

In v. 5a, the beast was given στόμα λαλοῦν μεγάλα καὶ βλασφημίας, "a mouth uttering haughty and blasphemous words," and again in v. 5b, it was given ἐξουσία ποιῆσαι μῆνας τεσσεράκοντα [καὶ] δύο, "authority to exercise for forty-two months" (cf. 11:2). The first phrase alludes to στόμα λαλοῦν μεγάλα, "a mouth speaking great things," ascribed to the little horn in LXX Theodotion Dan 7:8, 20,[82] which represents Antiochus IV Epiphanes.[83] The second phrase is expressed in the same durative sense as "one thousand two hundred and sixty days" in 11:3 and 12:6 and as "a time, and times, and half a time" in 12:14. It alludes to "a time, two times, and half a time" in Dan 7:25 and 12:7,[84] as well as the exact computation of the duration in Dan 8:14 and 12:11,[85] all of which, with "time" meaning one year,[86] refer to the period of time during which the Jews suffered from the persecution of Antiochus Epiphanes in approximately 167–164 BCE.[87] The reference to this length of time makes up the conventional view in apocalyptic literature that the antichrist's dominion would last three and a half years.[88] In this piece, the two main verbs are the same singular aorist passive ἐδόθη, "it was given."

In v. 7a, the beast was allowed ποιῆσαι πόλεμον μετὰ τῶν ἁγίων καὶ νικῆσαι αὐτούς, "to make war on the saints and to conquer them," and in v.

---

80. Caird, *Revelation*, 163; Harrington, *Revelation*, 140; Beasley-Murray, *Revelation*, 209.

81. Beale, *Revelation*, 687.

82. Aune, *Revelation*, 2:742; Charles, *Revelation*, 1:352; Mounce, *Revelation*, 249; Roloff, *Revelation*, 157; Harrington, *Revelation*, 138; Beasley-Murray, *Revelation*, 212.

83. Collins, *Daniel*, 299, 321; Montgomery, *Daniel*, 292–93; Lacocque, *Daniel*, 141.

84. Aune, *Revelation*, 2:743.

85. Lacocque, *Daniel*, 250, 154 nn. 142–43.

86. Collins, *Daniel*, 322; Lacocque, *Daniel*, 153–54; Aune, *Revelation*, 2:743.

87. Collins, *Daniel*, 321–22; Montgomery, *Daniel*, 313–14; Lacocque, *Daniel*, 153–54; Mounce, *Revelation*, 215 n. 77; Harrington, *Revelation*, 138.

88. Aune, *Revelation*, 2:742–43; Mounce, *Revelation*, 215.

7b, it was given ἐξουσία ἐπὶ πᾶσαν φυλὴν καὶ λαὸν καὶ γλῶσσαν καὶ ἔθνος, "authority over every tribe and people and tongue and nation." The first phrase alludes to Dan 7:21, where the little horn "made war with the saints, and prevailed over them."[89] The second reports that the authority given to the beast was universal extending over all areas of the world. Again, the two main verbs in this verse are the singular aorist passive ἐδόθη, "it was given."

In vv. 2b and 4a, it is clear that it was the dragon that ἔδωκεν, "gave," the power and authority to the beast from the sea. In vv. 5ab and 7ab, however, the four main verbs are the same aorist passive ἐδόθη, "it was given." Since this verb is passive, it does not disclose who gave the beast authority. Such a use of the divine passive is also found in Rev 9:1 and Jewish literature as well. Thus, a number of scholars argue that God is the best candidate here, and then conclude that whatever evil works the beast enacted, it was acting within the tolerance and permission of God.[90] The main difficulty, along with the exceptionality of the present passage from other places, however, is that the dragon seems to be the most likely figure for the one who grants the beast authority in vv. 5ab and 7ab, since the abovementioned solution does not explain why the beast, who had just received the power, the throne and great authority from the dragon (vv. 2b and 4a) should receive authority from something else, with no shift of power indicated in the entire scene, and especially between vv. 4a and 5a. Therefore, the one who granted the beast authority in vv. 5ab and 7ab was the same dragon who had just done the same thing to the beast in vv. 2b and 4a. The most plausible reason for the two verbal forms, ἔδωκεν and ἐδόθη, employed in the scene, is that the data in vv. 2b and 4a and those in vv. 5ab and 7ab derive from variant sources, as shown in the source analysis in the previous section.[91] To sum up, 13:2b, 4a, 5ab and 7ab demonstrate a clear hierarchical relationship between the dragon and the beast from the sea, which is original and not found in any other apocalyptic works.

Based on the hierarchical structure of the dragon and the beast from the sea, the vision is narrated with two thematic strata. The uppermost layer is the parodic theme, which consists of an earthly enthronement scene that

---

89. Aune, *Revelation*, 2:746; Charles, *Revelation*, 1:353; Harrington, *Revelation*, 139.

90. For instance, Aune, *Revelation*, 2:743; Roloff, *Revelation*, 157; Caird, *Revelation*, 167; Witherington, *Revelation*, 182; Beale, *Revelation*, 695; Mounce, *Revelation*, 249; Schüssler Fiorenza, *Revelation*, 82; Harrington, *Revelation*, 138, 141; Beasley-Murray, *Revelation*, 213.

91. See "The Link Between Revelation 12 and 13" on pp. 95–100.

An Examination of the Tripartite Ideology in Revelation 12 and 13

balances the heavenly investiture of the lamb in chapter 5.[92] The beast was granted power, the throne and great authority from the dragon (13:2), just as the lamb received the sealed scroll from the one seated upon the throne (5:7), and thereby received power, honor and glory (5:12).[93] The beast bore a mortal wound that had healed (13:3), just as the lamb had a mark of slaughter as a sign of recognition (5:6).[94] The inhabitants on earth fell prostrate before the beast, paid him homage with a song of praise (13:4), just as the cherubim and angelic beings around the heavenly throne offered their homage to the lamb (5:12).[95] The beast ruled over every tribe, people, tongue and nation (13:7), just as the lamb was the ruler over every tribe, tongue, people and nation purchased through his blood (5:9).[96] Also, the blasphemous name upon the heads of the beast (13:1) parodies the unknown name of Christ who is the Word of God (19:12–13).[97]

Furthermore, as part of the parody, there is a more fundamental principle that guides the author to narrate the vision in 13:1–10. War is the primary subject matter of the vision and the beast from the sea is a warlike figure. In chapter 12, combat takes place in a heavenly context, in which the dragon battles with the archangel Michael and his angels, and therefore, he does not appear to represent any persons on earth. Chapter 13 is different, however. In 13:2a, the seer reports that the beast was like a παρδάλει, "leopard," its feet were like those of a ἄρκου, "bear," and its mouth was like that of a λέοντος, "lion."[98] The portrayal is a pastiche blended with the characteristics of the four beasts found in Dan 7:1–9.[99] There, the four beasts are generally understood as representations of Babylonia, Media, Persia and the Greek kingdom of the Seleucid dynasty, corresponding to

---

92. Roloff, *Revelation*, 156–57; Aune, *Revelation*, 2:735.

93. Roloff, *Revelation*, 155.

94. Ibid.; Caird, *Revelation*, 164; Witherington, *Revelation*, 180; Schüssler Fiorenza, *Revelation*, 83; Harrington, *Revelation*, 138, 140; Beasley-Murray, *Revelation*, 210.

95. Roloff, *Revelation*, 155; Schüssler Fiorenza, *Revelation*, 83–84.

96. Roloff, *Revelation*, 155; Schüssler Fiorenza, *Revelation*, 83.

97. Witherington, *Revelation*, 180; Schüssler Fiorenza, *Revelation*, 83.

98. In Hos 13:7–8, God carries the three bestial images to wayward Israel. Collins notes that this passage is the closest parallel to the sequence of animals in Dan 7 (*Daniel*, 295 n. 154).

99. Aune, *Revelation*, 2:734; Charles, *Revelation*, 1:348; Caird, *Revelation*, 162; Mounce, *Revelation*, 244, 246; Witherington, *Revelation*, 181; Roloff, *Revelation*, 156; Schüssler Fiorenza, *Revelation*, 83; Harrington, *Revelation*, 138; Beasley-Murray, *Revelation*, 208–9.

the south, the north, the east and the west.¹⁰⁰ Here, therefore, the beast from the sea represents a kingdom on earth. In v. 3a, one of the heads of the beast seemed ἐσφαγμένην εἰς θάνατον, "to be mortally wounded," but ἡ πληγὴ τοῦ θανάτου αὐτοῦ ἐθεραπεύθη, "its mortal wound was healed." The way the beast was hurt is reported in v. 14c, that is, τῆς μαχαίρης, "by the sword." The expression describes a fight wound left on a warrior. In antiquity, warrior imagery is essential in the description of an emperor. In v. 4c, the belligerent sense is explicit in the parodic chanting incorporated into the gloss of the hierarchy of the dragon and the beast (v. 4a), "Who can fight against it?" Hence, in both the Danielic allusion and the glosses from the Nero's return legend, war is the underlying theme.

The war theme also underlies the two verses constructed using the aorist passive ἐδόθη, "it was given." In v. 5ab, both of the motifs of blasphemy and dominion for forty-two months are allusions to the specifics of the little horn in Dan 7, which in turn are references to the profanation of the temple by Antiochus Epiphanes (1 Macc 1:45; 4:54; 2 Macc 6:6).¹⁰¹ The belligerent attribute of the king is documented as he usurped Seleucid power by overthrowing several other claimants to the throne.¹⁰² The combat theme becomes more explicit in v. 7a, because the two infinitives ascribed to the beast, ποιῆσαι πόλεμον and νικῆσαι, "to make war" and "to conquer," are clearly related to war. Also, the entire phrase is an allusion to Dan 7:21, which is a reference to the persecution of the Jews by Antiochus Epiphanes.¹⁰³ In v. 7b, those who were under the beast's authority were every φυλὴν, "tribe," λαὸν, "people," γλῶσσαν, "language," and ἔθνος, "nation." Those who suffered under the beast's dominion were inhabitants and institutions on earth. The comprehensive list emphasizes the universal extent to which the beast exercised its authority.¹⁰⁴ Finally, the couplet explaining the vision (vv. 9–10) is an allusion to Jer 15:2 (cf. 43:11),¹⁰⁵ in which the apocalyptist left out of the natural disaster motif's judgments

100. Collins, *Daniel*, 166–70; Lacocque, *Daniel*, 139–42; Caird, *Revelation*, 162; Mounce, *Revelation*, 245 n. 8; Witherington, *Revelation*, 181; Roloff, *Revelation*, 154–55; Beasley-Murray, *Revelation*, 208.

101. Collins, *Daniel*, 321–22; Lacocque, *Daniel*, 153–54.

102. Lacocque, *Daniel*, 141.

103. Collins, *Daniel*, 320; Lacocque, *Daniel*, 153–54.

104. Aune, *Revelation*, 2:746.

105. Ibid., 2:749–50; Charles, *Revelation*, 1:355; Caird, *Revelation*, 169–70; Witherington, *Revelation*, 183; Roloff, *Revelation*, 158; Mounce, *Revelation*, 253; Harrington, *Revelation*, 139; Beasley-Murray, *Revelation*, 214.

"pestilence" and "famine,"[106] but retained αἰχμαλωσίαν, "captivity," μαχαίρῃ, "sword," ἀποκτανθῆναι, "to be slain," all of which are explicitly about battle. The double couplet begins with the tone of a military command (cf. 2:7, 11, 17, 29; 3:6, 13, 22),[107] and it closes with a call for endurance and faith from the believers (v. 10c), which in turn indicates that what was at stake was a matter of life and death on earth.

To sum up, war is the underlying theme in 13:1–10, since it is found as a principal idea in the various sources that constitute the vision. The beast from the sea is subordinate to the dragon. Whilst in chapter 12 the dragon battles with the supernatural beings in a mythical context with no allusions to any earthly figures, the beast from the sea represents an earthly figure and has to do with earthly war. He is described as a powerful person who heads a kingdom and he can make war. The best candidate for this beast is one of the Roman emperors.

Secondly, there is little doubt that the beast from the land in the second vision (13:11–18) alludes to Behemoth. The beast had κέρατα δύο ὅμοια ἀρνίῳ, "two horns like a lamb" (v. 11b), which echoes the ram with two horns in Dan 8:3, where the two horns symbolize the kings of Media and Persia (8:20).[108] Since the beast ἐλάλει ὡς δράκων, "spoke like a dragon" (v. 11b), it acted as the agent or plenipotentiary of the first beast.[109] The subordinate role of this second beast to the first beast becomes clear in the ensuing verses. In v. 12a, the beast exercises τὴν ἐξουσίαν τοῦ πρώτου θηρίου πᾶσαν, "all the authority of the first beast," ἐνώπιον αὐτοῦ, "in its presence,"[110] and, in v. 12b, it makes τὴν γῆν καὶ τοὺς ἐν αὐτῇ κατοικοῦντας, "the earth and its inhabitants,"[111] ἵνα προσκυνήσουσιν τὸ θηρίον τὸ πρῶτον, "to worship the first beast." Two descriptions outline the content of the worship (vv. 13–15). The beast deceives the inhabitants on earth through great miracles, including making fire come down from heaven to earth (v. 13), which it ἐδόθη, "was allowed," to perform ἐνώπιον τοῦ θηρίου, "on the authority of

---

106. Collins, *Apocalyptic Imagination*, 218.

107. Mounce, *Revelation*, 252.

108. Collins, *Daniel*, 330.

109. Aune, *Revelation*, 2:757.

110. Another translation is "by his authority." See Bauer, *Greek-English Lexicon*, 271.

111. The phrase, τὴν γῆν καὶ τοὺς ἐν αὐτῇ κατοικοῦντας, "the earth and its inhabitants," is only found here in the book. Bauckham argues that the expression is a subtle parallel to [οἱ] οὐρανοὶ καὶ οἱ ἐν αὐτοῖς σκηνοῦντες, "the heavens and those who dwell in them," in 12:12 (*Climax*, 240). In any case, it is a comprehensive designation for the entirety of the human race (Mounce, *Revelation*, 256 n. 11).

the beast" (v. 14a). Also, it ἐδόθη, "was allowed," to give breath to the cult image of the beast so that it could speak (v. 15ab). With these miracles, the second beast is assigned to make the entire world worship the first beast and to execute those who do not so do. It is clear from v. 12a that it is the first beast that gives permission for the second beast to carry out this mission. The subordination of this beast to the first beast is evident in the two occurrences of the aorist passive ἐδόθη (vv. 14a, 15a), and the idiomatic expression, ἐνώπιον τοῦ θηρίου, in v. 14a, and, ἐνώπιον αὐτοῦ, in v. 12a as well.

In the way it is portrayed, the worship in vv. 13–15 has parallels in the Hebrew Bible. The impressive signs (v. 13) are reminiscent of the spectacular miracle of fire Elijah performed at Mount Carmel (1 Kgs 18:38; 2 Kgs 1:10; cf. Luke 9:54). Since it carries out miracles of the same kind, the beast from the land seems to be a parody of the legendary prophet and it is referred to as the false prophet subsequently on many occasions (16:13; 19:20; 20:10). In v. 14b, having the people on earth make an image of the beast, echoes Dan 3:4, where King Nebuchadnezzar set up a golden image and ordered that all the subjects of his empire worship the image on pain of death.[112] On the other hand, the miraculous performances in worship lead many scholars to argue that the whole passage alludes to actual worship practices in the imperial cult in Asia.[113] According to Lucian of Samosata, there was liturgical technology that produced oracles in the first century CE (*Alex.* 26); for instance, the statues in the temple at Hierapolis could move and produce audible oracles at night (*De Syria dea* 10). Legends have it that Simon Magus persuaded people to follow him by performing miracles including giving life to statues or, at least, making them speak.[114] There are also reports that emperors like Caligula, who once tried to erect a statue of himself in the Jerusalem temple, had devices producing thunder and lightning that made them like Jupiter,[115] and that Roman ethicists condemned such acts of imitating gods by emperors.[116] Ventriloquism and sorcery had widespread influence in the New Testament world (Acts 8:6; 16:16; 19:13). Apelles, the miracle-monger of Ascalon, was a consultant in the court of

---

112. Aune, *Revelation*, 2:761; Roloff, *Revelation*, 163; Beale, *Revelation*, 710.

113. Aune, *Revelation*, 2:756; Charles, *Revelation*, 1:357–61; Caird, *Revelation*, 171–72; Mounce, *Revelation*, 255–56; Witherington, *Revelation*, 184; Schüssler Fiorenza, "Followers of the Lamb," 136.

114. Justin, *1 Apol.* 26; Irenaeus, *Haer.* 1.23.

115. Dio Cassius, *Hist. rom.* 59.28.6; Scherrer, "Signs and Wonders," 599–610.

116. Plutarch, *Mor.* 780E.

Caligula. Apollonius of Tyana was a friend of Nero, Vespasian and Titus. Tiberius had clairvoyants around him in his retreat on the island of Capri.[117]

Enough archaeological remains indicate the existence of the imperial cult in all seven cities mentioned in Rev 2–3 in the first century CE.[118] In ancient Rome religion did not exist as an independent sector with its own institutions, organizations and social activities but was integrated in all segments of society.[119] Since no emperors visited Asia in the first century CE, the imperial cult functioned as a network through which the inhabitants in Asia Minor might understand their relationships with the emperor on the one hand,[120] and, on the other, it worked as a bond that kept the disparate inhabitants of the far-flung empire together.[121] There was great competition among the cities of the province to be designated a *neokoros*, an official site of the imperial cult.[122] This is because being made a *neokoros* was a means by which to establish a personal link with the imperial family, which would in turn result in huge political and economic benefits for the local community.[123]

The imperial temple dedicated to Tiberius, Livia and the Senate at Smyrna best illustrates both the competitiveness and initiative used to achieve this status. The request to build the temple there was related to two court cases. In 22 CE, the province's lawyers accused their former proconsul, Gaius Silanus, of extortion, sacrilege against the divine essence of Augustus and contempt for the majesty of Tiberius. The proconsul was found guilty, then stripped of his property and exiled to an island.[124] After a year, the provincials of Asia accused Lucilius Capito of usurping the power of a military official by employing troops against them. He, too, was found guilty. Tiberius took an active role in both litigations seeking a guilty verdict. The two court cases led the cities of Asia to request permission to build an imperial temple for the emperor. Tacitus' accounts offer a great deal of information about the cases:

---

117. Caird, *Revelation*, 172.
118. Price, *Rituals and Power*, xviii–xxv, 252–64.
119. Elliott, *Social-Scientific Criticism*, 129.
120. Thompson, *Revelation*, 158.
121. Howard-Brook and Gwyther, *Unveiling Empire*, 102.
122. Price, *Rituals and Power*, 24–25, 249–74; for his definition of *neokoros*, 65 n. 47.
123. Slater, "Dating the Apocalypse," 254.
124. Tacitus, *Ann.* 3.66–69.

> So, after investigation of the business (against Lucilius Capito, the procurator of Asia), the defendant was condemned. In return for this vengeance, and because in the previous year there had been retribution against C. Silanus, the cities of Asia decreed a temple to Tiberius and his mother and the senate. And permission was given to build.[125]

Tiberius' initial approval for the request resulted in widespread criticism against his ambition.[126] This criticism led to the emperor having to defend his decision before the Senate where he explained that he had granted permission for the request following the precedent of *divus* Augustus and because the Senate was included in the dedication.[127] The request was pending for several years until it came before the Senate again. From 26 CE for three years eleven cities participated in an ongoing competition for the privilege of becoming *neokoros*. It came down to a contest between Sardis and Smyrna:

> With no great variety each pleaded national antiquity, and zeal for the Roman cause in the wars... But Hypaepa and Tralles, together with Laodicea and Magnesia, were passed over as inadequate to the task... The Pergamenes were refuted by their main argument: they had already a sanctuary of Augustus, and the distinction was thought ample. The state-worship in Ephesus and Miletus was considered to be already centered on the cults of Diana and Apollo respectively: the deliberations turned, therefore, on Sardis and Smyrna.[128]

Finally, Smyrna won.[129] The incident reveals two facts relating to the imperial cult. Firstly, the initiative for the spread of the imperial cult came from the cities of Asia Minor, not from Rome. More notably, the competition among the cities for establishing a temple to the imperial cult was intense.

On the other hand, one of the best examples to illustrate the link between the imperial cult and commerce is the system of guilds. Nelson

---

125. Ibid., 4.15.

126. Ibid., 4.37–38.

127. Both Suetonius and Tacitus state that Tiberius decided not to accept divine honors for himself from provinces (*Tib.* 26; *Ann.* 4.37). Suetonius, however, did not mention that Tiberius' policy was executed only after the approval of the cult of Tiberius, Livia, and the Senate (Friesen, *Twice Neokoros*, 6–17 n. 45).

128. Tacitus, *Ann.* 4.15.

129. Ibid., 4.56.

Kraybill argues with solid evidence for the connection of guilds, commerce and the imperial cult.[130] Trade guilds and merchant guilds were very common in the ancient world. They were voluntary and private associations and included people from various social strata such as Roman citizens, resident foreigners, freedmen and slaves. A prerequisite for membership was willingness to participate in the worship of a pagan deity.[131] Guilds normally owned a hall in which they conducted cultic ceremonies and discussed business.[132] These unions reflected a cross-section of the population, which in turn was an important setting for business interaction and relationships.[133] Thus, it was hardly possible for tradespeople to remain commercially viable without belonging to the guild relevant to their trade.[134] Enough inscriptions testify to the preeminence of trade guilds in Asia Minor, including the cities mentioned in Rev 2–3.[135] At Smyrna, silversmiths, porters and ferrymen had their guilds.[136] At Philadelphia, wool workers had their guild.[137] At Pergamum, there was a guild of dyers.[138] At Thyatira, there were guilds of bronze workers, leather workers, linen workers, dyers, bakers, wool dealers and slave dealers.[139] At Ephesus, there was a guild of money changers.[140] A tomb inscription for a certain silversmith and temple keeper buried in the city during the time of Claudius indicates that the guild had existed in the early first century CE.[141] Also, there was a fishery tollhouse built by the guild of fishermen and fish dealers in Ephesus during the reign of Nero, which was dedicated to Nero, his mother and wife, the demos of the Romans and

130. The very brief discussion of the guilds in this study basically follows Nelson Kraybill's analysis of the guilds in his work, *Imperial Cult and Commerce in John's Apocalypse*, 113–41. For the various Latin and Greek translations of "guilds," see 110 n. 44.

131. Ramsay, *Letters to the Seven Churches*, 54.

132. Kraybill, *Imperial Cult*, 115.

133. Thompson, *Revelation*, 119–20.

134. Kraybill, *Imperial Cult*, 111.

135. Ibid., 110–17.

136. *CIG* 3154 (silversmiths); Ramsay, "Notes and Inscriptions," 140–42 (porters); *IGRR* 4.1427 (ferrymen).

137. *IGRR* 4.1632.

138. *IGRR* 4.425.

139. *IGRR* 4.1259 (bronze workers); *IGRR* 4.1169 (leather workers); *IGRR* 4.1226 (linen workers); *IGRR* 4.1239, 1242, 1265 (dyers); *IGRR* 4.1244 (bakers); *IGRR* 4.1252 (wool dealers); *IGRR* 4.1257 (slave dealers).

140. *SEG* 4.541.

141. *IEph* 6.2212.

that of the Ephesians.[142] The cultic character of the house is evident in a statue of Isis and an altar which a woman belonging to the same fishermen's association, Cominia Junia, dedicated to Artemis, to Emperor Antoninus Pius, to the city of the Ephesians and to those who conducted business at the customs house for fishery when Tiberius Claudius Demostratos was civic president.[143] Many of these guilds were active before and during the New Testament era, whilst some began later. It appears that near the end of the first century guilds were booming in the Greco-Roman world.[144]

As a matter of fact, the guilds of shippers and merchants had existed as early as the third century BCE in the Mediterranean area. There is evidence, that, as early as 333 BCE, merchants from Cyprus established a temple to Aphrodite, and merchants from Egypt established one to Isis.[145] An inscription from 154–53 BCE indicates that there was a guild of the Tyrian merchants and shippers of Hercules, who worshiped and conducted business dealings regularly.[146] In a house belonging to ship owners at Nicomedia in Bithynia, there was an inscription from about 70 CE that reports that the structure, with a sanctuary incorporated, was dedicated to Vespasian.[147] Ruins at Ostia yield enough evidence of the mixing of cult and commerce.[148] The best example is an association in late first-century Ostia for this guild existed to promote the imperial cult. Its members took the title Augustales and were part of a larger association that appeared in many cities throughout the Roman Empire, composed of men of considerable financial means who were able to escalate quickly into leadership roles in various guilds.[149] By the late first or early second century, there was some form of expression of the imperial cult in nearly every guild.[150] There is evidence that a guild in Ephesus recognized the reigning emperor as its most revered patron.[151] Otherwise, patrons of trade guilds and merchant guilds were most likely to

---

142. *IEph* 1a.20.
143. *IEph* 5.1503.
144. Kraybill, *Imperial Cult*, 112.
145. Schürer, *History of the Jewish People*, 3:1:110.
146. Ibid., 3:1:108.
147. Magie, *Roman Rule*, 1:588.
148. Kraybill, *Imperial Cult*, 130–31.
149. Meiggs, *Roman Ostia*, 353, 335, 221.
150. Ibid., 327.
151. Petit, *Pax Romana*, 103.

An Examination of the Tripartite Ideology in Revelation 12 and 13

be wealthy imperial priests.[152] The mixture of cultic worship with trading in guilds put Christians and Jews in an intense dilemma since, if they adopted the radical stance of the apocalyptist, they had to withdraw from guilds and so from economic ties with Rome.[153] In so doing, they were likely to lose social and economic status.[154]

The economic theme becomes explicit after the allusion to the imperial cult. In 13:16, the beast from the land causes all people to receive a χάραγμα, "mark," on their right hand or on their forehead. The term χάραγμα occurs seven times in Revelation (13:16, 17; 14:9, 11; 16:2; 19:20; 20:4), always relating to the worship of the beast (13:16, 17; 14:11; 19:20; 20:4). The term is a parody of the σφραγίς, "seal," of God that is placed on the foreheads of his servants (7:3; 9:4).[155] Also, the position of the mark is a travesty of the use of phylacteries, which the rabbinic Jew, in the first century CE as now, wore on the left hand and on the forehead (Matt 23:5).[156] It is only in 13:16–17, however, that the motifs of the mark and the worship of the beast are connected in relation to the prohibition of buying and selling. In v. 17ab, unless he has τὸ χάραγμα, τὸ ὄνομα τοῦ θηρίου, "the mark, that is, the name of the beast," no one is able ἀγοράσαι, "to buy," πωλῆσαι, "to sell." The inability ἀγοράσαι, "to buy," πωλῆσαι, "to sell," refers to the prohibition of basic and essential commercial activities.[157] Therefore, not only does the "mark" here function to identify those who worship the beast, but it also allows them to participate in daily commercial transactions.[158]

As early as the beginning of the twentieth century, Adolf Deissmann argued, with solid evidence, that χάραγμα, "mark," is a technical term employed for the imperial seal on commercial documents since the stamp printed on deeds of sale with the name and year of the reigning emperor found on papyri is called χάραγμα.[159] The term also refers to the portraits and names of Roman emperors embossed on Roman coins.[160] With enough numismatic evidence, modern scholars are generally in favor of

---

152. Meiggs, *Roman Ostia*, 316.
153. Kraybill, *Imperial Cult*, 140.
154. Ibid.
155. Aune, *Revelation*, 2:768; Mounce, *Revelation*, 260; Harrington, *Revelation*, 143.
156. Charles, *Revelation*, 1:362–63.
157. Aune, *Revelation*, 2:768.
158. Mounce, *Revelation*, 260.
159. Deissmann, *Light from the Ancient East*, 345.
160. Caird, *Revelation*, 173.

Deissmann's view and believe that the term had a range of meanings that included an official stamp on documents and the impression on Roman coins.[161] These coins led some devout Christians and Jews to believe that the emperor had come to epitomize pagan worship.[162] There were certain groups that rebelled against the Roman Empire that rejected the use of Roman coins in order to be able to keep the law that prohibits the making of images, for instance, these included the Zealots and, later, Bar Kokhba. According to Hippolytus, some Essenes, too, had strict rules relating to not carrying a Roman coin bearing an image.[163] The anti-iconic ideology in Judaism reached its climax in the second half of the first century of the Christian era, at the time of the great revolt against Rome.[164] It is likely that the idea spread to the Christians in Asia Minor in a later period of the first century CE. In the present context, the refusal to use Roman coins is analogous to the Zealot refusal to handle, look at or produce coins bearing any sort of image.[165] The interpretation of the term χάραγμα as the imperial image is consistent with its meaning in v. 17b, where it is identified as the name of the beast written in its numerical equivalent.[166] The connection of this technical term with buying and selling is a reference to the use of Roman coins, which bear the portraits and names of Roman emperors.[167] Since the economic function of the mark is unique from all its occurrences in the Apocalypse, the account in v. 17ab is very likely a redactional text,[168] which the author employed to highlight the subject matter of the vision of the beast from the land. While the imperial cult is about political and economic benefits for local communities, the mark is a necessity for anyone who wants to be part of society and pursue basic business activities. Both accounts reflect the underlying theme of the second vision, that is, an economic concern.

To sum up, the beast from the land is subordinate to the beast from the sea. The beast is assigned to lead the people on earth to worship the

---

161. Kraybill, *Imperial Cult*, 136; Caird, *Revelation*, 173; Mounce, *Revelation*, 259; Witherington, *Revelation*, 184; Harrington, *Revelation*, 143.

162. Kraybill, *Imperial Cult*, 138 n. 169.

163. Hippolytus, *Haer.* 9.21.

164. Roth, "An Ordinance," 177.

165. Collins, *Crisis and Catharsis*, 126.

166. Mounce, *Revelation*, 260 n. 38; Charles, *Revelation*, 1:364.

167. Kraybill, *Imperial Cult*, 138–39.

168. Flusser, "Hystaspes," 58.

first beast by participating in the imperial cult, through which the people receive a mark, which in turn is a prerequisite for all who want to live in the society and pursue economic activities. Thus, the underlying theme of the second vision (13:11–18) is economic.

Having examined the primary concerns related to the dragon and the two beasts, the investigation in this part closes with several remarks. By reviewing three major perspectives concerning the structure of Revelation, the first section demonstrates that the position of chapters 12 and 13 is central to the entire Apocalypse and independent from its larger context in the narrative timeframe. Thus, it is appropriate to study the subject matter of the two chapters individually. In addition, since the different sections of the book are not arranged in a linear-temporal sequence but in different narrative contexts describing the same reality, the seven-headed beast from the sea in different passages (11:7; 13:1–18; 17:3–17; 19:17–21; 20:7–10) refers to the same monster. The second section demonstrates that, due to their shared attribute of having seven heads, the dragon in chapter 12 and the beast from the sea in chapter 13 derive from the same traditional source-the biblical Leviathan. In producing the two chapters, the apocalyptist allotted the bits and pieces to create two different entities, with the dragon being superior to the beast from the sea. Then, he went further and arranged the beast from the sea and the beast from the land according to the Leviathan-Behemoth template and assigned the same hierarchy to the pair, with the sea beast being superior to the land beast. The third section examines the notion that in this tripartite hierarchy, the three figures are found in different contexts and each takes a specific role in accordance with its context. The dragon is related to the ultimate sovereignty of the supernatural, mythical context. The sea beast takes the role of warrior and appears in a belligerent context. The land beast is related to the economic and profiteering aspects of earthly life.

In consequence, distinct from the Leviathan-Behemoth motif in the Second Temple apocalypses, the present account offers few implications for the two mythic figures; it only says that they return. If the Leviathan-Behemoth motif is at work here, it only informs the impending end-time. Therefore, the tripartite hierarchy of the three figures and their specific roles in the corresponding contexts come from a source distinct from the apocalyptic tradition. As the subsequent investigation carries on, it becomes clear that this structure reflects the influence of an ancient Indo-European ideology, that is, the tripartite ideology.

The Identities of the Beast from the Sea and the Beast from the Land in Revelation 13

THE TRIPARTITE IDEOLOGY IN THE ANCIENT WORLD

This part of the thesis explores the argument for the tripartite ideology in five sections. The first section briefly introduces the key idea of the tripartite ideology as proposed by Georges Dumézil. The second section reviews the primary literary evidence Dumézil employs to argue for a social tripartition of Rome through the generations. The third section examines the relics of a divine triad that had been most prominent in the Roman pantheon from the pre-Capitoline period up to the imperial period. Then, the next section investigates the major archaeological remains of the triad, that is, the great temple of the Capitoline Triad, Jupiter, Juno and Minerva. The final section studies the archaeological remains of Capitolia, the shrines of the Jupiter Capitolinus, which are found widely in the Mediterranean world.

The Hypothesis of the Tripartite Ideology of Georges Dumézil

Georges Dumézil, the key exponent of the theory, is a French philologist with expertise in comparative mythology. Dumézil argues that there was a common Indo-European cultural heritage in which the social structures and institutions were closely connected to and reflected in Indo-European myths. After studying the concepts and functions within several Indo-European mythological traditions, Dumézil discerns an all-encompassing structure of relationships underlying all these traditions, that is, a tripartite hierarchy.[169] The key to this structure is its three social-religious functions, which Dumézil illustrates with an analysis of four mythological traditions including the Indic, the Iranian, the Scandinavian and the Roman.[170]

The first function concerns the sovereignty of both the juridical and supernatural dimensions and is typically represented by a pair of gods. The Indic figures, Varuna-Mitra, the Iranian figures, Vohu Manah and Aša, the Scandinavian gods, Odin and Týr, and the Roman divinities, Jupiter and Dius Fidius, hold this superior position.[171] The second function concerns physical prowess and thus is represented by warlike figures. The Indic Indra and Maruts, the Iranian Xšathra, the Scandinavian Thor and the Roman

---

169. Littleton, *New Comparative Mythology*, 217, cf. 101.

170. For a precise diagram of the comparison of the four mythological traditions, see Larson, "Introduction: The Study of Mythology," 10.

171. Littleton, "Je ne suis pas," 152 n. 3.

Mars are the deities on this hierarchical level.[172] The third function governs physical well-being, fecundity and economic productivity and is normally represented by a pair of divinities. The Indic figures, Aśvins and the goddess Sarasvatī, the Iranian figures, Amərətāt-Haurvatāt and the goddess Armaiti, the Scandinavian Njördr-Freyr and the goddess Freyja and the Roman Quirinus satisfy this function.[173]

As a reconstruction, the tripartite ideology contains some peculiarities. First, the ideology integrates the total cultural experience of the Proto-Indo-Europeans, and therefore, it not only recurs in the Indo-European myths but also generates new myths under the pressure of historical circumstances.[174] Secondly, although the tripartite ideology reflects the archaic ideological system of Proto-Indo-European culture before its separation into nations and tribes, after the separation the ideology is still manifest in different strata of social and political life with many alterations.[175] Thirdly, and more importantly, the underlying principle behind these two features is the fact that the system is both rigorous and flexible in that the structure is more important and lasting than the individual constituents arranged in and throughout it. An example of this symbiotic nature is the replacement found in the Roman pantheon, in which to start with, Jupiter and Dius Fidius head the first function, but later, Dius Fidius recedes and becomes indistinct,[176] and also, in the later Roman pantheon, influenced by Etruscan culture, while the divine triad remains, its constituents become Jupiter, Juno and Minerva.[177]

The mythological traditions Dumézil employs to develop his tripartite ideology are ancient civilizations that had been in place over five hundred years prior to the Common Era. Dumézil argues that the ideology still existed in the Greco-Roman society of the imperial period because it is an underlying principle embedded and replicated in the underlying layers of different ancient cultures and thus all-encompassing in nature. In addition, the ideology sustained little alteration in the Greco-Roman world over time, since resistance to change is a primary characteristic of Romans.[178]

172. Ibid., 152.
173. Ibid.
174. Nagy, "Hierarchy," 201–2.
175. Ibid.
176. Littleton, *New Comparative Mythology*, 68–69.
177. Ibid., 69 n. 14, cf. 141.
178. North, *Roman Religion*, 13.

Evidence for the Tripartite Ideology in the Structure of Roman Society

My examination into how the tripartite ideology relates to the present thesis begins with its influence on the social structure of ancient Rome because that best demonstrates the general idea of this distinctive system. In the early stage of his scholarship, having discovered the evidence for a tripartite theology in the Roman pantheon, Dumézil once went further to surmise that social tripartition was a precondition for theological tripartition. Evidence for the social aspect of his argument is primarily literary.

First and foremost, it is necessary to examine who laid the foundation of the social structure. Already in the period of the Republic, two major versions of the legend of the founding of Rome existed side by side. Aeneas, the son of prince Anchises and the goddess Venus, appeared with Odysseus as the founder of Rome for the first time in a fragmentary piece by Hellanicus of Lesbos, a Greek historian in the fifth century BCE, reiterated by Dionysius of Halicarnassus (*Ant. rom.* 1.72.2),[179] in which Aeneas also named the city after one of the Trojan women accompanying him, Rhome, an equivalent to Roma in Greek, meaning strength.[180] But the later world knew him as the founder of the city primarily through the *Aeneid*,[181] an epic poem written in Latin by Virgil in the late first century BCE. According to this poem, having fled from the burning Troy at the end of the Trojan War, Aeneas began a long voyage with a band of refugees and finally landed in the city of Laurentum of Latium, where his son Ascanius later on founded a new city that he named Alba Longa.[182]

Romulus, known primarily through Livy's account to be the legendary founder of Rome, is a lot more familiar than Aeneas to the later world. By the time Livy put it in his composition, the legend of Romulus had long existed in its essentials, as a canonical mythic-historical account of

---

179. Some scholars argue that the passage is one of the eleven fragments preserved from Hellanicus of Lesbos' *Priestesses of Hera in Argos*. See Solmsen, "Aeneas Founded Rome," 93.

180. Baldi, *Foundations of Latin*, 106.

181. The account of the founding of Rome by Aeneas is mainly in book 12 of the *Aeneid*. But the founding of the city did not take place through the establishing of buildings or by instituting any laws or a political regime, but by making a peace settlement in Italy, which represented in microcosm the universal peace settlement to be concluded by Virgil's contemporaries, according to Adler, *Vergil's Empire*, 167.

182. Virgil, *Aen.* 1–2; also, a fragmentary account of Aeneas' odyssey by Hellanicus was reiterated in Dionysius, of Halicarnassus, *Ant. rom.* 1.46–48.

the founding of Rome, and thus was also found in the writings of many contemporaries, such as Ovid and Dionysius of Halicarnassus. However, variants, most of which are inconsequential, exist in the legend.[183] Romulus and his twin younger brother Remus were sons of the Vestal Virgin Rhea Silvia and the warlike god Mars and the grandsons of King Numitor of Alba Longa, and therefore, descendants of fugitives from Troy. Having been born miraculously from a virgin, the twins were thrown into the River Tiber to die in accordance with the order of Amulius, the usurper of Alba Longa, but were saved from death and then suckled by a *Lupa*, she-wolf.[184] Having grown up, the two decided to found their own city in the locality where they had been exposed shortly after they were born, but quarreled over the exact site for it. The sibling rivalry led Romulus to slay Remus. Eventually, Romulus founded Rome on the Palatine, named the city after himself, and served as its first king.[185]

During the period of the Republic, there were a number of dates proposed for the foundation of Rome, all of which were in the interval between 814 BCE and 728 BCE. Since Eratosthenes of Cyrene fixed a date of 1184 BCE for the fall of Troy in his *Chronographia*, and since 814 BCE was the earliest date proposed for the founding of Rome, the time gap between Aeneas and the origin of Rome was obvious. In the early second century BCE, by integrating the two legendary versions, the elder Cato came up with what the later world considered a canonical legend, with Aeneas settling down in Italy with his followers and Romulus founding the city of Rome.[186] Since Varro dated the foundation of Rome to April 21, 753 BCE, the date superseded many others from Emperor Claudius onwards,[187] and hence the

---

183. Here are only two examples of many. According to Livy, it was fratricide that killed the younger twin, Remus (1.7). Ovid, however, in his poem about the festivals of the Roman calendar, produced a new character as the murderer whom he named Celer (*Fast.* 4.807-59). According to Livy (1.4), Romulus' mother was a Vestal Virgin named Rhea Silvia, the daughter of King Numitor of Alba Longa. In Plutarch's account, however, Romulus' mother was a maidservant of King Tarchetius of Alba Longa (*Rom.* 2.3-5).

184. Livy (1.3-4) remained uncertain whether indeed Romulus was miraculously born and fathered by Mars, but such ambiguity did not exist in some variants of this tradition, for instance, Cicero, *Div. Caec.* 1.30. Another version is found in Plutarch's account, in which Romulus was miraculously born as a result of intercourse by a phantom phallus and a maidservant of the daughter of Tarchetius, the Alban king (*Rom.* 2.3-5). For the sources of the account of the infant twins, see Wiseman, *Remus*, ch. 1.

185. Livy, 1.6.3-7.3; Ovid, *Fast.* 4.807-59.

186. Dionysius, of Halicarnassus, *Ant. rom.* 1.73.4.

187. Alföldy, *Social History of Rome*, 2.

official date for *Ab Urbe Condita* in the Roman calendar. Like many other classicists, Dumézil accepts 753 BCE as the date of the foundation of Rome as well as Romulus as the founder of the city.

For the present examination, the significant point of the Romulus legend is the foundation of the social structure he established for Rome soon after he founded the city. This is because this structure is one of the keystones on which Dumézil develops his theory. Intellectuals from the Augustan period are in general agreement on the tribal combination of the original populace of Rome.[188] According to Varro (*Ling.* 5.55; 5.46), basing himself on the work of Junius Congus Gracchanus,[189] the initial inhabitants of the city consisted of the Latins, the Sabines and the Etruscans. The Latin community was named Ramnes after its leader Romulus. The Sabine community was named Tities after its leader Titus Tatius, and settled in Rome after the war and ensuing peace with the Latins. The Etruscan community was named Luceres after its warrior Lucumon, an ally of Romulus, who had led the community to fight against the Latins and then to settle in Rome. Cicero writes similarly of the origin of the city with an emphasis on the ethnic value of each tribe in accordance with its contribution in the making of Rome. He regarded the Ramnes as the companions of Romulus, the Luceres as the Etruscan allies led by Lucumon and the Titienses as the Sabines of Tatius (*Resp.* 2.8; also, 2.14). The tradition leads many to argue that the three tribes represent three ethnic groups that together constitute the original populace of Rome.[190]

A variant of the tradition is found in Livy (1.13.6–8), in which the Ramnes, the Tities, and the Luceres each formed ten smaller units called *curiae*, and each *curia* in turn formed a *decuria* and a *centuria*. Since a *decuria* contained ten equestrians and since a *centuria* a hundred infantrymen, the three tribes in total consisted of three hundred equestrians and three thousand infantrymen, which together constituted the original force of the legion.[191] In later times, Tarquinius Priscus doubled the size of the *decuriae* and so there were two hundred equestrians in each tribe, which in the *comitia centuriata* were divided into two levels known as *Ramnes priores, Ramnes posteriores, Tities priores, Tities posteriores, Luceres priores* and

---

188. Dumézil, *Archaic Roman Religion*, 2:164–65.
189. Cornell, *Beginnings of Rome*, 114 n. 94.
190. Ibid., 114 n. 95.
191. Ibid., 114 n. 93; Alföldy, *Social History of Rome*, 6 n. 14.

Luceres posteriores.[192] This institution was a surviving trace of the legend that retained the names of the three founding tribes until the period of the Republic.[193]

In the first Roman elegy of Sextus Propertius (4.1.9–32),[194] there is a picture of ancient Rome that contains three tableaux and Dumézil identifies in each of them a specific function of his tripartite system.[195] In the first tableau (ll. 9–14, 15–26), the fellows of Romulus and Remus are involved in senatorial, religious and ceremonial activities and thus perform the first function of the tripartite hierarchy. In the second tableau (ll. 27–29), Lucumon carries out the tasks of primitive warfare and, therefore, the second level. In the third (l. 30), Tatius is characterised by his wealth and hence represents the third sphere. Lines 31 and 32 conclude the elegy by describing Romulus as the leading figure who supervises the tribes of Ramnes, Tities and Luceres.[196] The Propertian elegy was so dominant in the early stage of Dumézil's argument that the philologist once concluded that a tripartite social structure was a precondition for a tripartite pantheon.[197]

This block of materials is the principle literary evidence with which Dumézil argues for the existence of social tripartition in ancient Rome.[198] It indicates the correlation between the division of the three founding tribes and the foundation of the city. Etymologically, the correlation is also reflected in the Latin word for tribe, *tribus*, since constructed with *tres*, a root denoting three, *tribus*, in its essential sense, refers originally to the tripartite ethnic division, which in turn is the foundation of the formation of Rome. Since each group provided a specific contribution at the birth of the city and accordingly had individual ethnic value, these three groups anticipated a tripartite social hierarchy.

---

192. Livy, 1.36.2–5; Dionysius, of Halicarnassus, *Ant. rom.* 3.71.1–5.
193. Cornell, *Beginnings of Rome*, 115.
194. Belier, *Decayed Gods*, 82 nn. 106, 109.
195. Ibid., 81.
196. Ibid.
197. Ibid., 82 n. 110.
198. Ibid., 80.

Evidence for the Divine Triad in the Roman Pantheon

There were numerous deities in the ancient Roman religion.[199] Since they have never appeared as an organized group of deities in a pantheon in which each held a specific status, there would be little agreement concerning their rankings and functions. Nevertheless, there would be little doubt that Jupiter, Juno, Mars and Apollo were the most important deities.[200] Enough evidence indicates that the idea of a divine triad lay behind this group consistently from the pre-Capitoline period up to imperial times.

In Festus's text that sets forth the *ordo sacerdotum* (299–300L2), there is an account of the order of Roman office, in which the most powerful is the *rex*, then come the *flamen Dialis*, the *flamen Martialis*, the *flamen Quirinalis* and, lastly, the *pontifex maximus*. Following the account, the report explains why the three flamines appear in the order they do for the hierarchy of the flamen relates to the position in the divine hierarchy that corresponds to the god their flamen serves. The *flamen Dialis* is the priest of the universe and thus the highest among the three flamines. The *flamen Martialis* takes the second seat because Mars is the father of the founders of Rome, who are Romulus and Remus.[201] The *flamen Quirinalis* holds the third position because Quirinus is summoned from Cures to be associated with the Roman Empire. Dumézil, citing Georg Wissowa as reference, discerns from this text that the order of the three flamines manifests the divine triad.[202]

One of the important rituals in which the three flamines participated was the annual sacrifice to Fides, the goddess of good faith. In enumerating the religious ceremonies the legendary King Numa instituted, Livy first reported the creation of the three flamines (20.1–2), and later recounted that, in the annual worship of Fides, the flamines proceeded in a two-horse hooded carriage to the sanctuary of the goddess to offer her sacrifice, with their right hands wrapped up as far as the fingers (21.4–5). There is general agreement that the flamines in the two passages were the same flamines who were those of Jupiter, Mars, and Quirinus, based on Livy's account.[203] This sacrifice had taken place in the sanctuary of Fides long before the

---

199. For a list of deities, see North, *Roman Religion*, 36.
200. Ibid., 35.
201. Ibid., 42.
202. Dumézil, *Archaic Roman Religion*, 2:141–44.
203. Ibid., 2:144; also, Beard et al., *Religions of Rome*, 2:4–5.

establishment of her temple on the Capitol, next to the temple of Jupiter, Mars and Minerva, around 250 BCE.[204] Hence, the triadic structure of the three flamines had been in place in the pre-Capitoline period and was still flourishing during the republican era.[205]

Another piece of evidence for the divine triad existed in the Regia of the Forum, also called the "house of the king," which was established from the seventh and sixth centuries BCE.[206] Its fundamental structure consisted of three consecutive divisions, a principle section and two smaller *sacraria* similar in size, which, during the republican era, became the seat of the Pontifex Maximus and the religious centre for many cultic ceremonies, including the sacrifice to Jupiter by the *flaminica Dialis* on every *nundinae* (Macrobius, *Sat.* 1.16.30), the sacrifice to Janus by the *rex* at the Agonalia (Ovid, *Fast.* 1.318; Varro, *Ling.* 312) and the sacrifice to Juno by the *regina sacrorum* every calends. In addition, every calends people would have come in to Rome from the country to transact affairs between the city and the country and to receive the laws and the acts that the leaders and the Senate had proclaimed on three consecutive *nundinae* (Macrobius, *Sat.* 1.16.33).[207] The monthly administration of the state, together with the weekly sacrifice to Jupiter, the sovereign deity of Rome, manifests the first function of the divine triad present in the Regia.[208]

One of the *sacraria* of the Regia is the *sacrarium Martis*, a shelter for the warlike talismans of Mars. Vestiges of the warrior god found in the *sacrarium* include the twelve shields, the *ancilia*, the spears and the *hastae Martis*.[209] When Rome declared war, the designated general came first to make the shields move, known as *commouebat*, and then the "spear of the statue," while uttering "*Mars uigila*" (Servius, *Commentary on the Aeneid of Virgil* 8.3.1; 7.603)! The talismans and the rite prove the warlike nature of Mars and thus his *sacrarium* signifies the second function of the divine triad.

Another *sacrarium* was dedicated to the goddess Ops Consiva, the personification of agricultural abundance, and was so sacred that only the Vestal virgins and the grand pontiff were allowed to enter, according to

204. Dumézil, *Archaic Roman Religion*, 2:141.
205. Ibid.
206. Ibid., 2:172 n. 39; Beard et al., *Religions of Rome*, 1:39 n. 115.
207. Michels, *Calendar of the Roman Republic*, 84–89.
208. Dumézil, *Archaic Roman Religion*, 2:173.
209. Ibid., 2:173–74.

Varro (*Ling.* 6.21) and the *ordo sacerdotum* by Festus (354 L2). According to another unique text from Tertullian (*Spect.* 5), the Vestal virgins and the *flamen Quirinalis* sacrificed to Consus, one of the old agrarian divinities of the valley of the Circus, at the underground altar that the god had in the Circus, on 21 August and 15 December. Four days following the two rites were the feasts of Ops Consiva, on 25 August and 19 December. The similarity between the nature of Ops Consiva and Consus and the proximity of their festivals reveal their close affiliation.[210] They were interdependent, both signified abundance and fecundity, and belonged to a group of deities, which, according to the canonical trilogy, were represented by Quirinus.[211] Therefore, this *sacrarium* represents the third function of the divine triad.

To summarize, in the ancient period, the original constituents of the triad were Jupiter, Mars and Quirinus. The three deities became Jupiter, Juno and Minerva later in the Capitoline period. These accounts were written approximately during the reign of Augustus by historians who were roughly contemporaneous with the emperor, such as Livy, Varro, and Dionysius of Halicarnassus, and so were reconstructions of the early Roman religion based on some earlier sources unknown to historians today. Therefore, although to what extent these reconstructions reflect the original contours of the ancient Roman religion is open to question, they indicate, at the very least, what it was supposed to be from the perspective of the writers on the one hand, and, on the other, reflect the importance of having a systematic religion that centers on the divine triad, particularly in the period during which Augustus began a series of revivals of religious practices and of temple restorations (*Res Gestae* 19–21).

The Great Temple of Capitoline Triad, Jupiter, Juno, and Minerva

Of the eighty-two temples Augustus claimed to have restored in his revival (*Res Gestae* 20.4), the most important evidence for the triadic divinity is the great temple of the Capitoline Triad, Jupiter, Juno and Minerva, which stood at the southern summit of the Capitoline Hill overlooking the Forum of Rome.[212] According to different traditions, it was the fifth king of Rome, Tarquin the Elder (616–579 BCE), who first laid the foundations of the

---

210. Ovid, *Fast.* 210–11.
211. Schilling, "Roman Religion," 62.
212. Stamper, *Architecture of Roman Temples*, 6.

Capitolinus,[213] and the last king, Tarquin the Proud (534–510 BCE), who then completed a large part of the project by the time of his fall.[214] Before the laying of the foundations, however, some shrines had existed on the same site. For instance, there was a small shrine dedicated to Jupiter Feretrius, which, according to some traditions, Romulus established to consecrate the loot of war from his victory over King Acron.[215] There may have been a small shrine dedicated to the triad Jupiter, Juno and Minerva as early as the late seventh century BCE.[216] In addition, there were some small shrines dedicated by the Sabine King Tatius, who had temporarily occupied a stronghold on the Capitoline Hill after a battle against Romulus.[217] These earlier structures constitute solid evidence for both the long and complicated history of the divine triad and the legend of the site at the Capitoline Hill as a religious and political center.

Surviving ruins reveal that the temple contained twenty-four columns in all and eighteen in the grand portico, which constituted a spectacular plan that was far greater than any plans of subsequent republican temples.[218] It was the center of the religious activities of the annual magistrates.[219] It was also in this Capitolinus where the victorious general laid laurel wreaths in the statue's lap.[220] The temple became a symbol of Roman religion and the apotheosis of sacred buildings across the whole of the Roman Empire hundreds of years later.[221]

Things related to the Jupiter Capitolinus always reflect the importance of the temple. For example, the privilege of restoring the temple after its destruction by fire in 83 BCE, during which the *Sibylline Oracles* were lost, was so important that many leading magistrates competed for the project. In 62 BCE, Julius Caesar, still a praetor then, tried to remove the privilege

---

213. Beard et al., *Religions*, 1:3.

214. Livy, 2.8; Cicero, *Dom.* 139; Dionysius, of Halicarnassus, *Ant. rom.* 5.35.3; Tacitus, *Hist.* 3.72.

215. Stamper, *Architecture of Roman Temples*, 6 n. 2.

216. Ibid., 6 n. 3.

217. Ibid., 6 n. 4.

218. Livy, 1.55.1; Dionysius, of Halicarnassus, *Ant. rom.* 4.61.

219. Beard et al., *Religions*, 1:59.

220. Coarelli, *Il foro romano*, 1:11–118.

221. Beard et al., *Religions*, 1:3.

of the upkeep of the temple from Quintus Lutatius Catulus and pass it to Pompey on the grounds that he was too slow in maintaining his privilege.[222]

Tensions existed between the Capitolinus and the new temples Augustus established in his revival.[223] The most spectacular edifice of the Augustan revival was probably the temple of Mars Ultor, also known as the Avenger,[224] which the first emperor gave permission for in 42 BCE, while he was still called Octavian, before he defeated his father's assassins in the battle of Philippi. Meanwhile Augustus established a temple next to his own house on the Palatine in the 20s BCE to Apollo, whom he considered to be responsible for his victory over Sextus Pompey in 38 BCE.[225] The two temples took over some privileges that had traditionally belonged to the Capitolinus, with the *Sibylline Oracles* going to the temple of Apollo in approximately 23–19 BCE and some military functions moving to the Forum of Augustus, part of the temple of Mars Ultor.[226]

According to Suetonius, Augustus had a dream in which Jupiter Optimus Maximus complained that the emperor's new shrine to Jupiter Tonans was drawing many of the worshippers from his own temple, and as the story carried on, the emperor explained that Jupiter Tonans was merely the doorkeeper of Jupiter Optimus Maximus.[227] Whatever the intention of the account, it does show the unrivaled status of the Jupiter Capitolinus. It also corresponds to the policy of the temple implemented by Augustus, who restored the temple after it had been destroyed by fire, made lavish offerings to it, and made an annual plea for the emperor's safety in it.[228] Therefore, although Augustus might have had his own proclivity towards some deities, particularly those who helped him win wars, the traditional divine triad with the Jupiter Capitolinus was still the center of Roman religion.

The Capitolinus was burning down during the course of the battle in 69 CE, when Vespasian fought to enter the city as emperor in the year of the four emperors. Tacitus described the destruction of the temple as the most lamentable and appalling disaster in the whole history of Rome.[229] To the

---

222. Suetonius, *Jul.* 15.
223. Beard et al., *Religions*, 1:125–34; North, *Roman Religion*, 58 n. 17.
224. North, *Roman Religion*, 42 n. 22.
225. Beard et al., *Religions*, 1:198–99.
226. Ibid., 1:201.
227. Suetonius, *Aug.* 91.2.
228. Beard et al., *Religions*, 1:201.
229. Tacitus, *Hist.* 3.72.

An Examination of the Tripartite Ideology in Revelation 12 and 13

Romans, the disaster resulted in a deep grieving, which in turn reflected the superior status of the Roman principle god as well as the Capitolinus. To the Diaspora, however, the disaster led to a humiliating policy that derided the Jewish god.

When Judaea was under direct Roman administration in 6 CE, the Roman governor restricted the potential power of the High Priest of the temple by having full authority to appoint the office annually, or dismiss the incumbent when necessary, and constrained the hand of the Jewish council, the Sanhedrin, by overseeing the finances of the temple. During this period, Jews in other provinces and in Italy were allowed to continue sending the temple in Jerusalem gifts and the regular annual temple tax,[230] in accordance with their traditions (Exod 30:13–16; Neh 10:32–33).[231] After the Romans quashed the Jewish revolt of 66–70 CE and demolished the Jerusalem temple, however, in 71–72 CE Vespasian imposed a new annual temple tax on all Jews throughout the Mediterranean, having them each pay two drachmae a year not towards Jerusalem, but to Rome in perpetuity for rebuilding the Jupiter Capitolinus, according to Josephus, Dio Cassius and Suetonius.[232]

Originally, the official name of this humiliating Roman tax was δίδραχμον,[233] as shown in Dio's account,[234] which implied that the Capitolinus replaced the Jerusalem temple in terms of social status because the same term had been used to designate the annual temple tax for Jerusalem (Matt 17:24). Traditionally, only men between the ages of twenty and fifty, including freed slaves and proselytes, paid the tax for the Jerusalem temple.[235] However, Vespasian extended the coverage of the new tax to both sexes, from the age of three to the sixty second birthday in the case of women, and perhaps for life in the case of men. The extension of liability made the tax a heavy burden for the head of a large family since then he had to pay for the women, children and slaves of the family, who had previously been exempt.[236]

---

230. Beard et al., *Religions*, 1:341.

231. Josephus, *Ant.* 18.9.1.

232. Josephus, *J.W.* 7.6.6; Dio Cassius, *Hist. rom.* 65.7.2; 68.1.2; Suetonius, *Dom.* 12.2; Cicero, *Flac.* 67.

233. Smallwood, *Jews under Roman Rule*, 372.

234. Dio Cassius, *Hist. rom.* 65.7.2.

235. Smallwood, *Jews under Roman Rule*, 373.

236. Josephus, *J.W.* 2.218; Dio Cassius, *Hist. rom.* 66.7.2; Tcherikover and Fuks, *CPJ*,

Since the new taxation applied to the Diaspora everywhere,[237] its effect was widespread. Its burden was not only financial but also psychological, because Judaism remained a *religio licita* only for those who declared allegiance to Rome by paying the annual tax to Jupiter, the god who triumphed over the Lord of Israel through Roman armies, and thus purchased the privilege to practice their religion,[238] and because the tax marked them out as members of a defeated race punished for their nationality.[239] Writing in the first century CE, Johanan b. Zakkai related this event to his note on Exod 19:1–2 in the Mishnah, arguing sarcastically that the Roman exaction was a recompense for Jewish sin.[240] Having the same Jewish tradition and also holding a monotheistic belief, though variant from Judaism, John of Patmos must have found the tax abhorrent.[241]

Two references to pagan religion occurring in Augustine's works reflect the importance of the divine triad and the Jupiter Capitolinus. In his *The City of God* (6.10–11), Augustine quoted the following words about the divine triad by Seneca:

> Jupiter has one special attendant to announce visitors and one to tell him the time; one to wash and another to oil him, who as a matter of fact is only miming the hand movements. Juno and Minerva each have a special female hairdresser, who works at some distance not just from the statue but from the temple; these mimic the finger-movements of hairdressers, while others again hold up mirrors. You find people praying to the gods to put up bail for them; and still others handing over writs and expounding the lawsuits they are engaged in. (Seneca, *On Superstition*, frr. 35–7 [Haase])

Apparently, the dramatic venue of the scenario is the Capitolinus on Capitol Hill. Augustine took this passage as evidence for an attack on pagan religion by Seneca, in order to suggest that even the leading pagan authority was opposed in the heart of pagan imperial Rome. Some scholars, however, point out that what Seneca was trying to attack here was not pagan religion

---

1:80–82; 2:204–5.
237. Josephus, *J.W.* 7.6.6.
238. Smallwood, *Jews under Roman Rule*, 345.
239. Ibid., 374.
240. Ibid., 345 n. 54.
241. Kraybill, *Imperial Cult*, 184.

but the popular expressions of piety by marking the nuance between proper religion and superstition, and therefore, Augustine distorted his meaning.[242] Whatever Seneca's original intention was, it does not affect the fact that the divine triad was central to the issue of pagan religion around the first century CE, the lifetime of Seneca, and even three centuries later in the time of Augustine.

In *The Harmony of the Evangelists* (1.22.30), Augustine used the following words to attack the incompetence of gentiles in understanding the Jewish god:

> But their own Varro (and they can find none of their people more learned than he) thought that the god of the Jews was Jupiter ... For because the Romans customarily worship nothing superior to Jupiter, as is sufficiently clearly attested by their Capitolium, and consider him to be king of all the gods, when he observed that the Jews worshipped a supreme god, he could not imagine that he was anything other than Jupiter.[243]

Augustine cited Varro's discussion of the Jewish god as part of his attack on the unintelligent identification of the Jewish god with Jupiter by the gentiles. Again, the passage clearly tells of the superiority of Jupiter the Capitolinus among other Roman deities. Additionally, the account reflects a situation in which the parallel between the two deities was a center of theological debate between Romans and Jews in the lifetime of Varro, around the beginning of the Common Era.

To summarize, the confluence of archaeological and literary evidence indicates that from the ancient era to the imperial period, the Jupiter Capitolinus was the most important religious and political center for Romans. It retained its preeminent role in the competitions with the temples established or renovated in the Augustan revival, such as the temples of Mars Ultor and of Apollo, two of Augustus's favorites. The references to the divine triad, Jupiter, Juno and Minerva with its Capitolinus in the works of Seneca and Varro, which was then cited by Augustine, reflect a competition between the triad and the Jewish god in the imperial period. The humiliating tax imposed by Vespasian on all Jews for rebuilding the Jupiter Capitolinus, is, in particular, a piece of striking evidence for the threat of the triad to Judaism and the early church as well.

---

242. North, *Roman Religion*, 82; Beard et al., *Religions*, 2:233–34.

243. Beard et al., *Religions*, 2:320

Capitolia: Shrines of Jupiter, Juno and Minerva

As the Roman Republic extended its power over the entire Mediterranean world, the Capitoline Triad increasingly became the preeminent deities for the communities both in the Latin west and in the Greek east before the imperial period. The communities' familiarity with the deity was manifest in the many treaties, statues and dedicatory inscriptions deposited in the Jupiter Capitolinus on the Capitol as well as in the proliferation of Capitolia, shrines to Jupiter, Juno and Minerva, established widely in the coastal cities of the Mediterranean. Many of the remains of these temples indicate a date approximately two centuries before the Common Era.

The custom of building Capitolia spread outwards from Rome to the Italian *coloniae* and then into the entire empire as well.[244] A Capitolium, a shrine to Jupiter, Juno and Minerva, on the Roman model established in a province, was of a mutual nature in the sense that on the one hand, it exhibited the allegiance of a *colonia* to Rome by means of mimicry, and on the other hand, it was a sign of independence to the *colonia* and hence a useful counter in the competition for prestige, honor and status that was one of the defining features of provincial culture across the Roman world.[245] Archaeological remains of Capitolia have been found in both the Latin west and the Greek east of the Roman world.

In Ostia, an ancient *colonia* in Italy, remains of a first-century synagogue was found along with an inscription, recording in Greek, the gift of an ark for keeping the scrolls of the Torah, prefaced by an invocation in Latin for the emperor's well-being.[246] There were also remains of a Capitolium at the north end of the forum, which was established by Hadrian to replace and to take over the cults of two older temples on the north side of the decumanus in the forum that had been destroyed, which were, too, a Capitolium,[247] and a temple of Jupiter,[248] established towards the end of the first century BCE.[249] These remains not only indicate an increased emphasis on the Capitoline Triad in the *colonia* throughout the period from

---

244. Beard et al., *Religions*, 2:244.
245. Ibid., 1:336.
246. Schürer, *History of the Jewish People*, 3:1:81–82; Meiggs, *Roman Ostia*, 587–88.
247. Meiggs, *Roman Ostia*, 352 n. 1.
248. Ibid., 352 n. 2.
249. Ibid., 380–81.

Augustus to Hadrian,[250] but also the interrelatedness, if not competition, between the imperial cult and the Capitoline Triad, as well as the tension between Judaism and the Roman cults.

Some second-century BCE *coloniae* in Spain established their own Capitolia immediately at the time of their foundations. For instance, recent excavations in Hispania unearthed ruins of a Roman temple with three chambers, each of which sheltered one of the Triad. It was established shortly after the foundation of Italica in 206 BCE and is the earliest Roman temple in Hispania.[251] About 100 BCE, in the new Roman town in Emporion there was a huge monumental complex enclosed on three sides by a porticoed passage, at the heart of which was a large, awe-inspiring Capitolium raised on a rectangular podium 19-metre in width and length.[252] The whole complex was the religious and commercial centre of town and the earliest known example of this Roman architectural type outside Italy.[253] By the middle of the first century CE, Capitoline worship had spread through major towns in many areas, for example, Tarraco, Clunia and Baelo.[254] In addition to Capitoline worship, the regulations from Urso specified major games in honor of the Capitoline Triad.[255]

From the second century CE onwards, *municipia* in North Africa began to establish their Capitolia. In Thubursicu Numidarum, a city in Algeria, there was a Capitolium dedicated in 113 CE. In Numluli, which lay in the territory of Carthage, some elite people dedicated a Capitolium for the local Roman citizens and for the village itself.[256] In neighbouring Thugga, in about the mid-second century CE, a group of Roman citizens dedicated a Capitolium in Roman-style to the Capitoline Triad for the well-being of Marcus Aurelius and Lucius Verus. On its pediment, there was a relief of an eagle bearing a man aloft, which symbolized that Jupiter, Juno and Minerva would protect the emperor in his earthly life and carry him to the heavens in his next life.[257] Tertullian reported that some Christians participated in the sacrifice to the Capitolium at Carthage, although many refused to do

250. Beard et al., *Religions*, 1:334 n. 58.
251. Keay, *Roman Spain*, 145 n. 2.
252. Ibid., 117 n. 2.
253. Ibid., 117.
254. Ibid., 148.
255. Ibid., 117, 145, 148.
256. *CIL* 8.26121.
257. *CIL* 8.15513.

so.²⁵⁸ Cyprian, the bishop of Carthage, employed the Capitolium as a metaphor for the enemy of the Christian church.²⁵⁹

The spread of the Capitoline Triad extended to the cities of the eastern Mediterranean. In Heliopolis, the modern Baalbek in Lebanon, which lay in the territory of the *colonia* of Berytus, there was a great new civic temple from the period of Augustus, in which the name of the chief god, Jupiter Optimus Maximus Heliopolitanus, indicated the influence of local culture on the Capitoline god.²⁶⁰

Converting Jerusalem into a Greco-Roman city had been Hadrian's most ambitious project concerning the city, according to Dio Cassius.²⁶¹ The plan for the project began in 130 CE,²⁶² and it rearoused the ongoing opposition of Jews to Romans that had long existed and eventually resulted in the revolt of Bar Kokhba, also known as the second Jewish war, which lasted for three and a half years, from the spring of 132 CE to the summer of 135 CE.²⁶³ The revolt turned into an upheaval that was at least as violent as the revolt in the time of Vespasian.²⁶⁴ Church fathers report consistently that Hadrian completely destroyed the vestiges of the Jewish capital that had survived the devastation by Titus.²⁶⁵ Approximately a year after Hadrian quashed the revolt, he laid the foundation of the new city, Aelia Capitolina, in which he erected the temples to Jupiter and to himself on the site of the Jerusalem temple and also the Jupiter Capitolinus in the forum in

---

258. Tertullian, *Cor.* 12.3.
259. Cyprian, *Ep.* 59.18.1.
260. Millar, *Roman Near East*, 281–85.
261. Dio Cassius, *Hist. rom.* 69.12.1–2.
262. According to Dio Cassius, *Hist. rom.* 69.12.1–2, the foundation of Aelia occurred during Hadrian's first visit to Syria in 130 CE. According to Eusebius, however, the conversion of Jerusalem into Aelia Capitolina was the punishment for the Bar Kokhba revolt and thus took place after the end of the revolt in 135 CE (*Hist. eccl.* 4.6.4). Smallwood argues with several reasons that the two authoritative accounts can be combined by supposing that Dio Cassius reported the inception of the project and Eusebius its fulfillment. Firstly, she explains that planning for the re-foundation of Jerusalem in 130 CE would harmonize with Hadrian's actions elsewhere. Secondly, she argues with plenty of evidence that it is logical to assume that the actual foundation of Aelia took place a year after the end of the revolt since reconstruction works could not have begun immediately. Moreover, she points out that Dio Cassius wrote by topics rather than annalistically in his report (*Jews under Roman Rule*, 433; 459 n. 122; 432 n. 16).
263. Smallwood, *Jews under Roman Rule*, 441 n. 51.
264. Schürer, *History of the Jewish People*, 1:543.
265. Ibid., 1:550 n. 162.

the city center.²⁶⁶ An image of a plow guided by Hadrian appeared on a coin of Aelia, and the ploughing up of Jerusalem and the temple became the last of the five national disasters commemorated annually on 9 Ab, according to the Mishnah.²⁶⁷ The symbolism of ploughing up the city was employed by both sides. To the Jews, it represented the devastation of Jerusalem, and to the Romans, the inauguration of the new Greco-Roman city.²⁶⁸ In addition, standing on the ruins of the heart of Jerusalem, the new structures symbolized both the punishment meted out to the mutinous Jews and the suppression of Yahweh by Jupiter, which in turn represented the tenacity of Roman control over the city.²⁶⁹

The failure of the revolt of 66–70 CE resulted in the destruction of the Jerusalem temple and a disparaging temple tax paid by Jews for rebuilding the Capitolinus in Rome. The failure of the revolt of Bar Kokhba in 132–135 CE resulted in the conversion of Jerusalem into a pagan city in whose center stood the Jupiter Capitolinus. Therefore, there was an increased emphasis on the Capitoline Triad as a means by which the Romans bolstered their control over Palestine from the second half of the first century to the second century CE.

Finally, the most germane locale for the present study is Asia Minor, the home of the seven Christian communities mentioned in Rev 1–3. In order to let their devotion be memorialized in the capital, many eastern communities honored Roma and the Romans by establishing dedications and statues on the Capitol.²⁷⁰ Moreover, since the Greeks understood Jupiter to be the guardian of oaths and treaties,²⁷¹ many Greek cities and kings

---

266. Dio Cassius reported only a temple of Jupiter on the temple site, not a Capitolinus (*Hist. rom.* 69.12.1). Eusebius, however, mentioned a temple of Venus on the site of Christ's tomb (*Vit. Const.* 3.25–26), and Jerome spoke of statues of Jupiter and Venus there and on the site of the cross (*Ep.* 58.3). The two accounts are probably references to the Capitolium in the forum, provided the historian confused Minerva with Venus. Remnants of the Capitolium survive below the Russian Hospice of Alexander near the Church of the Holy Sepulchre (Kenyon, *Jerusalem*, 190). For an analysis of the literary sources on the three temples, see Smallwood, *Jews under Roman Rule*, 459–60 n. 125. In addition, Schürer argues that the main cult of the city was that of Jupiter Capitolinus (*History of the Jewish People*, 1:554 n. 186).

267. Schürer, *History of the Jewish People*, 1:551 n. 163.

268. Ibid., 1:551 n. 164.

269. Smallwood, *Jews under Roman Rule*, 459.

270. Mellor, *Worship of the Goddess Roma*, 203; Beard et al., *Religions*, 1:158.

271. Mellor, *Worship of the Goddess Roma*, 130 n. 144.

The Identities of the Beast from the Sea and the Beast from the Land in Revelation 13

deposited oaths and treaties in or around the Jupiter Capitolinus on the Capitol.[272]

Among the remains of these deposits, there is a series of dedicatory inscriptions inscribed in roughly similar letter forms on travertine blocks approximately 57 cm in height with the same moldings, which, therefore, constitute a homogeneous group of contemporary texts.[273] Of these texts, one was dedicated by a king Ariobarzanes of Cappadocia,[274] and another one by the Tabaeans.[275] Since the first Ariobarzanes came to the throne in 95 BCE, and since on historical grounds the Tabaean text was most likely produced after the three Mithridatic Wars, many scholars date the two texts to the period shortly after the defeat of Mithridates by Sulla and the peace of Dardanus (84 BCE) and so date the other deposits to the first century BCE.[276]

In addition to the group of first century remains, there are pieces of dedicatory inscriptions and statues dated to the second century BCE. One of them was dedicated by a man whose surname was "Philopator and Philadelphus."[277] According to numismatic evidence, the man was Mithridates IV Philopator Philadelphus, who was a son of Mithridates III and hence the sixth king of Pontus, who ruled the kingdom from 170–150 BCE.[278] This identification is also agrees with the restoration of the dedicator's name from the bilingual text.[279] Since Mithridates IV came to the throne shortly after 160 BCE,[280] it is likely that the dedication took place during the short reign of the king in the 150s BCE.[281]

Another famous inscription contains a bilingual text that records the dedication of a statue of Roma to Capitoline Jupiter and the Romans by Lycia, a group of cities on the western coast of Asia bound together in the Lycian League. The dedicatory letters, "in recognition of their goodness,

---

272. Lintott, "Capitoline Dedications," 137–44.
273. Mellor, *Worship of the Goddess Roma*, 203 n. 1.
274. *CIL* I2 731.
275. *CIL* I2 730.
276. Mellor, *Worship of the Goddess Roma*, 203–4.
277. *CIL* I2 730; *ILS* 30 = *ILLRP* 180; *ILLRP* 181.
278. Mellor, *Worship of the Goddess Roma*, 204 n. 6; 84 n. 370.

279. Neither the Greek text nor the Latin leaves the king's name. But Mellor points out that because this dynasty retained the name for generation after generation, it is easy to restore it from the remains (*Worship of the Goddess Roma*, 84 n. 368).

280. Mellor, *Worship of the Goddess Roma*, 204 n. 6.
281. Ibid., 204.

benevolence and favour towards the Lycians,"[282] refers to the aftermath of the defeat of Rhodes by the Romans in the battle of Pydna in 168 BCE, in which the Lycians had their freedom restored from the subjugation of their traditional enemies whom they had been fighting against for over twenty years,[283] since they had been assigned to the Rhodians at the Treaty of Apamea in 188 BCE.[284] Both the phrasing and tone of the text indicate a date shortly after 167 BCE for the dedication of the statue,[285] and it was probably the only such statue on the Capitol then.[286] The inscription was preserved in Renaissance copies and found on the Capitoline Hill in the sixteenth century CE.[287]

To the north of Lycia was the Cibyrate Federation, a group of thriving trading communities of which Cibyra was the leading one and thus the federation was usually so called. At the Treaty of Apamea, Cibyra had its freedom restored from the rule of Moagetes, a tyrant who was notorious in his savage and deceitful character.[288] According to the text of the treaty between Rome and Cibyra, the settlement was a mutual assistance treaty.[289] Copies of it were inscribed on bronze tablets that were set up both on the base of the gold statue of Roma in Cibyra and in the temple of Jupiter Capitolinus in Rome.[290] Hence, it is likely that the treaty was ratified and the statue erected in 188 BCE, shortly after the deposition of Moagetes.[291] Additionally, the peculiarities of the letter forms and the orthography of the text support this date.[292]

---

282. *CIL* I2 725 = *CIL* 6.372; *ILS* 31 = *ILLRP* 174.

283. Livy, 41, 25, 8 (174 BCE); 42, 14, 8 (172 BCE); Mellor, *Worship of the Goddess Roma*, 38 n. 61.

284. Mellor, *Worship of the Goddess Roma*, 37, 204. In addition, since Antiochus III took control of Lycia in 197 BCE, the Lycians loyally supported the king in his war against Rome (Magie, *Roman Rule*, 1:524; 2:1380 nn. 30–31). Later on, at the Treaty of Apamea in 188 BCE, Rome gave Lycia to the Rhodians, which the Rhodian embassy had not even requested (Livy, 37, 56, 5).

285. Mellor, *Worship of the Goddess Roma*, 204.

286. Ibid., 153 n. 144.

287. *CIL* I2 725 = *CIL* 6.372.

288. Mellor, *Worship of the Goddess Roma*, 40 n. 68.

289. Ibid., 40 n. 71; 150 n. 125.

290. Ibid., 40, 150.

291. Ibid., 40 n. 71.

292. Ibid.

Ephesus was the most important city on the Ionian coast and, among the seven cities of Asia mentioned in Rev 1–3, the nearest one to Patmos. The city was assigned to Eumenes of Pergamum in the Treaty of Apamea in 188 BCE,[293] and under Pergamene control, the chief port of Asia flourished and became the second capital of the Attalids. The city had its freedom restored either shortly after the death of Attalus in 133 BCE and the bequest of his kingdom to Rome or soon after the Roman commissioners organized the new province of Asia in, and after, 129 BCE.[294] Hence, the Ephesians dedicated a statue to the Romans in gratitude for the restoration of their freedom from Attalid control.[295] In any case, the Ephesian dedication on the Capitoline took place more than a century before the Common Era.

At the southwest corner of Phrygia lay Laodicea on the Lycus River, where the Christian community was one of the seven, along with Ephesus, mentioned in Rev 1–3. The city was assigned to Pergamum in the Treaty of Apamea. The Laodiceans dedicated a statue of Populus Romanus on the Capitoline at Rome,[296] in gratitude for the city's freedom granted by Rome, which took place shortly after Attalus bequeathed the territory to Rome in 133 BCE, either after the quashing of the uprising led by Aristonicus of Pergamum in 131 BCE or at the time of the organization of the province of Asia in 129 BCE.[297] In addition to the Laodicean inscription, on the same monument on the Capitoline, was found a tiny fragment, which, according to the few inscribed letters that are left, populus Ie[rapolitanus . . .],[298] was dedicated by the citizens of Hierapolis, another Phrygian city situated about seven miles down the Lycus from Laodicea.

These dedicatory inscriptions and statues were deposited in the Jupiter Capitolinus on the Capitol, since Jupiter had been the guardian of oaths and treaties for the Romans long before the imperial period, and since the Jupiter Capitolinus was a repository for important oaths, treaties and dedications.[299] The great temple, however, was destroyed by a conflagration in July 83 BCE, which caused the Capitolinus to lose its function for over a decade until its rededication in 69 BCE. Therefore, there is a suggestion that

---

293. Ibid., 56 n. 192.
294. Ibid., 57, 204.
295. *CIL* I2 727–28.
296. *CIL* I2 728; *CIL* 6.374.
297. Mellor, *Worship of the Goddess Roma*, 204.
298. *CIL* I2 729.
299. Mellor, *Worship of the Goddess Roma*, 130 n. 143.

soon after 83 BCE, following Sulla's return to Rome, a separate monument was established on the Capitol to store these inscriptions and statues while the Capitolinus was in ruins.[300] Since the minimum perimeter of the extant fragments of these inscriptions is sixty feet, it is reasonable to argue that once there was a separate monument established for storing these inscriptions and statues.[301]

In addition to the statues and inscriptions deposited in the Jupiter Capitolinus, many cities in Asia Minor also established Capitolia locally as did other coastal cities on the Mediterranean. In the Greek city of Nicaea in Bithynia, there were statues of the Capitoline Triad to the local god, albeit with a Greek inscription, dedicated by an Italian merchant.[302]

In Alabanda, one of the principle cities of Caria with a reputation for affluence, there was a cult of Roma that included a temple and a festival, according to epigraphic and numismatic evidence.[303] Remains of the Capitoline Triad were apparent in the Romaia, in which during an ambassadorial trip to Rome in 170 BCE, the Alabandan envoys presented a gold crown to Jupiter, contributed armor for the Roman forces in Macedon, together with a dedicatory inscription.[304] The cult was established either in 189 BCE, soon after the battle of Magnesia and before the dispatch of the first ambassadorial trip to Rome, or after Apamea in 188 BCE, at which the city was granted freedom.[305] The Roma in Alabanda is the only report of such a cult in the extant writings of Livy (43.6.5), and the Romaia in the city are considered the earliest example of a festival in such a cult.[306]

In the three Ionian cities, Miletus, Teos and Smyrna, evidence for Capitoline influence is varied. One of the wealthy coastal communities, the Milesians, had been loyal to the Romans in their campaigns against Antiochus,[307] and before that against Perseus.[308] As a reward of their loyalty they were granted freedom at Apamea,[309] at which the Milesians also had

---

300. Ibid., 205.
301. Ibid.
302. Beard et al., *Religions*, 1:337 n. 64.
303. Mellor, *Worship of the Goddess Roma*, 42 n. 83.
304. Ibid., 42.
305. Ibid., 43.
306. Ibid., 37–38 n. 56; 42 n. 84.
307. Livy, 37.16.2.
308. Ibid., 43.6.4.
309. Mellor, *Worship of the Goddess Roma*, 54.

Myus, or some parts of it, that is the territories they had lost a decade earlier, restored to them.[310] An inscription from the temple in the city contains the regulations for the priesthood of Roma and for the sacrifices to the goddess as well as details of the festival of the Romaia.[311] The regulation for the first priest's tenure, a partial term of three years and eight months instead of the full term of four years, indicates that the cult was established about 130 BCE.[312] Additionally, these sacrifices marked regular turning points in civic life, because the sacrifices to Rome and its people were also performed at the entry into office of new magistrates and other regular official events.[313]

At Teos, there was an altar to Zeus Ktesios, Zeus Kapetolios, Roma and Agathos Daimon.[314] After the Apamea settlement, Teos was under the control of Eumenes of Pergamum.[315] Although the Greek city subsequently appealed to Rome,[316] which was a sign of diplomatic autonomy,[317] the city did not have its freedom restored until it was granted by Rome in 167 BCE or probably after the bequest of Attalus.[318] The altar was dedicated in gratitude to Rome for the city's freedom.[319] Since Zeus appeared both in his domestic semblance as the city guardian and in his public guise as the securer of treaties, the altar indicated knowledge of the Jupiter Capitolinus in the Greek community.[320]

Like Ephesus and Laodicea, Smyrna is one of the seven cities mentioned in Rev 1–3. Smyrna had been loyal to Rome in the campaigns against Mithridates through the years,[321] and therefore, after Apamea the city had its freedom restored and its territory increased.[322] As early as 195 BCE, the Smyrnaeans established a temple to Roma.[323] Smyrnaean coins

310. Ibid., 52 n. 159.
311. Beard et al., *Religions*, 1:159.
312. Magie, *Roman Rule*, 1:167; 2:1056 n. 28.
313. Beard et al., *Religions*, 1:159 n. 131.
314. *IGRR* 4.1556.
315. Mellor, *Worship of the Goddess Roma*, 55 n. 183.
316. Ibid., 56 n. 184.
317. Ibid., 56 n. 185.
318. Ibid., 56.
319. Ibid., 155 n. 161.
320. Ibid., 155.
321. Ibid., 52 n. 152.
322. Livy, 38.39.11.
323. Tacitus, *Ann.* 4.56.

that were embossed with the image of the temple were still current in the third century of the Empire.[324] The Romaia were still celebrated four centuries after the establishment of the cult.[325] More importantly, a Capitolium was found in Smyrna.[326]

To sum up, enough archaeological and epigraphic evidence demonstrates that throughout the imperial period, the Capitoline Triad not only played a preeminent role among the many deities in the Roman pantheon by dwelling in the Jupiter Capitolinus in Rome, but also influenced the whole Mediterranean world, from Italy to Spain, North Africa, Jerusalem, and Asia Minor, through the extensive establishment of Capitolia. The annual temple tax Vespasian imposed on Jews in 71–72 CE for rebuilding the Capitolinus in Rome apparently stirred up the tension between the Capitoline Triad and the gospel of the early church. The conversion of Jerusalem into Aelia Capitolina Hadrian carried out in 132–135 CE manifests the increasing significance of the Capitoline Triad as a means of dominion over the Jews from the first to the second century CE. A variety of archaeological remains of the Capitoline Triad has been found in Asia Minor, including many cities mentioned in Rev 1–3.

CONCLUSION

This chapter aims to argue that the tripartite ideology is the underlying principle according to which John stratifies the dragon and the beast from the sea and the beast from the land in Rev 12–13. The first part of this chapter has demonstrated that in producing Rev 12–13, the author arranged the dragon and the two beasts in a hierarchical relationship, in which the beast from the land is subordinate to the beast from the sea, which in turn is subordinate to the dragon. In this hierarchy, the three figures are found in different contexts and each takes a specific role in accordance with its context. The dragon is related to the ultimate sovereignty of the supernatural, mythical context. The sea beast takes the role of warrior and appears in a belligerent context. The land beast is found as a figure relating to the economic theme. This distinctive hierarchical relationship of the dragon and the two beasts is not found in biblical and extra-biblical writings but is found exclusively in Rev 12 and 13.

324. Mellor, *Worship of the Goddess Roma*, 51 n. 151.
325. Ibid., 51 n. 150.
326. Ibid., 130 n. 146.

The second part of this chapter studies the tripartite ideology that Dumézil discerns in many Indo-European mythological traditions, including the Indic, Scandinavian, Iranian and Roman. According to Dumézil, in this tripartite hierarchy, the figure on the top level relates to ultimate sovereignty in a supernatural sphere; the figure on the second level is a warlike figure; the figure on the third level relates to economics and productivity. A variety of evidence exists for both the social and theological tripartitions in Roman society from the ancient period to the imperial age. The Capitoline Triad, Jupiter, Juno and Minerva, are of critical importance, since the Jupiter Capitolinus was the central issue in both the first and second Jewish wars.

There is a striking parallel between the hierarchy of the three figures in Rev 12 and 13 and the tripartite ideology Dumézil has discovered in the Indo-European traditions. In Rev 12 and 13, the dragon and the sea beast and land beast in the hierarchy display the same functions as the three figures of the tripartite system argued by Dumézil. Thus, the relationship between the dragon and the two beasts in Rev 12 and 13 fits well with this tripartite ideology not only in terms of the underlying structure of the relationship but also in terms of the function of each figure on its corresponding hierarchical level. Therefore, this tripartite ideology can explain the hierarchical relationship of the three figures in Rev 12 and 13. It is plausible that the relationship between the dragon and the two beasts reflects the influence of this tripartite ideology.

5

The Identities of the Two Beasts

CHAPTER 4 HAS DEMONSTRATED that the tripartite ideology is the underlying principle with which the apocalyptist put together the dragon and the two beasts in Rev 12–13, assigning each figure a specific role in its corresponding context. The dragon is about ultimate sovereignty in the supernatural realm, and thus tops the tripartite hierarchy, just as does Jupiter in the Capitoline Triad. The beast from the sea is of a belligerent nature, and, hence, holds the second position in the structure like Juno in the Roman system. The beast from the land belongs to the economic sphere, and accordingly takes the third seat of the order like Minerva. In accordance with this arrangement, the sea beast represents one of the Roman emperors and the land beast is a key figure relating to the imperial cult. Based on these findings, this chapter goes further to probe the exact referents of the two beasts in two sections. The first section identifies the beast from the sea by studying the related passages, and then, in correspondence with those, seeks to date the Apocalypse by examining the related evidence. The second section identifies the beast from the land by exploring the evidence for the establishment of the imperial cult.

THE IDENTITY OF THE BEAST FROM THE SEA

Revelation 13 contains two pieces of information concerning the beast from the sea. Firstly, one of its heads seemed to have sustained a mortal wound caused by a sword, but this wound had healed (vv. 3a, 12c, 14c). Secondly, the number of the name of the beast is 666 (13:18). This information points consistently towards Nero being the most plausible candidate for this beast. While the descriptions of the mortal wound that had healed in vv. 3a, 12c, 14c fit the legend of Nero's return in a pictorial way,[1] the number 666 in 13:18 functions as a cryptic game to confirm this identification. Nero was the emperor of Rome from 54–68 CE. Rumors of his return from the dead are well-documented. On 8 June 68, the Senate deposed him and declared that he was a public enemy. He committed suicide on the following day, but since there was a paucity of witnesses who indeed saw his corpse and his burial, rumors spread widely that he was still alive and would come back.[2] Since, during his lifetime, Nero maintained a good relationship with the Parthians in the east, the rumors resulted in a legend that he had sought asylum with the Parthians and would come back with them to retake the imperial throne of Rome (*Sib. Or.* 4.137–39). The legend became the myth of Nero *redux*, that is, "Nero returned," which held that the emperor had not died at all but was still alive and would return.[3] A variant version was the myth of Nero *redivivus*, that is, "Nero revived," which expressed the notion that, although he was dead, the emperor would return to life and come back.[4] Either version of the legend fits the imagery of the mortal wound that had healed.

The number 666 is most likely a gematria riddle as most commentators have remarked.[5] Gematria is a form of coded wordplay applicable to both Greek and Hebrew, in which the letters of the alphabet are assigned numerical values based on their positions in the alphabet. The popularity of the game in both the Jewish and Greek communities of the Greco-Roman world is well-documented.[6] When the name "Nero Caesar" is transliter-

---

1. While one of the heads of the beast seemed to have a mortal wound (v. 3a), it was the beast that recovered from the wound on its head (vv. 12c, 14c). It appears that there are two source variants here, with one describing the beast's head and the other the beast. See ch. 4, pp. 98–99.

2. Suetonius, *Nero*, 57; Tacitus, *Hist.* 2.8.

3. Aune, *Revelation*, 2:738.

4. Ibid.

5. Charles, *Revelation*, 1:367; Collins, *Combat Myth*, 174; Bauckham, *Climax*, 387 n. 10; Witherington, *Revelation*, 176–77, 185; Roloff, *Revelation*, 166; Harrington, *Revelation*, 144; Krodel, *Revelation*, 258–59.

6. In his work, *Light from the Ancient East*, 276, Deissmann cites two graffiti from Pompeii as examples, both in Greek: "I love the girl whose number is 545 [ΦΜΕ]," and "The number of her honorable name is 45 (or 1035)." In the *Sibylline Oracles*, the Roman emperors from Julius Caesar to Hadrian are referred to by numerals equivalent to their

ated into Hebrew from the Greek to form קסר נרון, the numerical value of the letters is 666.[7] A close parallel to this case occurs in an Aramaic document from Wadi Murabbaʻat dated to the second year of Nero, in which the Greek form of the emperor's name is transliterated along with the title as קסר נרון, which, too, comes to the same numerical value—666.[8] Although here the Hebrew spelling is defective, that is, omits the yod from קיסר, the defective spelling is attested in rabbinic literature and so is acceptable in some instances.[9] Another support for this solution is the variant reading 616 found in the MS tradition, since when the Latin form of Nero is transliterated into Hebrew it yields קסר נרו, with the omission of the final nun, the numerical value of which is 616.[10] The entire text in 13:18 confirms this view too. The apocalyptist says that the one who has understanding should reckon τὸν ἀριθμὸν τοῦ θηρίου, ἀριθμὸς γὰρ ἀνθρώπου ἐστίν, "the number of the beast, for it is a human number." The term ἀνθρώπου functions in a nongeneric rather than a generic sense, and thus refers to a specific, present and historical figure on earth.[11] The beast and the man are identical,[12] and so are the number of the beast and that of the man.[13] This twofold equivalence confirms that the beast is a representation of Nero, because when the Greek word θηρίον, "beast," is written in Hebrew as תריון, the numerical value of these letters is 666.[14] Bauckham concludes that "the gematria does not merely assert that Nero is the beast: it demonstrates that he is."[15] For these reasons, until any new discoveries are made, gematria appears to be

---

initial letters on many occasions, especially in the later books (5:12–51; cf. 11:256, 266; 12:16–271).

7. Charles, *Revelation*, 1:367; Collins, *Combat Myth*, 174–75; Bauckham, *Climax*, 387; Witherington, *Revelation*, 177; Roloff, *Revelation*, 166; Harrington, *Revelation*, 144; Krodel, *Revelation*, 258–59.

8. Aune, *Revelation*, 2:770.

9. Bauckham, *Climax*, 388 n. 14; cf. Charles, *Revelation*, 1:367.

10. Charles, *Revelation*, 1:367; Bauckham, *Climax*, 387; Collins, *Combat Myth*, 175; Witherington, *Revelation*, 177; Roloff, *Revelation*, 166; Harrington, *Revelation*, 144; Krodel, *Revelation*, 258–59.

11. Aune, *Revelation*, 2:769; Charles, *Revelation*, 1:364–65; Collins, *Combat Myth*, 174 n. 106; Mounce, *Revelation*, 261 n. 43.

12. Charles, *Revelation*, 1:366.

13. Bauckham, *Climax*, 389.

14. Ibid., 389 n. 19; Witherington, *Revelation*, 177; Roloff, *Revelation*, 166; Krodel, *Revelation*, 258–59.

15. Bauckham, *Climax*, 389.

the most convincing resolution to the mysterious number, and accordingly, Nero is the beast.

Having reviewed the beast from the sea in chapter 13, the investigation turns to the beast in chapter 17. There are several points of resemblance between the two beasts in the way they are depicted. Firstly, it is only in its first usage in both accounts that the beast appears anarthrously, ἐκ τῆς θαλάσσης θηρίον ἀναβαῖνον, "beast rising out of the sea" (13:1), and θηρίον κόκκινον, "scarlet beast" (17:3). Secondly, since in both cases, the beast has the same physical features, seven heads, as the biblical Leviathan, the ultimate prototype for the beast is Leviathan. Thirdly, similarly, since in both occurrences, the beast has ten horns (13:1; 17:3) just as does the fourth beast in Dan 7 (vv. 7, 20, 24), it reflects the same influence of Daniel. In addition, the introductory phrases, ὧδε ἡ σοφία ἐστίν, "this calls for wisdom," in 13:18a and, ὧδε ὁ νοῦς ὁ ἔχων σοφίαν, "this calls for a mind with wisdom," in 17:9a are in close parallel.[16] Just as the phrase in 13:18a is a redactional addition to its context,[17] the latter one appears to be the same to its. This point of parallel indicates that the data in 13:18 and those in 17:8–11 are related in the final literary setting.[18]

Although an independent unit contextually, Rev 17 functions as the beginning part of a larger section describing the fall of Babylon (17:1—19:10), which is generally understood as an independent unit,[19] since the judgment of the great harlot promised by the angel at the beginning (17:1) is the motif of the entire section.[20] The passage in question is the interpretation of the scarlet beast (vv. 7–14). The interpretation of the "seven heads" is twofold. They are "seven mountains" (v. 9b) and also "seven kings" (v. 9c). The second expression is complex since it implies different layers as found in the final form of the passage. Taking out the first interpretive piece (v. 9b), the passage reveals how the second interpretive cluster (vv. 9c–11) delineates the "seven heads" symbol with reference to the beast "that you

---

16. Aune, *Revelation*, 2:769; 3:941; Charles, *Revelation*, 2:68; Bauckham, *Climax*, 394; Mounce, *Revelation*, 315; Roloff, *Revelation*, 198; Harrington, *Revelation*, 144; Richard, *Apocalypse*, 131.

17. Aune, *Revelation*, 2:769; cf. Charles, *Revelation*, 2:68.

18. Cf. Bauckham, *Climax*, 394–96; Roloff, *Revelation*, 198; Richard, *Apocalypse*, 131.

19. Aune, *Revelation*, 3:915; Collins, *Combat Myth*, 19; Bauckham, *Climax*, 3–5; Witherington, *Revelation*, 216; Roloff, *Revelation*, 15; Harrington, *Revelation*, 20; Schüssler Fiorenza, *Revelation*, 95; Richard, *Apocalypse*, 33–34, 127–28; Beasley-Murray, *Revelation*, 248; Beale, *Revelation*, 114, 847.

20. Aune, *Revelation*, 3:915; cf. Charles, *Revelation*, 2:55.

saw" (v. 8a). First, the beast is described with the following sequential elements twice in v. 8ac:

> ἦν καὶ οὐκ ἔστιν, καὶ μέλλει ἀναβαίνειν ἐκ τῆς ἀβύσσου, καὶ εἰς ἀπώλειαν ὑπάγει;
> ἦν καὶ οὐκ ἔστιν καὶ παρέσται;
>
> was, and is not, and is to ascend from the bottomless pit and go to perdition;
> was and is not and is to come;

The same temporal characteristics of the beast are reported separately in v. 11ab as follows:

> καὶ τὸ θηρίον ὃ ἦν καὶ οὐκ ἔστιν ... καὶ εἰς ἀπώλειαν ὑπάγει;
> As for the beast that was and is not ... and it goes to perdition;

These fragments appear to originate from the same cluster of materials since they report the same sequential details of the beast.

On the other hand, when juxtaposing the reckoning data in v. 10a and the first phrase in v. 11b in the following way, the two pieces appear to originate from the same group of materials since they report details of the same kind:

> οἱ πέντε ἔπεσαν, ὁ εἷς ἔστιν, ὁ ἄλλος οὔπω ἦλθεν;
> καὶ αὐτὸς ὄγδοός ἐστιν καὶ ἐκ τῶν ἑπτά ἐστιν;
>
> five of whom have fallen, one is, the other has not yet come;
> it is an eighth but it belongs to the seven;

The first fragment deals with the beast's heads, not the beast, and so does the second piece, since they have the same origin. Finally, the enumeration of the beast's heads and the chronological data of the beast make up the final form of the riddle (v. 11ab) with the former piece being sandwiched in the middle of the entire verse as follows:

> καὶ τὸ θηρίον ὃ ἦν καὶ οὐκ ἔστιν, καὶ αὐτὸς ὄγδοός ἐστιν καὶ ἐκ τῶν ἑπτά ἐστιν, καὶ εἰς ἀπώλειαν ὑπάγει;
>
> As for the beast that was and is not, it is an eighth, but it belongs to the seven, and it goes to perdition;

This analysis demonstrates that the information in the interpretation is a mélange of two source variants. Firstly, the accounts in vv. 8ac and 11ab come from the same source, not including the first phrase in v. 11b, since both verses deal with the beast, not its heads, and describe in a similar manner the sequential features of the beast, which "was and is not and is to go to perdition."[21] Secondly, the numerical data in v. 10a, "five of whom have fallen, one is, the other has not yet come," and the first phrase in v. 11b, "it is an eighth but it belongs to the seven," are very likely to come from a variant source, since they engage in the heads of the beast, not the beast. The two source variants exhibit their own characteristics. The sequential elements related to the beast (vv. 8ac, 11ab) function as a parody of the Christ, since God is described as "the One who is and who was and who is coming" many times (1:4, 8; 4:8; also, 11:17; 16:5).[22] Since the parody of God is a typical feature found in different parts and contexts of/in the Apocalypse, the source appears to be the work of the final editor produced in line with the parodic style of the Apocalypse at a later stage of its composition.

By contrast, the enumeration of the seven heads (vv. 10a, 11b) is found only once in the book here. In recent studies, there has been an increasingly popular perspective that the seven heads in the riddle do not refer to seven specific Roman emperors, but rather function as an apocalyptic symbol designating the complete series of the rulers of Rome.[23] A number of pieces of evidence support this view. First and foremost, the apocalyptist was working with the mythic figure of biblical Leviathan, the distinctive sign of which is its seven heads. Thus, it is the mythic tradition that is responsible for the number seven here. Secondly, seven is a symbol of completeness or totality.[24] This symbolic number occurs fifty-three times in Revelation to reflect the divine arrangement of the universe, for instance, the seven seals, the seven trumpets and the seven bowls.[25] Thirdly, there are cases in other apocalyptic writings that the number of ages or world periods conforms to different numerical schemes. In *4 Ezra* 14:11, history is divided into twelve parts, nine of which have already passed. In the *Apocalypse of Weeks*, Enoch divides history into ten periods, seven of which are already past (*1*

---

21. In arguing that 17:11–17 belongs to a source referring to the return of Nero in the interpretation of the vision (17:8–18), Charles notes that the expression, "which was and is not and is to come" (vv. 8ac, 11), is an addition to the source (*Revelation*, 2:67–68, 70). His argument, though with different focus, is in agreement with the present analysis with respect to the origin of the sequential expression (vv. 8ac, 11).

22. Aune, *Revelation*, 3:939–40.

23. Ibid., 3:948; Caird, *Revelation*, 218–19; Mounce, *Revelation*, 315; Harrington, *Revelation*, 172; Beasley-Murray, *Revelation*, 256–57; Bauckham, *Climax*, 405.

24. Bauckham, *Climax*, 405; Aune, *Revelation*, 3:948.

25. Aune, *Revelation*, 3:948.

En. 93), and three are yet to come leading to eschatological judgment (*1 En.* 91:12-17). Fourthly, there have been attempts to identify the seven kings with seven historical Roman emperors and, based on that, to propose a specific date for the composition of the book.[26] These attempts, however, rarely result in a satisfactory outcome because, no matter how one counts the emperors, a conclusion is not arrived at that makes sense of the passage and the whole Apocalypse as well.[27] Basically, this is because the way in which the ancient Greeks and Romans counted the Roman emperors is not certain.[28] Fifthly, according to the canonical Roman tradition, there were exactly seven kings in Rome from the founding of the city (753 BCE) to that of the Republic (509 BCE): Romulus, Numa Pompilius, Tullus Hostilius, Ancus Marcus, Tarquinius Priscus, Servius Tullius and Tarquinius Superbus.[29] There is evidence, however, that there were more than seven kings historically during this period, and that Roman and Etruscan historians identified minor figures with major ones in order to maintain the canonical number.[30] For all these reasons, the seven heads are more likely to function to symbolize the entire series of the emperors of Rome as the whole Roman imperial power than to refer specifically to seven historical rulers. Following this reckoning, the verse culminates with how far the time of Revelation is from the end of the sequence of seven, that is, the full sequence of the emperors of Rome. The distance is stated as "only a little while" (v. 10b), a conventional timeframe used to designate apocalyptic imminence (cf. 6:11). Thus, the primary concern of v. 10 is the nearness of the end rather than the tabulation of the past.[31]

The beast is "an eighth, but it belongs to the seven" (v. 11b). In early Judaism, eight carries eschatological implications since it represents the eighth day of the new creation after the seven-day creation had been completed (*2 En.* 33:1-2; *Barn.* 15:9). In early Christian tradition, occasionally, the eighth day represents Sunday (*Barn.* 15:9). There are cases in Hebrew idiom where the consecutive numbers seven and eight are found in parallel

---

26. For instance, Bell, "Date of John's Apocalypse," 93-102; Wilson, "Domitianic Date," 587-605.

27. Bauckham, *Climax*, 405. For the results of the different ways of counting the seven emperors, see Aune, *Revelation*, 1:lxi-lxii.

28. See ch. 1, pp. 7-9.

29. Aune, *Revelation*, 3:948.

30. Ibid.

31. Mounce, *Revelation*, 317; Bauckham, *Climax*, 406-7.

to form a "graded numerical saying" (Eccl 11:2).³² In Mic 5:4[5], in "the seven shepherds and eight princes of men," the consecutive seven and eight appear to indicate indefinite but adequate numbers.³³ Thus, the cardinal eighth is symbolic as is the numeral seven. The symbolic function of the two numbers is consistent with the larger context, since the phrase in which the number is found is independent from the parodic fragments that enclose it.

Having studied the passages relating to the "seven kings," the investigation turns back to the "seven mountains" (17:9b). This first interpretive piece very likely originates from another source. Verse 9b reads αἱ ἑπτὰ κεφαλαὶ ἑπτὰ ὄρη εἰσίν, ὅπου ἡ γυνὴ κάθηται ἐπ' αὐτῶν, "the seven heads are seven mountains on which the woman is seated." The portrayal of the woman sitting occurs four times in chapter 17 (vv. 1, 3, 9, 15), and it signifies enthronement in each case.³⁴ The phrase "seven hills" is frequently found as a symbol of Rome in various works by Roman writers from the mid-first century BCE onwards.³⁵ In this usage, the terms *mons*, "mountain," and *collis*, "hill," are normally interchangeable.³⁶ On the reverse of a specific sestertius, minted during the reign of Vespasian (69–79 CE), Dea Roma dressed in military garments is depicted sitting on the Seven Hills of Rome, with a parazonium in her left hand resting on her left knee.³⁷ A similar image of the goddess sitting on the Seven Hills is found on an inscription from Corinth on the base of a statue erected during the first half of the second century CE.³⁸ Hence, the imagery of "seven mountains" was far from enigmatic, but rather instantly recognizable as a metaphor for the city of Rome in the Greco-Roman world. It is likely that the "seven mountains" fragment is a later interpolation,³⁹ which the final editor inserted

32. Bauckham, *Climax*, 405.

33. Ibid.

34. Aune, *Revelation*, 3:930.

35. Among many others, some examples are Ovid, *Tr.* 1.5.69; Pliny, *Nat.* 3.66–67. According to Varro, the location of Rome was called the *Septimontium*; in his list, the Seven Hills are Capitol (previously called Tarpeian and earlier Saturnian), Aventine, Caelian, Esquiline, Quirinal, Viminal, and Palatine (*Ling.* 5.41–54). Since Varro, this list can be found as the standard for the Seven Hills of Rome in many works, for instance, Strabo, 5.3.7.

36. Livy, 1.44.3.

37. Aune, *Revelation*, 3:920.

38. Robinson, "Monument of Roma," 470–84, pl. 101–6.

39. Charles, *Revelation*, 2:68–69.

into the block before the "seven heads" as an additional clue to the ensuing apocalyptic reference to the symbol, which suggests that the beast is not a supernatural being, but a representation of an earthly power in Rome.

Consequently, having examined the passages related to the seven-headed beast in chapters 13 and 17, this part closes with two points. Firstly, Rev 13 contains two pieces of information concerning the sea beast. One includes the fragments in vv. 3a, 12c and 14c, which together tell of the mortal wound upon one of the heads of the beast that had healed. The other contains the number of the name of the beast, namely, 666 (v. 18). They point to Nero as the most plausible candidate for the beast from the sea. The descriptions of the beast's mortal wound (vv. 3a, 12c, 14c) fit the legend of the return of Nero in a metaphorical way. The number 666 (v. 18) functions as a cryptic word game to confirm this identification.

Secondly, two groups of materials exist in the interpretation block of the beast in 17:8–11. One group contains the fragments describing the temporal elements of the beast (vv. 8ac, 11ab), which in their present literary setting function to parody the divine name.[40] Since the parody of Christ is a preeminent feature found in different parts of the Apocalypse, it is likely that this source reflects work of a later stage by the apocalyptist in order to make it fit in with the overall style of Revelation. The other group contains the reckoning data of the seven heads of the beast (vv. 10a, 11b). Both the numeral seven and the cardinal eighth are symbolic. Seven symbolizes the entire series of the emperors of Rome, designating imperial power as a whole. Eight carries eschatological implications. Functioning in tandem, the two clusters produce the final form of the riddle (v. 11ab). The "seven mountains" fragment (v. 9b) comes from another source. This imagery was a widespread reference to the city of Rome in Roman writings.

The Date of Revelation

There are two opinions concerning the date of Revelation. A number of scholars argue for a date between 68–70 CE shortly after the reign of Nero.[41] Most modern scholars, however, are in favour of a Domitianic date.[42] While both views contain aspects of a potential solution, there are several reasons

---

40. The same temporal expression in three tenses is found with reference to God in 1:4, 8; 4:8; 11:17; 16:5, the latter two of which are shorter variations.

41. Bell, "Date of John's Apocalypse," 93–102; Wilson, "Domitianic Date," 587–605.

42. Aune, *Revelation*, 1:lviii.

why the Domitianic reign is more likely to be the period during which the Apocalypse was composed. This section of the thesis briefly reviews these reasons.

The first and foremost reason is Irenaeus' witness, as it is the only piece of external evidence for the date of Revelation. Writing approximately a century after the Domitianic reign, Irenaeus reported that the book was written πρὸς τῷ τέλει τῆς Δομετιανοῦ ἀρχῆς, "near the end of the reign of Domitian."[43] In this account, what is reported as being "near the end" of the Domitianic reign is the Apocalypse, not John, since the logical subject of the main passive verb ἑωράθη, "it was seen," is more likely to be τὴν ἀποκάλυψιν, "the Apocalypse," than τοῦ καὶ τὴν ἀποκάλυψιν ἑορακότος, "the one who also saw the Apocalypse," that is, ὁ Ἰωάννης, John of Patmos.[44] About two centuries after Domitian's reign, Eusebius, having reported the Neronian persecution in detail,[45] adapted Irenaeus' testimony and stated that the emperor was the successor of Nero with respect to his hostility to God since he organized persecution against the early church.[46] With this report, Eusebius preserved the Greek version of Irenaeus' dating in two different passages.[47] Irenaeus' dating of Revelation was broadly accepted in the ancient church.[48] Secondly, there is a wide consensus that the beast's mortal wound and the 666 conundrum in chapter 13 (vv. 3a, 12c, 14c, and 18) are references to the legend of Nero's return, as aforementioned. It is unlikely that the Nero *redivivus* or Nero *redux* myth was widely circulated until the end of the first century CE.[49] Thirdly, the name "Babylon" is found six times in the Apocalypse (14:6; 16:19; 17:4; 18:2, 10, 21). In each case, it is clearly a symbol for Rome. Also, "Babylon" is found many times in Jewish apocalyptic literature with the same symbolic reference (*4 Ezra* 3:1–2, 28–31; *2 Bar.* 10:1–3; 11:1; 67:7; *Sib. Or.* 5.143, 159) and each such usage was composed after 70 CE, near the end of the first century. Occasionally, the enemy, Rome, is designated Edom, Kittim or Egypt, as well as Babylon

---

43. Irenaeus, *Haer.* 5.30.3.
44. Robinson, *Redating the New Testament*, 221.
45. Eusebius, *Hist. eccl.* 2.25.
46. Ibid., 3.17.1.
47. Ibid., 3.18.3; 5.30.3.
48. Clement of Alexandria, *Quis div.* 42; Victorinus, *Comm. Apoc.* 10.11; 17.10; Origen, *Comm. Matt.* 16.6; Jerome, *Vir. ill.* 9.
49. Mounce, *Revelation*, 19; Aune, *Revelation*, 1:lxi.

in Jewish literature.[50] And Babylon, as a code name for an ungodly, evil power, represents the Syrian empire in Daniel and *Sib. Or.* 3.300–309, both of which are generally dated in the second century BCE.[51] For the most part, however, Babylon is found as a code name for Rome representing the second destroyer of Jerusalem in 70 CE from the latter decades of the first century to the early decades of the second century.[52] This is because just as Babylon captured Jerusalem and demolished the temple in 587 BCE (2 Kgs 25), so Rome captured Jerusalem and destroyed the second temple in 70 CE.[53] The employment of "Babylon" as a symbol for Rome in the Apocalypse points to a date post-70 CE after the first Jewish revolt.[54] The same rationale applies to the description of Jerusalem being like Sodom (11:8), the ancient city destroyed by fire.[55]

Fourthly, the historical circumstances of the seven churches in Roman Asia, reflected in Rev 2–3, provide evidence for a date later rather than earlier in the first century CE. The Laodicean congregation is condemned since it said, "I am rich, I have prospered, and I need nothing" (3:17). While the wealth the community claimed to have may refer to a spiritual richness, indeed the town of Laodicea was famous for its banks and medical school.[56] During the Neronian reign, the city was suffering from an earthquake that almost completely destroyed the whole city around 60–61 CE. The city refused to accept imperial assistance to rebuild the city after the disaster.[57] The arrogant claim of the Laodiceans, however, makes more sense if it is taken to reflect the affluence the community achieved decades later after it recovered from the disaster than if it is taken to refer to the pride held by the congregation after rebuilding itself after the catastrophe that left it almost in ruins. Hence, the wealth of the Laodicean church, if taken literally, seems to refer to a period towards the end of the first century rather than a period during the reign of Nero.[58] On the other hand, the church at Smyrna is described as having been steadfast for a certain time (2:8–11).

50. Thompson, *Revelation*, 14.
51. Collins, "Sibylline Oracles," 1:354–57.
52. Thompson, *Revelation*, 14.
53. Aune, *Revelation*, 1:lxi.
54. Collins, "Dating the Apocalypse of John," 35.
55. Witherington, *Revelation*, 4 n. 9.
56. Strabo, 12.8.20.
57. Ramsay, *Letters to the Seven Churches*, 428.
58. Aune, *Revelation*, 1:lxiii; Mounce, *Revelation*, 19; Roloff, *Revelation*, 11.

There is evidence that the Smyrnaean church did not exist in 60–64 CE, a time when Paul was boasting about the church in Philippi (Polycarp, *Phil.* 11:3).[59] The overall conditions of the churches reflect the fact that they had existed for a period of time that was long enough for them to suffer various trials and defections in the case of Smyrna, and to experience a decline in zeal and faithfulness in the cases of Ephesus, Sardis and Laodicea.[60]

Fifthly, it is reported in 21:14 that on the twelve foundations of the New Jerusalem were inscribed δώδεκα ὀνόματα τῶν δώδεκα ἀποστόλων τοῦ ἀρνίου, "the twelve names of the twelve apostles of the Lamb." The closet parallel to the phrase is τῶν δὲ δώδεκα ἀποστόλων τὰ ὀνόματά, "the names of the twelve apostles" found in Matt 10:2. Elsewhere in the New Testament the expression οἱ δώδεκα ἀπόστολοι, "the twelve apostles," is only found as a variant reading of Luke 9:1; 22:14. The phrase οἱ δώδεκα, "the twelve," was a technical term that originated before Easter (cf. 1 Cor 15:5), while οἱ ἀπόστολοι, "the apostles," originated later, since in the phrase οἱ δώδεκα ἀπόστολοι, the adjectival use of δώδεκα refers to the group of twelve around the pre-Easter Jesus, thus excluding Paul.[61] The idea of this technical phrase developed in the second Christian generation.[62] Since the earliest attestation of the phrase οἱ δώδεκα ἀπόστολοι, "the twelve apostles," is found in the Gospel of Matthew, and since that Gospel was most likely written in the period 80–95 CE,[63] the use of the same phrase in Rev 21:14 suggests a date no earlier than 80 CE.[64]

Sixthly, as the previous chapters have demonstrated, participation in the imperial cult is a major issue in the Apocalypse (13:11–18; 14:9, 11; 15:2; 16:2; 19:20; 20:4). The imperial cult began to flourish in Asia Minor with the first temple established for Augustus in Pergamum in 29 BCE after his defeat of Mark Antony and his allies.[65] Recent studies have argued with solid evidence that it was the provincial league that initiated the request for the establishment of the imperial temple, which in turn needed the approval of the Senate and the emperor, and that participation in the cult was

---

59. Charles, *Revelation*, 1:xciv; Mounce, *Revelation*, 19; Roloff, *Revelation*, 11.
60. Mounce, *Revelation*, 19; Witherington, *Revelation*, 4.
61. Aune, *Revelation*, 1:lxiv.
62. Roloff, *Revelation*, 243.
63. Kümmel, *Introduction to the New Testament*, 119–20.
64. Aune, *Revelation*, 1:lxiv.
65. Dio Cassius, *Hist. rom.* 51.20.6–9; also, Tacitus, *Ann.* 4.37.

not mandatory.⁶⁶ From Augustus onwards, the title θεός, "god," in a dedication was limited to only deceased emperors who had been officially deified by the Senate.⁶⁷ Yet the tradition underwent certain significant changes in the reign of Domitian, as the emperor demanded divine worship in Rome itself in the form of sacrifices.⁶⁸ In addition, there is sufficient evidence for enthusiastic promotion of the imperial cult and simultaneous repression of non-supporters of this cult in Asia during the time of Domitian, which put Christians under significant social pressure to conform to the imperial cult system.⁶⁹ Many scholars believe that the imperial cult had not been a critical threat to the Christian communities until the last decade of the first century CE during the reign of Domitian.

Seventhly, according to Dio Cassius, Domitian ordered that his cousin Flavius Clemens be executed and his wife Domitilla be exiled on a charge of ἀθεότης, "atheism," which Dio equated with τὰ τῶν Ἰουδαίων ἤθη.⁷⁰ Since in the latter half of the nineteenth century, Joseph Lightfoot argued for a widespread persecution in the reign of Domitian with this piece of Dio's work as major evidence,⁷¹ the Domitianic persecution had been an important assumption that commentators adopted for dating the Apocalypse.⁷² This view had undergone little significant challenge until in the latter half of the twentieth century some scholars pointed out that what was the point in Dio's account was the couple's conversion to Judaism in accordance with the context,⁷³ not Christianity, the difference between which would not be a problem to a third-century historian, and that this piece of work is only extant in the eleventh-century epitome of Xiphilinus and a twelfth-century summary by Zonarus, the quality of which are questionable.⁷⁴ Since Xiphilinus' epitome is not completely reliable, however, it cannot be used conclusively to invalidate Dio's argument. Also, Eusebius described

---

66. Price, *Rituals and Power*, 24–25, 249–74.
67. Friesen, *Twice Neokoros*, 22–23.
68. Pliny, *Pan.* 52.1.7.
69. Slater, "On the Social Setting," 238; Price, *Rituals and Power*, 123–26, 197–98.
70. Dio Cassius, *Hist. rom.* 67.14.2.
71. Lightfoot, *Apostolic Fathers*, 1:1:34–37.
72. For example, Charles, *Revelation*, 1:xcv n. 1.
73. Dio Cassius, *Hist. rom.* 67.13.1–3.
74. In his work, "Date of John's Apocalypse," 94, Bell notes that in translating his history, Earnest Cary comments that Xiphilinus' epitome, the chief source for the reign of Domitian, was produced "very carelessly"; also, Wilson, "Domitianic Date," 590–91.

Flavius Clemens and Flavia Domitilla as Christians.[75] On the other hand, in more recent times, by examining the epigraphical and literary evidence, Leonard Thompson argues that the Latin literalists whose writings were primary sources of Dio Cassius, including Pliny the Younger, Tacitus and Suetonius, belonged to a circle of political-writers in association with the senatorial aristocracy that was frequently in conflict with the emperor, and thus denigrate nearly every aspect of Domitian's career and achievements for propagandistic reasons and for ingratiating themselves to Trajan and his new imperial family as well, and that in contrast to these writers, Quintilian, Statius, and Martial other Latin writers contemporaneous with Domitian, described the emperor more positively, emphasizing his military achievements and his modesty. Above all, there is no solid evidence that Domitian inaugurated an empire-wide persecution of Christians.[76] It appears that Geoffrey de Ste. Croix provides a more balanced view in arguing that between 64 and 250 CE, there were only isolated local persecutions, though the total number of victims was quite considerable.[77]

There is clear internal evidence for persecution in Revelation. In the opening of the fifth seal in 6:9–11, the seer saw under the altar "the souls of those who had been slain for the word of God and for the witness they had borne," who were told to wait until the number of their fellow servants and brothers should be complete, "who were to be killed as they themselves had been." In 14:13, a heavenly voice announced that "blessed are the dead who die in the Lord henceforth." In 16:6, the angel of water said that God has given blood to drink to those who have shed "the blood of saints and prophets." In 17:6, the woman is described as drunk "with the blood of the saints and the blood of the martyrs of Jesus." In 18:24, in Babylon were found "the blood of prophets and of saints and of all who have been slain on earth." In 11:3–13, the two prophetic witnesses were killed by the beast. It is debatable whether these and other passages in Revelation are occasions of Christian suffering that had taken place in the past or prophecies of the persecution that would happen in the future, or perhaps combinations of the two.[78] The death of Antipas who is described as a faithful martyr (2:13), however, is clearly a reference to persecution that had occurred in Asia Minor.

75. Eusebius, *Hist. eccl.* 3.18.4.
76. Thompson, *Revelation*, 95–115.
77. Ste. Croix, "Why Were the Early Christians Persecuted?," 211.
78. Aune, *Revelation*, 1:lxv–lxvi.

Finally, the reference to the temple in 11:1-2 is critical for the pre-70 CE dating. Some scholars interpret it literally and thus argue that the temple was still standing when Revelation was written.[79] There is a general consensus that the short fragment originates from a source independent from that of the ensuing passage.[80] The seer was commanded not to measure the court outside the temple (v. 2a),[81] because it was given over to the Gentiles, who would trample over the city for forty-two months, a formulaic period of eschatological tribulation derived from the length of time during which Antiochus Epiphanes took over Jerusalem (Dan 7:25; 12:7).[82] The details of the imminent threat to the outer court lead many scholars to relate the brief account to the destruction of Jerusalem in 70 CE, and to go further to argue that it was a fragment of a Zealot oracle from the weeks before the fall of Jerusalem, predicting that the Romans would take over the temple court but would fail to take its inner parts where the Zealots had been in control (Josephus, *J.W.* 6.3.122), which in its present literary setting is a spiritualized reinterpretation.[83] It is unlikely that a Christian writer would use a zealot oracle such as this because the course of history overtook the oracle's original prediction and the Romans sacked the whole temple.[84]

A symbolic interpretation appears to make more sense here. Elsewhere in Revelation the temple is found in the heavenly context and described as a structure in heaven, not a literal building on earth (3:12; 7:15; 11:19; 14:14-18; 15:5-8; 21:9-10). Also, in Ezek 40:1-4, on which Rev 11:1-2 is modeled, there is a heavenly prototype of the temple too.[85] In early Christian literature, the temple is frequently used as a symbol for the Christian community which worships God (1 Cor 3:10, 16-17; 2 Cor 6:16; Eph 2:19-22; Gal 2:9; Matt 16:18; 1 Pet 2:5). The measuring of not only the temple and the altar but also of worshippers underlines the fact that

---

79. Wilson, "Domitianic Date," 604-5; Slater, "Dating the Apocalypse," 257.

80. Collins, *Combat Myth*, 195 n. 60.

81. Most scholars agree that literally, the odd expression in v. 2a, καὶ τὴν αὐλὴν τὴν ἔξωθεν τοῦ ναοῦ ἔκβαλε ἔξωθεν, refers to the court outside the temple (Aune, *Revelation*, 2:606-7; Charles, *Revelation*, 1:278; Mounce, *Revelation*, 214 n. 68; Roloff, *Revelation*, 128; Harrington, *Revelation*, 118-19; Beasley-Murray, *Revelation*, 182; Richard, *Apocalypse*, 90).

82. See ch. 2, pp. 54-56.

83. Charles, *Revelation*, 1:270-73; Beasley-Murray, *Revelation*, 37-38.

84. Caird, *Revelation*, 131; Roloff, *Revelation*, 129.

85. Aune, *Revelation*, 2:603; Caird, *Revelation*, 130-31; Mounce, *Revelation*, 213; Roloff, *Revelation*, 128; Harrington, *Revelation*, 118; Witherington, *Revelation*, 157.

readers are dealing with symbols here.[86] The temple and the outer court represent, respectively, the church in its inward being and the church in its earthly, empirical existence.[87] Just as Ezekiel was brought in a vision to see how an angelic being measured the temple in heaven with a measuring reed (40:1–3ff.), the apocalyptist was told to measure the temple with a measuring rod, not including the court outside the temple. In Ezekiel, the symbolic measuring was for the restoration of the temple as, at that time, it was lying in ruins. In the present passage, the measuring signifies the preservation of the Christian community from spiritual harm.[88] Hence, the protection was not security against bodily suffering and death of the Christian community but against damage to their faith in the crucified Lord.[89] The holy city is just another designation for the church.[90] The trampling of the holy city symbolizes the great martyrdom, as the symbolic apocalyptic number "forty-two months," ultimately derived from Dan 7:25, refers to the duration of the persecution of Antiochus Epiphanes and hence represents a time of great tribulation.[91]

To summarize, the enumeration of the seven heads of the beast (17:8–11) is more likely to be a symbol for imperial power as a whole than it is to be a source for dating the Apocalypse. There is some other evidence for dating Revelation, for instance, Irenaeus' witness, the name "Babylon" as a code for Rome (14:6; 16:19; 17:4; 18:2, 10, 21), "the twelve names of the twelve apostles of the Lamb" (21:14), the historical circumstances of the seven churches, the increasing influence of the imperial cult in the Domitianic reign. While the interpretation of the temple reference in 11:1–2 is debatable, the rest of the evidence appears to indicate that Revelation is more likely to have been written during the time of Domitian than at an earlier period around 70 CE.

---

86. Harrington, *Revelation*, 119.

87. Ibid.; Mounce, *Revelation*, 214; Caird, *Revelation*, 132; Witherington, *Revelation*, 157–58.

88. Caird, *Revelation*, 132; Mounce, *Revelation*, 213; Witherington, *Revelation*, 157–58.

89. Caird, *Revelation*, 132; Mounce, *Revelation*, 213–15; Harrington, *Revelation*, 119; cf. Bauckham, *Climax*, 272.

90. Ibid.

91. Ibid.

THE IDENTITY OF THE BEAST FROM THE LAND

Chapter 4 has argued that the beast from the land represents a figure related to the imperial cult. This section attempts to identify the exact referent. It will briefly review the archaeological evidence for the imperial temples in the seven cities mentioned in Rev 2–3. Then, it will study the larger system to which the referent of the land beast belongs. The review begins with the following important data provided by Dio Cassius:

> At that time Caesar (i.e., Octavian) was attending to general matters, and he permitted the establishment of precincts to Rome and to (his) father Caesar—calling him the hero Julius—in Ephesos and in Nicea, for these were then the most distinguished cities in Asia and in Bithynia respectively. He ordered the Romans who had settled among them to honor these two. But he allowed the foreigners—whom he called Hellenes—to consecrate precincts to him, the Asians in Pergamon and the Bithynians in Nicomedia. Beginning there, this (practice) continued under other emperors, not only among the Hellenic nationalities but also among the others, in so far as they are subject to the Romans. For in the city (of Rome) and in the rest of Italy there is no one who dared to do such a thing, however worthy of renown. Yet even there, various godlike honors are given after their death to those who rule uprightly; and heroic shrines are even built (to them). These things occurred in winter, and the Pergamenes also received (the right) to hold games called "sacred" in honor of his temple.[92]

This account is found in the context of a discussion about events that took place around 29 BCE. In the winter of 32 BCE, Mark Antony, who had controlled the eastern Mediterranean area and was recognized as the New Dionysus as early as 41 BCE,[93] gathered forces with Cleopatra VII and three hundred senators at Ephesus and prepared to make war on Octavian,[94] the adopted son of Julius Caesar. In the following year, Octavian defeated the mutinous forces. Having lost its former ruler, the provincial council of the cities of Asia declared its allegiance to Octavian by requesting permission

---

92. Dio Cassius, *Hist. rom.* 51.20.6–9 (Cary, LCL); see also, Tacitus, *Ann.* 4.37. In studying the imperial cult in Asia Minor, most scholars use this piece of Dio's work as major evidence. Scholars rarely question the reliability of this piece of Dio's work. In addition, there is archaeological and numismatic evidence that supports the existence of the precincts mentioned in this account, as shown in the present section of this thesis.

93. Plutarch, *Ant.* 24.4; 60.3–5.

94. Ibid., 56, 58.

to establish a cult for him in Pergamum. It was in this social situation that the imperial cult began to flourish in Asia Minor through a system that the province took the initiative in establishing.[95]

The provincial imperial cult in Pergamum was established for the use of the foreign Hellenes. Few direct archaeological remains of the temple have been unearthed.[96] However, its existence is evidenced through a number of epigraphic pieces on which the title of a temple "of goddess Roma and of Emperor Caesar Augustus, son of God" is engraved.[97] The double dedication accords with Suetonius' report that Augustus refused cultic honors for himself unless Rome was included in the dedication.[98] Of a group of Augustan cistophori issued between June 20 BCE and June 18 BCE, one reverse type of these coins indicates the provincial temple recognized by the inscriptions, "ROM.ET.AUGUST," on its architrave and, "COM.ASIAE," on each side.[99] The temple was the meeting place of the annual assembly of the koinon of Asia,[100] and therefore also the related sacred games, the great Sebasta Romaia,[101] as shown in the citation from Dio.[102] The precinct also functioned as a repository for important documents and various decrees of the koinon.[103] The first provincial temple at Pergamum became the center of the imperial cult in Asia Minor and the religious and political center of the koinon of Asia as well.[104]

The phrase, "the establishment of precincts to Rome and to (his) father Caesar—calling him the hero Julius—in Ephesos," indicates that there was a provincial imperial cult dedicated to Rome and Julius Caesar in Ephesus. The temple was established for the use of the expatriate Romans. Archaeological evidence for this includes a podium that once supported either a double altar or a double temple near the meeting place of the city council.[105]

95. Friesen, *Twice Neokoros*, 7–8.

96. Schäfer reports "a room which served for the cult of the emperor," but mentions no archaeological remains of it, in his work, "Pergamon Mysia," 688–91, especially 689; Mellor, *Worship of the Goddess Roma*, 141.

97. *IEph* 7.2.3825, ll. 11–13; *IGRR* 4.1611.

98. Suetonius, *Aug.* 52.

99. Sutherland, *Cistophori of Augustus*, 36, 103, pl. 12–14, 77–78, 32–34.

100. Tacitus, *Ann.* 4.37.

101. *IGRR* 4.498 (Pergamum).

102. Dio Cassius, *Hist. rom.* 51.20.9.

103. Mellor, *Worship of the Goddess Roma*, 141.

104. Ibid., 80.

105. Mitsopoulou-Leon, "Ephesos," 306–10.

There are remains of monumental steps at one side of the structure and remnants of the temple near the back wall of a peristyle courtyard. The design is distinctively Italian known earliest in Asia, which allows students to date the cult to the last half of the first century BCE.[106] Apart from this vestige of the foundation, there is little trace of the cult left.[107] Moreover, evidence exists for a municipal imperial cult dedicated to Augustus at the Artemision.[108] Within the precincts of Artemis outside the city, two copies of an inscription from 6/5 BCE have been found,[109] recording in both Greek and Latin that the temple of Artemis and the Sebasteion had been walled in with public financial support from the city of Artemis.[110] Since the text implies that a wall was built for the Artemision and the Sebasteion in a single operation,[111] the peribolos on which the copies were discovered was a common wall of the two precincts, making each a sacred enclosure. This architectural vestige has parallels in the Acropolis of Athens.[112] Furthermore, there is substantial evidence for another municipal cult dedicated to Augustus in the upper agora of the city. Archaeological remains unearthed in this area include a three-aisled monumental basilica,[113] a life-sized head of Augustus and fragments of two seated statues about a third larger than life-size, one of Augustus and another of Livia.[114] With enough pieces of the exterior architrave, a significant portion of the dedication inscription has been restored, reporting bilingually in Latin and in Greek that the basilica was dedicated in part to the emperor.[115] The inscription allows scholars to date the dedication to the years 11–13 CE.[116]

In addition to these three temples, there is a more notable example of the provincial imperial cult of the Sebastoi discovered near the upper agora of the city. It is different from previous provincial cults in Asia because the

106. Friesen, *Imperial Cults*, 26–27 n. 5.

107. Fishwick comments that the cult of Rome and Julius appears to have quickly disappeared (*Imperial Cult*, 1:130 n. 234).

108. Tertullian generally employs the term *municipali consecratione* to refer to civil cults (*Apol.* 24.8).

109. Wood, *Discoveries at Ephesus*, 130–34.

110. *IEph* 5.1552.

111. Price, *Rituals and Power*, 254.

112. Nock, *Essays on Religion*, 1:225.

113. Scherrer, *Ephesos*, 82–84.

114. Alzinger, "Das Regierungsviertel," 264–65.

115. *IEph* 2.404.

116. Friesen, *Imperial Cults*, 96 n. 68.

temple did not include in the veneration the corporate figures of Rome or the Senate but rather only the imperial family, ὁ Σεβαστός, the Sebastoi.[117] Ruins unearthed from the site reveal that the temple was set atop an artificial terrace on the slopes of Mount Korresos.[118] Thirteen inscriptions from the dedication of the temple have been discovered.[119] All the inscriptions begin with a formulaic dedication to Αὐτοκράτορι [[Δομι-]] [[τιανῶι]] Καίσαρι Σεβαστῶι [[Γερμανικῶι]], "Emperor Domitian Caesar Sebastos Germanicus,"[120] with the variations in the later words depending on the status of the cities that commissioned the inscriptions. Since the dates of all the inscriptions are within the range 88 CE–90 CE, except the two engraved with the term νεωκόρος, "neokoros," it is likely that the imperial cult of the Sebastoi was dedicated in 89/90 CE.[121] On the other hand, the Sebastoi is particularly noteworthy because of it Ephesus was granted "neokoros" status. The earliest known attestation of a city called "neokoros" is found on the Kyzikos inscription from 38 CE,[122] on which the city calls itself the neokoros of the imperial family of Gaius.[123] In describing Paul's visit to Ephesus, the author of Acts assumed that the city of the Ephesians was well-known throughout the world as the neokoros of Artemis and accordingly responsible for the protection of the prominent Ephesian deity (19:27, 35, 37).[124] Only after the Sebastoi did the term "neokoros" function as a title for a city with an imperial cult.[125] The term is engraved on the last two of the thirteen inscriptions, one dedicated by the city of Stratonikeia in 90 CE and the other by the city of Tmolos in 90/91 CE.[126] Since the Sebastoi was dedicated in 89/90 CE, it is likely that the temple had become fully functional by the year 90 CE, which was the time it acquired the title "neokoros."[127] On the reverse of two coins issued during the reign of Domitian, the carved

117. Ibid., 46.

118. Keil, "XVI," 53–61.

119. Friesen, *Twice Neokoros*, 46–47.

120. An example is the inscription dedicated by the city of Aphrodisias (*IEph* 2.233).

121. Friesen, *Twice Neokoros*, 48–49.

122. *IGRR* 4.146.

123. For a partial translation of the restored text, see Friesen, *Twice Neokoros*, 54 n. 21.

124. Brown comments that the best date for Acts would appear to be 85, within the range between 80 and 100 CE (*Introduction to the New Testament*, 274).

125. Friesen, *Twice Neokoros*, 50 n. 1.

126. *IEph* 2.237, 241.

127. Friesen, *Twice Neokoros*, 48.

phrases, Ἐφεσίων Β Νεοκόρων, or, Ἐφεσίων Δ[ὶς Νε]οκόρων, appear.[128] The phrases mean that the city is "twice neokoros," that is, to Artemis and to the Sebastoi. This prestigious honor did not become a regular civic title shown on Ephesian inscriptions, however, until the city received its second provincial imperial cult under Hadrian.[129]

Numismatic evidence exists for a municipal imperial cult for Domitian and Domitia in Laodicea. Groups of coins issued from the city during the Domitianic reign bear images of royal family members on the obverses, including Domitian in military attire,[130] his wife Domitia,[131] or both.[132] On the reverses are several variations of the front elevation of a temple dedicated to Domitian with three or four steps. Of these, one has the temple with four columns, the architrave frieze of which carries the inscription ΕΠΙΝΕΙΚΙΟΣ, "warlike," with Domitian standing on the left in military dress and Domitia on the right between the columns.[133] Since the theme emphasized in this numismatic imagery is the emperor's military victory, and since the term ΕΠΙΝΕΙΚΙΟΣ carved on the frieze seems to be an alternate spelling of Ἐπινίκιος, which means "victorious," it is likely that the temple was dedicated to Domitian in 84 CE, in honor of the victories that led him to take the title Germanicus.[134]

At Smyrna, there was a provincial imperial cult dedicated to Tiberius, Livia and the Senate. The structure of the temple is portrayed on a bronze coin from Smyrna issued while Petronius was proconsul (26–35 CE). The reverse of the coin indicates a temple on a stepped crepidoma, in the center of which stands a statue of Tiberius sacrificing as a priest in the middle of four columns. The obverse contains the bust of Livia on the right and that of the personified Senate on the left facing each other.[135] The numismatic imagery demonstrates that the cult was of a triple dedication that venerated not only Tiberius but also the Senate and Augustus and Livia. The establishment of the cult was related to two court cases, according to Tacitus,[136]

---

128. Keil, "Die erste Kaiserneokorie," 118.
129. Price, *Rituals and Power*, 65 n. 47; Friesen, *Twice Neokoros*, 57.
130. *BMC*, 25:307, nos. 181–82.
131. Ibid., 25:308, nos. 187–88.
132. Ibid., 25:307, no. 185, pl. 37.6.
133. Imhoof-Blumer, *Monnaies Grecques*, 404–5.
134. Ibid., 405.
135. Friesen, *Imperial Cults*, 38; Price, *Rituals and Power*, 258 nn. 45–46.
136. Tacitus, *Ann.* 3.66—4.56.

which is solid evidence for the amount of competition building the imperial temple generated.

To summarize, recent studies have clearly demonstrated some valid points relating to the imperial cult. Firstly, from the beginning, it was the province of Asia Minor that initiated the establishment of the imperial cult to the emperor. Augustus approved the establishment only when it was in Ephesus, Pergamum, Nicaea, and Nicomedia, and only when its dedication included Rome. Secondly, Roman emperors generally avoided initiating any cults for themselves, with only a few exceptional cases.[137] In the establishment of the imperial cult for Tiberius, Livia and the Senate in Smyrna, Tiberius even had to defend himself before the Senate as to why he approved the request from the cities of Asia. More strikingly, the Senate denied Tiberius' approval for the establishment of a cult dedicated to him there. In addition, the case reflects the fact that there was strong competition among the cities in Asia for building imperial cults to emperors. Neokoros status was rigorously contested.

Having reviewed the evidence for the imperial cult in Asia Minor, the investigation will now study the key figure in its establishment, that is, the provincial imperial high priest. A number of commentators agree that the beast from the land represents the high priesthood.[138] It is exceedingly difficult to provide details as to how the office functioned in the koinon, because there is a dearth of information on this office. The little evidence that remains is, however, sufficient to provide a general contour of the priesthood.

The earliest evidence for the provincial high priest is found in the first provincial imperial cult of Asia in Pergamum. There, on an inscription from Sardis dated to 4 BCE, the official is referred to as ὁ ἀρχιερεὺς θεᾶς Ῥώμης καὶ Αὐτοκράτορος Καίσαρος θεοῦ υἱοῦ Σεβαστο[ῦ], "the high priest of goddess Roma and of Emperor Caesar Augustus, son of God."[139] At

---

137. A piece of literary evidence claims that Hadrian dedicated the temple to Zeus Olympios and also an altar to himself at Athens, and in the same manner consecrated temples to himself, which could be the temples at Smyrna, Ephesus and Cyzicus, for which he was otherwise known to have given permission or funds (Price, *Rituals and Power*, 68–69 n. 61; 147).

138. Aune, *Revelation*, 2:756; Witherington, *Revelation*, 184; Beasley-Murray, *Revelation*, 216.

139. IGRR 4.1756, ll. 75–76. The same reference to the high priest of the temple is also found in a copy of a koinon decree from Hypaipa dated from 2 BCE to 14 CE (*IEph* 7.2.3825, ll. 11–13 = *IGRR* 4.1611).

Smyrna, the second provincial cult in Asia established in 26 CE, the temple official is referred to in a similar manner on an inscription as the ἀρχιερεὺς τῆς Ἀσίας ναοῦ το[ῦ ἐν] Σμ[ύρ]νῃ, "high priest of Asia of the temple in Smyrna."[140] On an inscription dated from 37–41 CE relating to the provincial cult of Gaius in Miletus, the text describes the emperor's service as high priest of the temple in Asia for the third time with the terms, ἀρχιερέως, "of a high priest," and Ασίας, "of Asia."[141] Then, in epigraphic traces, the term ἀρχιερεὺς Ἀσίας, "high priest of Asia," is found more typically as the title of the provincial high priest.[142] On the other hand, in many cases, the phrase is related to the title of a specific imperial cult. For example, in a later period, the provincial high priest in Pergamum is not referred to by his earlier title but by Ἀρχιερεὺς Ἀσίας ναῶν τῶν, or ναοῦ τοῦ, ἐν Περγάμῳ.[143] The same priestly reference is also found at Ephesus, Ἀρχιερεὺς Ἀσίας ναῶν τῶν ἐν Ἐφέσῳ;[144] at Smyrna, Αρχιερεὺς Ἀσίας ναῶν τῶν, or ναοῦ τοῦ, ἐν Σμύρνῃ;[145] and at Sardis, Ἀρχιερεὺς Ἀσίας ναῶν τῶν ἐν Σάρδεσιν.[146] Hence, it appears that from the establishment of the cult in Smyrna, the provincial high priest was in general referred to as the ἀρχιερεὺς Ἀσίας, "high priest of Asia."[147] In many occurrences, the phrase appears with the title of the related provincial imperial cult. The two expressions are variants of the same title for the same office.[148]

Since the second provincial cult in Asia established in 26 CE in Smyrna, there had been one provincial cult in each city of the province, and accordingly, there was one provincial high priest elected annually for each cult in each city as well.[149] Beginning in the second century CE, some cities established a second and a third imperial cult. In these cities, the provincial high priest served all the cults of that city.[150] With this arrangement, these high priests were not assigned in any hierarchical order but were of equal

---

140. *IGRR* 4.1524.
141. Robert, "Le cult de Caligula," 206–7.
142. *IEph* 7.2.3801; *IGRR* 4.1323.
143. Magie, *Roman Rule*, 2:1601–3 nn. 10, 13, 15, 19, 31, 33, 39, 43 and 66.
144. Ibid., 2:1601–3 nn. 9, 14, 26, 41, 42, 58 and 62, and Ἀρχιέρειαι, nn. 11 and 22.
145. Ibid., 2:1601–2 nn. 24, 28 and 61, and Αρχιέρειαι, nn. 5 and 20.
146. Ibid., 2:1602 n. 49.
147. Friesen, *Twice Neokoros*, 80.
148. Magie, *Roman Rule*, 2:1297–98 n. 59; Friesen, *Twice Neokoros*, 77.
149. For example, the dedicatory inscriptions *IEph* 2.232–35, 237–41; 5.1498.
150. Deininger, *Die Provinziallandtage*, 38–39 n. 10; 49.

status.¹⁵¹ During the approximately three centuries duration of the provincial imperial cults in Asia, eighty different names of provincial high priests are attested from the numismatic and epigraphic evidence, and a number of them served more than one term. In addition to this group of named high priests, there are eighteen other references to officials whose names are unknown.¹⁵² In addition to the provincial high priests, there were high priestesses in the province. Of a group of fifteen high priestesses from Ephesus from the late first century to the third century CE shown in inscriptions, some had husbands who were priests of the imperial cult of the province, while some had husbands who were not high priests, or whose husbands' details were not known.¹⁵³ This group of epigraphic evidence indicates that provincial high priestesses were not necessarily dependent on their consorts for their titles and so were not likely to be honorary officials but rather functional ones.¹⁵⁴

The creation of the provincial high priesthood was closely related to the koinon in Asia in many ways. The koinon had long existed for various purposes before being adapted as a vital mechanism that initiated imperial cults in the imperial period. For instance, an inscription from Klazomenai states that the koinon offered to local Hellenes a cult to Antiochus I Soter between 268 BCE and 262 BCE.¹⁵⁵ In the republican period, it protested against the unreasonable tax demands by the Senate on the farmers, and in 42–41 BCE. Mark Antony confirmed certain privileges to athletes through that body.¹⁵⁶ The koinon of Asia had been organized in 29 BCE for propagating the provincial imperial cult of the goddess Roma and of Emperor Caesar Augustus in Pergamum. From this time onwards, the provincial assembly of over a hundred delegates met annually for the worship of the new deities and for business transactions, at first in Pergamum, then at Smyrna, Ephesus, Sardis, Cyzicus, Philadelphia, Laodicea and so forth.¹⁵⁷ That meeting was called ἐκκλησία ἀρχαιρετική, or ἀρχαιρεσίαι, which implies that the main concern of the assembly was the election of officers.¹⁵⁸ In his earliest

---

151. Ibid., 18, 37–41.
152. Friesen, *Twice Neokoros*, 78 n. 4; for the list of the provincial high priests, 172–84.
153. Kearsley, "Asiarchs," 186–87.
154. Friesen, *Twice Neokoros*, 85; for the list of the provincial high priestesses, 185–88.
155. *OGI* 222.
156. Millar, *Emperor in the Roman World*, 385–86, 456.
157. Magie, *Roman Rule*, 1:448.
158. Ibid., 2:1295 n. 55.

occurrence in attestation, the high priest of the provincial cult at Pergamum was found to be the one who appointed individuals to honorary offices.[159] There are also cases where the high priest was the author of correspondence from the koinon to a city.[160]

There is little doubt that those who received the provincial high priesthoods were preeminent in age and reputation as well as wealth.[161] The office, which in itself it did not bring with it political advantages, normally entailed many benefits since the endowment of the office of priest was a sign that the emperor appreciated the talents and character of that person.[162] For example, the office was a stepping-stone to senatorial status in Rome,[163] and a priest's son would typically receive equestrian status and his grandson senatorial or consular status.[164] The prominence of the priesthood is also indicated in its role in the major imperial festivals. One of the great festivals was the Ῥωμαῖα Σεβαστά, "Romaia Sebasta," in honor of the goddess Roma and the deified emperor.[165] It was the koinon of Asia that established the games in conjunction with the first provincial imperial cult in Asia at Pergamum.[166] The games were the first and only provincial games for over fifty years.[167] An inscription dated to about 5 CE records the victory of a pentathlete from Kos in the games.[168] The provincial high priest was the official at these games and sometimes served as the "agonothete for life" of them,[169] while his principal duty was to conduct the worship of the goddess Roma and the deified emperor.[170]

The official's preeminence is also evident in his participation in the major imperial festivals. According to an inscription concerning the Pergamene hymnodes,[171] the most important festival days included the birthday

159. *IEph* 7.2.3825 (Hypaipa).
160. *Sardis*, 7.8 (VII and VIII, pp. 21–22).
161. Plutarch, *Oth.* 1.2.
162. Suetonius, *Vit.* 5.1.
163. Millar, *Emperor in the Roman World*, 389.
164. Bowersock, "Greek Intellectuals," 182.
165. Magie, *Roman Rule*, 1:448 n. 57.
166. Friesen, *Twice Neokoros*, 115.
167. Price, *Rituals and Power*, 104.
168. *IGRR* 4.1064.
169. *IEph* 7.2.3825.
170. Magie, *Roman Rule*, 1:449.
171. *IGRR* 4.353.

of Augustus, celebrated as part of a three-day festival, and Livia's birthday.[172] At the city of Gytheum in the Peloponnese, there was a six-day festival with each day assigned to honor a different member of the imperial house and with two additional days in honor of two distinguished Spartans.[173] The key feature of these imperial festivals was the procession. In the festivals, the provincial high priest marched with a crown and purple garb, leading the procession with the incense bearers, who were young males, around him.[174] There was great competition for the right to head the procession, *propompeia*, as the post was very honorable.[175] This point can be illustrated more clearly from the funeral of Augustus. According to Dio Cassius, at the imperial funeral, once the emperor's corpse had been placed on the funeral pyre, all the priests walked round it first, followed by the knights, the cavalry and the infantry.[176] Hence, the provincial high priest normally took precedence in processions over those with military titles.

In summary, the provincial high priest is found for the first time in connection with the first provincial imperial cult in Asia at Pergamum. A number of provincial high priests and high priestesses are attested in the epigraphic evidence. These people were prominent in reputation as well as affluence. The prestigious status of the official is evident in its position in the procession at imperial festivals such as the Romaia Sebasta and the celebration of Augustus' birthday. The official is a key figure of the imperial cult system and functions as a mediator between the emperor and the people in the promotion of the imperial cult.

CONCLUSION

There are two sets of information concerning the beast from the sea in Rev 13. The first set includes the fragments in 13:3a, 12c and 14c, which in turn reflect two source variants, with one describing the beast's head (v. 3a) and one the beast itself (vv. 12c, 14c). The combination of the source variants results in the fact that in the final form of the passage, while one of the beast's heads seems to have a mortal wound (v. 3a), it is the beast that is healed (vv. 12c, 14c). The second set contains the number of the name

172. Pleket, "Aspect of the Emperor Cult," 341.
173. Price, *Rituals and Power*, 106.
174. Dio Chrysostom, *Or.* 35.10.
175. Ibid., 38.38.
176. Dio Cassius, *Hist. rom.* 56.42.2.

of the beast, namely, 666 (13:18), which is most likely a gematria riddle. The two clusters point to Nero as the most plausible candidate for the sea beast. Secondly, there is enough archaeological evidence for the existence of the provincial high priest. The office functions as a mediator between the emperor and the people in the promotion of the imperial cult. The role of provincial high priest corresponds to that of the land beast reported in Rev 13:11–18, in which the land beast is subordinate to the sea beast and makes the world and its inhabitants worship the sea beast. Therefore, it appears that the provincial high priest is the best candidate for the beast from the land.

6

Summary

THIS THESIS AIMS TO identify the beast from the sea and the beast from the land in Rev 13. Unlike most modern scholarly approaches, the present thesis studies the topic by examining the underlying structure of the relationship between the dragon and the two beasts in Rev 12 and 13. The thesis argues that there is a tripartite hierarchical relationship that links the three figures, in which the dragon is superior to the sea beast, which in turn is superior to the land beast. This hierarchical structure is not found in biblical or extra-biblical writings but only in the book of Revelation. According to Dumézil, there was an all-encompassing structure of relationships underlying most Indo-European mythological traditions, including the Indic, Scandinavian, Iranian and Roman, namely, the tripartite ideology. Dumézil states that, in this tripartite structure, each figure carries a specific role and function corresponding to its hierarchical level. Having studied the hierarchical structure linking the dragon and the two beasts and each creature's function in its context in Rev 12 and 13, the present thesis points out that there is a striking parallel between the hierarchy of the three creatures in the Apocalypse and the tripartite ideology Dumézil has discovered in the Indo-European traditions. Thus, it is plausible that the relationship of the dragon and the two beasts reflects the influence of the tripartite ideology. In addition, in Dumézil's tripartite system, the figure on the second level is a warlike figure found in a war context, and the figure on the third level is concerned with economics and productivity. In Rev 13, the sea beast and land beast are found, respectively, as a warlike figure in a context with a

Summary

war theme and as a figure relating to an economic theme, just as the second and third figures on the corresponding levels in the tripartite system are. Therefore, on the one hand, the tripartite ideology could explain the hierarchical relationship of the three creatures in Rev 12 and 13. On the other hand, the characteristics of the second and third constituents in the tripartite system are an important source in identifying the sea beast and land beast in Rev 13.

Chapter 2 first reviews the recent scholarship of the *Chaoskampf* tradition, which is the ultimate mythological background of Dan 7 and Rev 13. Then it reviews scholarship on the reference to the "son of man." Apocalyptic literature from around the first century CE, both canonical and extracanonical, consistently describes heavenly, angelic beings using expressions like "one like a son of man" or similar. In Dan 7:13, the phrase is most likely to refer to the archangel Michael. In Rev 1:13 and 14:14, the same idiom is used to designate the risen Christ. In addition, chapter 2 studies the use of Dan 7 in Rev 13. The sea beast in Rev 13 shares features with those of the four beasts in Dan 7, such as a lion's mouth, bear's feet and looking like a leopard. The sea beast in Rev 13 has ten horns like the fourth beast in Dan 7. The allusion to the "little horn" of the fourth beast in Dan 7 is particularly explicit. In Rev 13:5a, the sea beast is described as having "a mouth uttering haughty and blasphemous words," which is a clear allusion to the motif of arrogant speech in Dan 7:8, 20. In Rev 13:7a, it is reported that the sea beast "made war on the saints," just as the little horn in Dan 7:21 did. In Rev 13:5b, the duration of the war is reported as lasting for "forty-two months," which is clearly a reference derived from Dan 7:25. These allusions to Dan 7 cannot explain the hierarchical relationship of the dragon and the sea beast and land beast in Rev 13.

Chapter 3 examines the account of Leviathan and Behemoth, or Leviathan alone, in *4 Ezra, 2 Baruch, 1 Enoch, Apocalypse of Abraham* and the *Ladder of Jacob*. The enormity of the beasts is common to all passages, but the emphases differ in each case. The first three accounts of the pair agree about the principal themes with respect to the two monsters, that their separation signifies the beginning of the world, their return the end-time and that they are being preserved to become food for the righteous at the messianic banquet. *Fourth Ezra* and *1 Enoch* are, in particular, informative in their accounts concerning the abodes and origins of the two figures with Leviathan of watery origin and Behemoth of earthly origin. On most occasions, Leviathan and Behemoth are above all creatures, through his control of which, God exhibits his ultimate sovereignty. On the other hand, in each case, there are contextual nuances in the use of the Leviathan-Behemoth motif. In *4 Ezra*, the two beasts are incorporated in the *Hexaemeron* with a comprehensive description of their enormous size showing the supremacy of God, who takes charge of them, in order to highlight the contrast with God's inertia at the fall of Jerusalem reported at the contextual climax (6:59). In *2 Baruch*, being the first element of the nourishment theme, the pair prompts the messianic banquet scenario. In *1 Enoch*, in the second of the three eschatological visions, the occurrence of the pair enhances the end-time theme. In each occurrence, the two monsters, or Leviathan alone, stand in a strategic position in the eschatological context in order to highlight a specific theme. The characteristics of the two beasts commonly found in the Second Temple apocalypses under examination do not occur in the vision of the sea beast and land beast in Rev 13. Also, the information about the pair in these writings cannot explain the hierarchy between the pair in Rev 13: namely, the sea beast being superior to the land beast.

Chapter 4 is the center of this thesis. It contains two parts. The first part of this chapter begins by briefly reviewing three major perspectives on the structure of Revelation. The chapter then demonstrates that, due to their shared feature of having seven heads, the dragon in chapter 12 and the beast from the sea in chapter 13 derive from the same traditional source-the biblical Leviathan. In producing the two chapters, the apocalyptist allotted the various attributes to create two different entities, with the dragon being superior to the sea beast. Then, he went further and arranged the sea beast and the land beast according to the Leviathan-Behemoth template and assigned the same hierarchy to the pair, with the sea beast being superior to the land beast. This distinctive relationship between the dragon and the sea beast and land beast is not found in biblical and extra-biblical writings but is found exclusively in Rev 12 and 13. The first part of the chapter concludes by examining the notion that in this tripartite hierarchy, the three figures are found in different contexts and each takes a specific role in accordance with its context. The dragon is related to the ultimate sovereignty of the supernatural, mythical context. The sea beast takes the role of warrior and appears in a belligerent context. The land beast is related to the economic and profiteering aspects of earthly life.

The second part of chapter 4 studies the tripartite ideology that Dumézil discerns in the Indo-European mythological tradition. According to Dumézil, in this tripartite hierarchy, the figure on the top level relates to

Summary

ultimate sovereignty in a supernatural sphere; the figure on the second level is a warlike figure; the figure on the third level relates to economics and productivity. Having introduced the hypothesis of the tripartite system, the second part of this chapter examines the related literary and archaeological evidence. Among the many remains, the Jupiter Capitolinus in Rome is the most illustrative, and it plays an important role in the two Jewish wars. In Rev 12 and 13, the dragon and the beast from the sea and the beast from the land in the hierarchy display the same functions as the three figures of the tripartite system argued by Dumézil. Therefore, this tripartite ideology can explain the hierarchical relationship of the three figures in Rev 12 and 13. In addition, the characteristics of the second and third constituents in the tripartite system are an important source in identifying the two beasts in Rev 13.

Chapter 5 identifies the referents of the sea beast and land beast, based on the findings of the previous chapters. The book of Revelation 13 contains two sets of information concerning the beast from the sea. The first set includes the fragments in 13:3a, 12c and 14c, which in turn reflect two source variants, with one describing the beast's head (v. 3a) and one the beast itself (vv. 12c, 14c). The combination of the source variants results in the fact that in the final form of the passage, while one of the beast's heads seems to have a mortal wound (v. 3a), it is the beast that is healed (vv. 12c, 14c). The second gloss contains the number of the name of the beast, namely, 666 (13:18). The two clusters point to Nero as the most plausible candidate for the sea beast. The references to the beast's mortal wound (vv. 3a, 12c, 14c) fit the legend of the return of Nero in a metaphorical way. The number 666 (v. 18) functions as a cryptic word game to confirm this identification. Furthermore, the tripartite ideology supports this identification. In the tripartite system, the figure on the second level is a warlike figure. Nero fits this criterion well. The number "seven" in 17:8–11 symbolizes the entire series of the emperors of Rome, representing the whole Roman Empire. On the other hand, internal evidence supports the likelihood that Revelation was written during the reign of Domitian near the end of the first century CE.

There is enough archaeological evidence for the existence of the provincial high priest. The office is a key figure in the imperial cult system, as it functions as a mediator between the emperor and the people in the promotion of the imperial cult. The role of provincial high priest corresponds to the function of the land beast reported in Rev 13:11–18, in which the land beast is subordinate to the sea beast and makes the world and its inhabitants worship the sea beast. It appears that the provincial high priest is the best candidate for the land beast. Also, this identification corresponds to the figure on the third level in the tripartite system, since the imperial cult is about political and economic benefits for local communities.

In consequence, it appears that until any new findings, the tripartite ideology Dumézil proposes is a helpful way to explain the hierarchical relationship of the dragon and the two strange beasts in Rev 12 and 13. The system appears to explain both the relationship of the three figures and the function of each figure in its corresponding context. Since the dragon and the two beasts are central to the book, and since they are beyond the time and space of other series in the book, the three figures in their hierarchical relationship also fit the all-encompassing nature of the tripartite system. It is possible that the tripartite hierarchy of the dragon and the two beasts reflects the lower layer of the worldview in the book.

Using the tripartite ideology to study the two beasts in Rev 13 is a new angle on the topic. There may be other elements in Revelation that reflect vestiges of this system. Studying the influence of the tripartite ideology on other parts of Revelation may be the next topic for investigation.

Bibliography

Adler, Eve. *Vergil's Empire: Political Thought in Aeneid*. Oxford: Rowman and Littlefield, 2003.
Albright, William F. "New Light on Early Canaanite Language and Literature." *BASOR* 46 (1932) 15–20.
Alföldy, Géza. *The Social History of Rome*. Translated by David Braund and Frank Pollock. London: Croom Helm, 1985.
Alzinger, Wilhelm. "Das Regierungsviertel." *JÖAI* 50 (1972–75) 229–300.
Augustine. *The City of God Against the Pagans*. Translated by George E. McCracken et al. 7 vols. Loeb Classical Library. London: Heinemann, 1957–1972.
Aune, David E. *Revelation*. Word Biblical Commentary 52ABC. 3 vols. Dallas: Word, 1997–98.
―――. "The Social Matrix of the Apocalypse of John." *BR* 28 (1981) 16–32.
Baldi, Philip. *The Foundations of Latin*. Trends in Linguistics: Studies and Monographs 117. New York: De Gruyter, 1999.
Barr, David L., ed. *Reading the Book of Revelation: A Resource for Students*. Atlanta: Society of Biblical Literature, 2003.
Barton, George. "Tiamat." *JAOS* 15 (1893) 1–27.
Bauckham, Richard. *The Climax of Prophecy: Studies on the Book of Revelation*. Edinburgh: T. & T. Clark, 1993.
―――. "Son of Man: 'A Man in my Position' or 'Someone'?" *JSNT* 23 (1985) 23–33.
Bauer, Walter. *A Greek-English Lexicon of the New Testament and Other Early Christian Literature*. 2nd ed. Chicago: University of Chicago Press, 1979.
Beale, Gregory K. *The Book of Revelation: A Commentary on the Greek Text*. New International Greek Testament Commentary. Grand Rapids: Eerdmans, 1999.
―――. *The Use of Daniel in Jewish Apocalyptic Literature and in the Revelation of St. John*. Lanham, MD: University Press of America, 1984.
Beard, Mary, John North, and Simon Price. *Religions of Rome*. 2 vols. Cambridge: Cambridge University Press, 1998.
Beasley-Murray, George R. *The Book of Revelation*. New Century Bible. London: Marshall, Morgan & Scott, 1981.
Belier, Wouter W. *Decayed Gods: Origin and Development of Georges Dumézil's "idéologie tripartie."* Leiden: Brill, 1991.
Bell, Albert. "The Date of John's Apocalypse: The Evidence of Some Roman Historians Reconsidered." *NTS* 25 (1979) 93–102.

Bibliography

Biguzzi, G. "Ephesus, Its Artemision, Its Temple to the Flavian Emperors, and Idolatry in Revelation." *NovT* 40 (1998) 276–90.

Black, Matthew. "The Apocalypse of Weeks in the Light of 4QEng." *VT* 28 (1978) 464–69.

Black, Matthew, James C. VanderKam, and Otto Neugebauer, eds. *The Book of Enoch or 1 Enoch: A New English Edition: with Commentary and Textual Notes*. Leiden: Brill, 1985.

Blenkinsopp, Joseph. *Ezekiel*. Interpretation. Louisville: John Knox, 1990.

Bogaert, Pierre-Maurice. *Apocalypse de Baruch, introduction, traduction du Syriaque et commentaire*. 2 vols. Sources Chrétiennes 144. Paris: Cerf, 1969.

Boring, Eugene. *Revelation*. Interpretation. Louisville: John Knox, 1989.

Bornkamm, Günther. "Die Komposition der apokalyptischen Visionen in der Offenbarung Johannes." *ZNW* 36 (1937) 132–49.

Bousset, Wilhelm. *Die Offenbarung Johannis*. Göttingen: Vandenhoeck & Ruprecht, 1906.

Bowersock, Glen W. "Greek Intellectuals and the Imperial Cult in the Second Century A.D." In *Le culte des souverains dans l'Empire Romain*, edited by W. den Boer, 177–206. Vandoeuvres, Geneva: Foundation Hardt, 1973.

Bowman, John. "The Background of the Term 'Son of Man.'" *ExpTim* 59 (1948) 283–88.

Box, George Herbert. *The Ezra-Apocalypse: Being Chapters 3–14 of the Book Commonly Known as 4 Ezra (or II Esdras)*. London: Sir Isaac Pitman & Sons, 1912.

Box, George Herbert, and J. I. Landsman, eds. *The Apocalypse of Abraham*. Translations of Early Documents 1: Palestinian Jewish Texts (Pre-Rabbinic). New York: Macmillan, 1919.

Breech, Earl. "These Fragments I Have Shored Against My Ruins: The Form and Function of 4 Ezra." *JBL* 92 (1973) 267–74.

Brekelmans, C. H. W. "The Saints of the Most High and Their Kingdom." *OTS* 14 (1965) 305–29.

Brown, Raymond E. *An Introduction to the New Testament*. The Anchor Bible Reference Library. New York: Doubleday, 1997.

Caird, George B. *A Commentary on the Revelation of St. John the Divine*. Black's New Testament Commentaries. London: Adam & Charles Black, 1984.

Callahan, Allen. "Language of the Apocalypse." *HTR* 88 (1995) 453–70.

Caragounis, Chrys. *The Son of Man: Vision and Interpretation*. Tübingen: Mohr-Siebeck, 1986.

Casey, Maurice. *The Solution to the "Son of Man" Problem*. Library of the New Testament Studies 343. London: T. & T. Clark, 2007.

———. *Son of Man: The Interpretation and Influence of Daniel 7*. London: SPCK, 1979.

Cassius, Dio Cocceianus. *Roman History*. Translated by Earnest Cary. Loeb Classical Library. 9 vols. Cambridge, MA: Harvard University Press, 1914–1969.

Charles, R. H. *The Apocalypse of Baruch*. London: Adam and Charles Black, 1896.

———. *The Book of Enoch or 1 Enoch*. Oxford: Clarendon, 1912.

———. *A Critical and Exegetical Commentary on the Revelation of St. John*. 2 vols. International Critical Commentary 44. Edinburgh: T. & T. Clark, 1920.

———, ed. *The Apocrypha and Pseudepigrapha of the Old Testament in English: with introductions and critical and explanatory notes to the several books*. 2 vols. Oxford: Clarendon, 1913.

Charlesworth, James H., ed. *The Old Testament Pseudepigrapha*. 2 vols. New York: Doubleday, 1983–85.

———. "The SNTS Pseudepigrapha Seminars at Tübingen and Paris on the Books of Enoch." *NTS* 25 (1979) 315–23.
Cicero. *On the Orator*. Books 1–2. Translated by E. W. Sutton and H. Rackham. Loeb Classical Library 348. Cambridge, MA: Harvard University Press, 1948.
———. *In Catilinam 1-4. Pro Murena. Pro Sulla. Pro Flacco*. Translated by C. Macdonald. Loeb Classical Library. Cambridge, MA: Harvard University Press, 1976.
———. *Pro Archia. Post Reditum in Senatu. Post Reditum ad Quirites. De Domo Sua. De Haruspicum Responsis. Pro Plancio*. Translated by N. H. Watts. Loeb Classical Library. Cambridge, MA: Harvard University Press, 1923.
———. *The Verrine Orations*. Translated by L. H. G. Greenwood. 2 vols. Loeb Classical Library. Cambridge, MA: Harvard University Press, 1928/1935.
Clifford, Richard J. "Cosmogonies in the Ugaritic Texts and in the Bible." *Orientalia* 53 (1984) 188–93.
———. *God's Conflict with the Dragon and the Sea: Echoes of a Canaanite Myth in the Old Testament*. Cambridge: Cambridge University Press, 1985.
Coarelli, Filippo. *Il foro romano*. 2 vols. Rome: Periodo arcaico, 1983–85.
Collins, Adela Yarbro. *The Combat Myth in the Book of Revelation*. Harvard Dissertations in Religion 9. Missoula, MT: Scholars, 1976.
———. "Dating the Apocalypse of John." *BR* 26 (1981) 33–45.
———. *Cosmology and Eschatology in Jewish and Christian Apocalypticism*. New York: Brill, 1996.
———. *Crisis and Catharsis: The Power of the Apocalypse*. Philadelphia: Westminster, 1984.
Collins, Adela Yarbro, and John J. Collins. *King and Messiah as Son of God*. Grand Rapids: Eerdmans, 2008.
Collins, John J. *The Apocalyptic Imagination: An Introduction to Jewish Apocalyptic Literature*. 2nd ed. Grand Rapids: Eerdmans, 1998.
———. *Daniel: A Commentary on the Book of Daniel*. Hermeneia. Minneapolis: Fortress, 1993.
———. "The Son of Man and the Saints of the Most High in the Book of Daniel." *JBL* 93 1 (1974) 50–66.
———. "The Son of Man in First-century Judaism." *NTS* 38 (1992) 448–66.
———. "The Sibylline Oracles." In *The Old Testament Pseudepigrapha*, edited by James H. Charlesworth, 1:317–472. 2 vols. New York: Doubleday, 1983–85.
Cornell, Tim J. *The Beginnings of Rome: Italy and Rome from the Bronze Age to the Punic Wars (c. 1000–264 BC)*. London: Routledge, Taylor & Francis, 1995.
Cross, Frank Moore. *Canaanite Myth and Hebrew Epic: Essays in the History of the Religion of Israel*. Cambridge, MA: Harvard University Press, 1973.
Cuss, Dominique. *Imperial Cult and Honorary Terms in the New Testament*. Paradosis: Contributions to the History of Early Christian Literature and Theology. Fribourg: Fribourg University Press, 1974.
Cyprian. *The Letters of St. Cyprian*. 4 vols. Ancient Christian Writers. Mahwah, NJ: Paulist, 1983.
Dahood, Mitchell. *Psalms II 51–100*. Anchor Bible 17. Garden City: Doubleday, 1968.
Davies, Philip R. *Daniel*. Sheffield: JSOT, 1985.
Day, John. *God's Conflict with the Dragon and the Sea: Echoes of a Canaanite Myth in the Old Testament*. Cambridge: Cambridge University Press, 1985.
———. "Leviathan." In *ABD* 4:295–96.

Bibliography

de Moor, Johannes C. "An Incantation Against Evil Spirits (Ras Ibn Hani 78/20)." *UF* 12 (1980) 429–32.

de Ste. Croix, Geoffrey E. M. "Why Were the Early Christians Persecuted?" In *Studies in Ancient Society*, edited by M. I. Finley, 210–49. Past and Present. Boston: Routledge & Kegan Paul, 1974.

Deininger, Jürgen. *Die Provinziallandtage der römischen Kaiserzeit von Augustus bis zum Ende des dritten Jahrhunderts n. Chr.* Munich: Beck, 1965.

Deissmann, Gustav Adolf. *Light from the Ancient East*. Translated by Lionel Strachan. London: Hodder and Stoughton, 1910.

Dequeker, Luc. "The 'Saints of the Most High' in Qumran and Daniel." *OTS* 18 (1973) 133–62.

Di Lella, Alexander A. "The One in Human Likeness and the Holy Ones of the Most High in Daniel 7." *CBQ* 39 (1977) 1–19.

Dio Chrysostom. *Discourses 1–80*. Translated by H. Lamar Crosby and J. W. Cohoon. 5 vols. Loeb Classical Library. Cambridge, MA: Harvard University Press, 1932–1951.

Dionysius, of Halicarnassus. *Roman Antiquities*. Translated by Earnest Cary. 7 vols. Loeb Classical Library. Cambridge, MA: Harvard University Press, 1937–1950.

Duff, Paul. *Who Rides the Beast? Prophetic Rivalry and the Rhetoric of Crisis in the Churches of the Apocalypse*. New York: Oxford University Press, 2001.

———. "Wolves in Sheep's Clothing: Literary Opposition and Social Tension in the Revelation of John." In *Reading the Book of Revelation: A Resource for Students*, edited by David L. Barr, 65–79. Atlanta: SBL, 2003.

Dumézil, Georges. *Archaic Roman Religion: With an Appendix on the Religion of the Etruscans*. Translated by P. Krapp. 2 vols. Chicago: University of Chicago Press, 1970. Translation of *La religion romaine archaique*. 2 vols. Paris: Payot, 1966.

Edmunds, Lowell, ed. *Approaches to Greek Myth*. Baltimore: Johns Hopkins University Press, 1990.

Eichrodt, Walther. *Ezekiel*. Translated by Cosslett Quin. Old Testament Library. Philadelphia: Westminster, 1970.

Eissfeldt, Otto. *Baal Zaphon, Zeus Kasios und der Durchzug der Israeliten durchs Meer*. Halle: Niemeyer, 1932.

Elliott, John. *Social-Scientific Criticism of the New Testament*. London: SPCK, 1995.

Emerton, J. A. "Leviathan and *LTN*: The Vocalization of the Ugaritic Word for the Dragon." *VT* 32 (1982) 327–31.

Eusebius. *Ecclesiastical History*. Translated by Kirospp Lake. 2 vols. Loeb Classical Library. Cambridge, MA: Harvard University Press, 1926/1932.

Farrer, Austin. *A Rebirth of Images: The Making of St. John's Apocalypse*. Westminster: Dacre, 1949.

Finley, M. I., ed. *Studies in Ancient Society*. Boston: Routledge & Kegan Paul, 1974.

Fishwick, Duncan. *The Imperial Cult in the Latin West*. 2 vols. Etudes préliminaires aux religions orientales dans l'empire romain 108. Leiden: Brill, 1987.

Fitzmyer, Joseph. "The New Testament Title 'Son of Man' Philologically Considered." In *The Semitic Background of the New Testament Volume II: A Wandering Aramean: Collected Aramaic Essays*, 143–60. Grand Rapids: Eerdmans, 1997.

Flusser, David. "Hystaspes and John of Patmos." In *Irano-Judaica: Studies Relating to Jewish Contacts with Persian Culture throughout the Ages*, edited by Shaul Shaked, 12–75. Jerusalem: Ben-Zvi, 1982.

Bibliography

Fontenrose, Joseph. *Python: A Study of Delphic Myth and Its Origins*. Berkeley and Los Angeles: University of California Press, 1959.

Forsyth, Neil. *The Old Enemy: Satan and the Combat Myth*. Princeton: Princeton University Press, 1987.

Frank, Tenney, ed. *An Economic Survey of Ancient Rome*. Vol. 4. Baltimore: Johns Hopkins University Press, 1938.

Friesen, Steven J. *Imperial Cults and the Apocalypse of John: Reading Revelation in the Ruins*. New York: Oxford University Press, 2001.

———. *Twice Neokoros: Ephesus, Asia and the Cult of the Flavian Imperial Family*. Edited by R. Van den Broek et al. Religions in the Graeco-Roman World 116. Leiden: Brill, 1993.

Gibson, John C. L. *Canaanite Myths and Legends*. 2nd ed. Edinburgh: T. & T. Clark, 1977.

———. "The Theology of the Ugaritic Baal Cycle." *Orientalia* 53 (1984) 202–19.

Ginsberg, Harold L. "Ugaritic Myths, Epics, and Legends." In *Ancient Near Eastern Texts Relating to the Old Testament*, edited by James B. Pritchard, 129–55. 3rd ed. Princeton: Princeton University Press, 1969.

Ginzberg, Louis. *The Legends of the Jews*. 7 vols. Philadelphia: Jewish Publication Society of America, 1909–38.

Gordon, Cyrus H. *Ugaritic Textbook: Grammar, Texts in Transliteration, Cuneiform Selections, Glossary, Indices*. Rev. ed. Analecta orientalia 38. Roma: Pontificio Istituto Biblico, 1998.

Gray, John. *The Legacy of Canaan: The Ras Shamra Texts and their Relevance to the Old Testament*. 2nd ed. Vetus Testamentum Supplements 5. Leiden: Brill, 1965.

Gunkel, Hermann. *Creation and Chaos in the Primeval Era and the Eschaton: A Religio-Historical Studies of Genesis 1 and Revelation 12*. Translated by K. William Whitney. Grand Rapids: Eerdmans, 2006.

Habel, Norman. *The Book of Job*. Old Testament Library. London: SCM, 1985.

Halperin, David J. *The Faces of the Chariot: Early Jewish Responses to Ezekiel's Vision*. Tübingen: Mohr, 1988.

Harrington, Wilfrid J. *Revelation*. Sacra pagina 16. Collegeville, MN: Liturgical, 1993.

Heidel, Alexander. *The Babylonian Genesis*. Chicago: University of Chicago Press, 1951.

Hengel, Martin. *Judaism and Hellenism: Studies in Their Encounter in Palestine During the Early Hellenistic Period*. Translated by John Bowden. 2nd ed. 2 vols. London: SCM, 1981.

———. *The Zealots*. Translated by David Smith. Edinburgh: T. & T. Clark, 1989.

Herodotus. *The History*. Translated by David Grene. Chicago: University of Chicago Press, 1988.

Herr, Moshe David. "Pirkei de-Rabbi Eliezer." In *EncJud* 13:558–59.

Hippolytus. *Refutation of All Heresies*. Translated by M. David Litwa. Writings from the Greco-Roman World. Atlanta: SBL Press, 2016.

Hoberman, Barry. "BA Portrait: George Smith (1840–1876) Pioneer Assyriologist." *BA* 46 1 (1983) 41–42.

Howard-Brook, Wes, and Anthony Gwyther. *Unveiling Empire: Reading Revelation Then and Now*. Maryknoll, NY: Orbis, 1999.

Imhoof-Blumer, F. *Monnaies Grecques*. Amsterdam: Johannes Müller, 1883.

St. Irenaeus of Lyons: Against the Heresies (Books 1–3). 3 vols. Ancient Christian Writers. Translated by Dominic J. Unger et al. Mahwah, NJ: Paulist, 1992–2012.

Bibliography

Isaac, E. "1 (Ethiopic Apocalypse of) Enoch." In *The Old Testament Pseudepigrapha*, edited by James H. Charlesworth, 1:5-89. 2 vols. New York: Doubleday, 1983-85.

Jerome. *On Illustrious Men*. Translated by Thomas P. Halton. The Fathers of the Church: A New Translation (Patristic Series). Vol. 100. Washington, DC: The Catholic University of America Press, 1999.

———. *Select Letters*. Translated by F. A. Wright. Loeb Classical Library. Cambridge, MA: Harvard University Press, 1933.

Josephus. Translated by H. St. J. Thackeray et al. 10 vols. Loeb Classical Library. Cambridge, MA: Harvard University Press, 1926-1965.

St. Justin Martyr. *The First Apology, The Second Apology, Dialogue with Trypho, Exhortation to the Greeks, Discourse to the Greeks, The Monarchy of the Rule of God*. Translated by Thomas B. Falls. The Fathers of the Church: A New Translation (Patristic Series). Vol. 6. Washington, DC: The Catholic University of America Press, 2008.

Kaiser, Otto. *Isaiah 13-39*. Old Testament Library. Philadelphia: Westminster, 1974.

Kearsley, Rosalinde A. "Asiarchs, *Archiereis*, and the *Archiereiai* of Asia." *GRBS* 27/2 (1986) 183-92.

Keay, Simon J. *Roman Spain*. Berkeley: University of California Press, 1988.

Keil, Josef. "XVI. Vorläufiger Bericht über die Ausgrabungen in Ephesos." *JÖAI* 27 (1932) 5-72.

———. "Die erste Kaiserneokorie von Ephesos." *NZ* 12 (1919) 115-20.

Kenyon, Kathleen M. *Jerusalem: Excavating 3000 Years of History*. London: Thames and Hudson, 1967.

Klijn, A. F. J. "2 (Syriac Apocalypse of) Baruch." In *The Old Testament Pseudepigrapha*, edited by James H. Charlesworth, 1:615-52. 2 vols. New York: Doubleday, 1983-85.

———. "The Sources and the Redaction of the Syriac Apocalypse of Baruch." *JSJ* 1 (1970) 65-76.

Knibb, Michael A. "The Date of the Parables of Enoch: A Critical Review." *NTS* 25 (1979) 345-59.

———. *The Ethiopic Book of Enoch: A New Edition in the Light of the Aramaic Dead Sea Fragments*. 2 vols. Oxford: Clarendon, 1978.

Kraus, Hans-Joachim. *Psalms*. Translated by Hilton C. Oswald. 2 vols. Continental Commentaries. Minneapolis: Fortress, 1993.

Kraybill, J. Nelson. *Imperial Cult and Commerce in John's Apocalypse*. Journal for the Study of the New Testament: Supplement Series 132. Sheffield: Sheffield Academic, 1996.

Krodel, Gerhard A. *Revelation*. Minneapolis: Augsburg, 1989.

Kugel, James L. *The Ladder of Jacob: Ancient Interpretations of the Biblical Story of Jacob and His Children*. Princeton: Princeton University Press, 2006.

Kümmel, Werner Georg. *Introduction to the New Testament*. Translated by Howard Clark Kee. London: SCM, 1975.

Lacocque, André. *The Book of Daniel*. Translated by David Pellauer. London: SPCK, 1979.

Larson, Gerald James, ed. *Myth in Indo-European Antiquity*. Berkeley: University of California Press, 1974.

Lietzmann, Hans. *Der Menschensohn*. Freiburg: Mohr, 1896.

Lightfoot, Joseph. *Apostolic Fathers: Clement, Ignatius, and Polycarp: Revised Texts with Introduction, Notes, Dissertations, and Translations*. 5 vols. 1890. Reprint, Grand Rapids: Baker, 1981.

Lindars, Barnabas. *Jesus Son of Man*. London: SPCK, 1983.

Bibliography

Lintott, Andrew W. "The Capitoline Dedications to Jupiter and the Roman People." *ZPE* 30 (1978) 137–44.

Littleton, Covington Scott. "'Je ne suis pas . . . structuraliste': Some Fundamental Differences between Dumézil and Lévi-Strauss." *JAS* 34 1 (1974) 151–58.

———. *The New Comparative Mythology: An Anthropological Assessment of the Theories of Georges Dumézil.* Rev. ed. Berkeley: University of California Press, 1973.

Livy. *History of Rome.* Translated by B. O. Foster et al. 14 vols. Loeb Classical Library. Cambridge, MA: Harvard University Press, 1919–1959.

Lunt, Horace G. "Ladder of Jacob." In *The Old Testament Pseudepigrahpa*, edited by James H. Charlesworth, 2:401–11. 2 vols. New York: Doubleday, 1983–85.

Magie, David. *Roman Rule in Asia Minor to the End of the Third Century after Christ.* 2 vols. Princeton: Princeton University Press, 1950.

Margalit, Baruch. *A Matter of "Life" and "Death": A Study of the Baal-Mot Epic (CTA 4-5-6).* Alter Orient und Altes Testament 206. Neukirchen-Vluyn: Neukirchener, 1980.

Meadowcroft, Tim J. *Aramaic Daniel and Greek Daniel: A Literary Companion.* Journal for the Study of the Old Testament: Supplement Series 198. Sheffield: Sheffield Academic, 1995.

Mearns, Christopher L. "Dating the Similitudes of Enoch." *NTS* 25 (1978–79) 360–69.

Meier, Sam. "Baal's Fight with Yam (KTU 1.2.1, IV): A Part of the Baal Myth as Known in KTU 1.1, 3–6?" *UF* 18 (1986) 241–54.

Meiggs, Russell. *Roman Ostia.* Oxford: Clarendon, 1973.

Mellor, Ronald. ΘΕΑ ΡΩΜΗ: *The Worship of the Goddess Roma in the Greek World.* Hypomnemata. Heft 42. Gottingen: Vandenhoeck & Ruprecht, 1975.

Michels, Agnes Kirsopp. *The Calendar of the Roman Republic.* Princeton: Princeton University Press, 1967.

Milik, Józef T., and Matthew Black, eds. *The Books of Enoch: Aramaic Fragments of Qumrân Cave 4.* Oxford: Clarendon, 1976.

Milik, Józef T., and James C. VanderKam. "Jubilees." In *Qumran Cave 4. VIII: Parabiblical Texts Part 1*, edited by H. Attridge et al., 1–185. Discoveries in the Judaean Desert 13. Oxford: Clarendon, 1994.

Millar, Fergus. *The Emperor in the Roman World.* Ithaca: Cornell University Press, 1977.

———. *The Roman Near East 31 BC—AD 337.* Cambridge, MA: Harvard University Press, 1993.

Miller, Patrick D. *The Divine Warrior in Early Israel.* Harvard Semitic Monographs 5. Cambridge, MA: Harvard University Press, 1973.

Mitsopoulou-Leon, Veronika. "Ephesos." In *The Princeton Encyclopedia of Classical Sites*, edited by Richard Stillwell et al., 306–10. Princeton: Princeton University Press, 1976.

Momigliano, Arnaldo. *Claudius: The Emperor and His Achievement.* Westport, CT: Greenwood, 1981.

Montgomery, James A. *A Critical and Exegetical Commentary on the Book of Daniel.* International Critical Commentary 23. Edinburgh: T. & T. Clark, 1927.

Mosca, Paul G. "Ugarit and Daniel 7: A Missing Link." *Biblica* 67 (1986) 496–517.

Mounce, Robert H. *The Book of Revelation.* New International Commentary on the New Testament. Grand Rapids: Eerdmans, 1998.

Murphy, Frederick J. *The Structure and Meaning of Second Baruch.* Atlanta: Scholars, 1985.

Myers, Jacob M. *I and II Esdras.* Anchor Bible 42. Garden City, NY: Doubleday, 1974.

Bibliography

Nagy, Joseph Falaky. "Hierarchy, Heroes, and Heads: Indo-European Structures in Greek Myth." In *Approaches to Greek Myth*, edited by Lowell Edmunds, 200–238. Baltimore: Johns Hopkins University Press, 1990.

Nickelsburg, George W. E. *Jewish Literature between the Bible and the Mishnah: A Historical and Literary Introduction*. Philadelphia: Fortress, 1981.

Nock, Arthur Darby. *Essays on Religion and the Ancient World*. Edited by Zeph Stewart. 2 vols. Cambridge, MA: Harvard University Press, 1972.

North, John A. *Roman Religion*. Greece and Rome: New Surveys in the Classics 30. Oxford: Oxford University Press, 2000.

Noth, Martin. "The Holy Ones of the Most High." In *The Laws in the Pentateuch and Other Essays*, 215-28. London: Oliver and Boyd, 1966. Reprint, London, SCM, 1984.

Ovid. *Fasti*. Edited and Translated by A. J. Boyle and R. D. Woodard. London: Penguin, 2000.

———. *Tristia. Ex Ponto*. Translated by A. L. Wheeler. Revised by G. P. Goold. Loeb Classical Library. Cambridge, MA: Harvard University Press, 1924.

Pennington, A. "The Ladder of Jacob." In *The Apocryphal Old Testament*, edited by Hedley F. D. Sparks, 453–63. London: Oxford University Press, 1983.

Petersen, David, and Kent Harold Richards. *Interpreting Hebrew Poetry*. Minneapolis: Fortress, 1992.

Petit, Paul. *Pax Romana*. Translated by James Willis. Berkeley: University of California Press, 1976.

Philo. *The Works of Philo*. Translated by C. D. Yonge. New updated edition. Peabody, MA: Hendrickson, 2013.

Pleket, Henri W. "An Aspect of the Emperor Cult: Imperial Mysteries." *HTR* 58 4 (1965) 331–47.

Pliny. *Natural History*. Translated by H. Rackham et al. 10 vols. Loeb Classical Library. Cambridge, MA: Harvard University Press, 1938–1963.

Pliny the Younger. *Letters*. Translated by Betty Radice. Loeb Classical Library. Cambridge, MA: Harvard University Press, 1969.

Plutarch. *Lives. Aratus. Artaxerxes. Galba. Otho*. Translated by Bernadotte Perrin. Loeb Classical Library. Cambridge, MA: Harvard University Press, 1926.

———. *Lives. Demetrius and Antony. Pyrrhus and Gaius Marius*. Translated by Bernadotte Perrin. Loeb Classical Library. Cambridge, MA: Harvard University Press, 1920.

———. *Moralia*. Translated by Frank Cole Babbitt et al. 15 vols. Loeb Classical Library. Cambridge, MA: Harvard University Press, 1927–1976.

Price, Simon R. F. *Rituals and Power: The Roman Imperial Cult in Asia Minor*. Cambridge: Cambridge University Press, 1984.

Pritchard, James B., ed. *Ancient Near Eastern Texts Relating to the Old Testament*. 3rd ed. Princeton: Princeton University Press, 1969.

Raabe, Paul R. "Daniel 7: Its Structure and Role in the Book." *HAR* 9 (1985) 267–75.

Ramsay, William Mitchell. *The Letters to the Seven Churches of Asia*. New York: Hodder & Stoughton, 1905.

———. "Notes and Inscriptions from Asia Minor." *AJA* 1 (1885) 138–51.

Reade, Julian. "Hormuzd Rassam and His Discoveries." *Iraq* 55 (1993) 39–62.

Richard, Pablo. *Apocalypse: A People's Commentary on the Book of Revelation*. Maryknoll, NY: Orbis, 1995.

Rissi, Matthias. *Time and History: A Study of the Revelation*. Richmond, VA: John Knox, 1966.

Bibliography

Rives, James B. *Religion in the Roman Empire*. Malden, MA: Blackwell, 2007.
Robert, Louis. "Le cult de Caligula a Milet et la province d'Asie." *Hellenica* 7 (1949) 206–38.
Robinson, H. S. "A Monument of Roma at Corinth." *Hesperia* 43 (1974) 470–84.
Robinson, J. T. *Reading the New Testament*. Philadelphia: Westminster, 1976.
Roloff, Jürgen. *The Revelation of John*. Translated by John E. Alsup. Continental Commentaries. Minneapolis: Fortress, 1993.
Roth, Cecil. "An Ordinance against Images in Jerusalem." *HTR* 49 (1956) 169–77.
Rowland, Christopher. *The Open Heaven: A Study of Apocalyptic in Judaism and Early Christianity*. London: SPCK, 1982.
———. "The Vision of the Risen Christ in Rev 1.13 ff: The Debt of an Early Christian Christology to an Aspect of Jewish Angelology." *JTS* 31 (1980) 1–11.
Royalty, Robert. *The Streets of Heaven: The Ideology of Wealth in the Apocalypse of John*. Macon, GA: Mercer University Press, 1998.
Rubinkiewicz, R., and Horace G. Lunt. "Apocalypse of Abraham." In *The Old Testament Pseudepigrahpa*, edited by James Charlesworth, 1:681–705. 2 vols. New York: Doubleday, 1983–85.
Russell, David Syme. *The Method and Message of Jewish Apocalyptic: 200 BC—AD 100*. Old Testament Library. London: SCM, 1964.
Sayler, Gwendolyn B. *Have the Promises Failed? A Literary Analysis of 2 Baruch*. Society of Biblical Literature Dissertation Series 72. Chico, CA: Scholars, 1984.
Schäfer, Jörg. "Pergamon Mysia, Turkey." In *The Princeton Encyclopedia of Classical Sites*, edited by Richard Stillwell et al., 688–91. Princeton: Princeton University Press, 1976.
Schäfer, Peter. *Jesus in the Talmud*. Princeton: Princeton University Press, 2007.
Scherrer, Peter, ed. *Ephesos: Der Neue Führer*. Vienna: Österreichisches Archäologisches Institut, 1995.
Scherrer, S. J. "Signs and Wonders in the Imperial Cult." *JBL* 103 (1984) 599–610.
Schilling, Robert. "Roman Religion." In *Roman and European Mythologies*, edited by Yves Bonnefoy, 61–67. Translated under the direction of Wendy Doniger by Gerald Honigsblum et al. Chicago: University of Chicago Press, 1991.
Schmidt, Nathaniel. "The 'Son of Man' in the Book of Daniel." *JBL* 19 1 (1900) 22–28.
Scholem, Gershom G. *Jewish Gnosticism, Merkabah Mysticism, and Talmudic Tradition*. New York: Jewish Theological Seminary, 1965.
Schürer, Emil. *The History of the Jewish People in the Age of Jesus Christ (175 BC—AD 135)*. Edited by M. Black et al. 3 vols. Edinburgh: T. & T. Clark, 1973–87.
Schüssler Fiorenza, Elisabeth. *The Book of Revelation: Justice and Judgment*. Philadelphia: Fortress, 1984.
———. "The Eschatology and Composition of the Apocalypse." *CBQ* 30 (1968) 537–69.
———. "The Followers of the Lamb: Visionary Rhetoric and Social-Political Situation." *Semeia* 36 (1986) 123–46.
———. *Revelation: Vision of a Just World*. Minneapolis: Fortress, 1991.
Scott, R. B. Y. "Behold, He cometh with Clouds." *NTS* 5 (1958–59) 127–32.
Segal, Alan F. *Two Powers in Heaven: Early Rabbinic Reports about Christianity and Gnosticism*. Studies in Judaism in Late Antiquity 25. Leiden: Brill, 1977.
Shaked, Shaul, ed. *Irano-Judaica: Studies Relating to Jewish Contacts with Persian Culture throughout the Ages*. Jerusalem: Ben-Zvi, 1982.
Slater, Thomas B. "Dating the Apocalypse to John." *Biblica* 84 (2003) 252–58.

———. "*HOMOION HUION ANTHRŌPOU* IN REV 1.13 AND 14.14." *BT* 44 3 (1993) 349–50.

———. "One Like a Son of Man in First-Century CE Judaism." *NTS* 41 (1995) 183–98.

Smallwood, E. Mary. *The Jews under Roman Rule: From Pompey to Diocletian*. Studies in Judaism in Late Antiquity 20. Leiden: Brill, 1976.

Smith, Mark S. "Interpreting the Baal Cycle." *UF* 18 (1986) 313–39.

———. "The 'Son of Man' in Ugaritic." *CBQ* 45 (1983) 59–60.

Snyder, Barbara W. "Combat Myth in the Apocalypse: The Liturgy of the Day of the Lord and the Dedication of the Heavenly Temple." PhD diss., Graduate Theological Union and University of California, 1991.

Solmsen, Friedrich. "Aeneas Founded Rome with Odysseus." *HSCP* 90 (1986) 93–110.

Stamper, John. *The Architecture of Roman Temples: The Republic to the Middle Empire*. Cambridge: Cambridge University Press, 2005.

Stillwell, Richard, et al., eds. *The Princeton Encyclopedia of Classical Sites*. Princeton: Princeton University Press, 1976.

Stone, Michael E. "Apocalyptic Literature." In *Jewish Writings of the Second Temple Period: Apocrypha, Pseudepigrapha, Qumran, Sectarian Writings, Philo, Josephus*, edited by Michael E. Stone, 383–441. Compendia rerum iudaicarum ad Novum Testamentum 2.2. Philadelphia: Fortress, 1984.

———. *Armenian Apocrypha relating to the Patriarchs and Prophets*. Jerusalem: Israel Academy of Sciences and Humanities, 1982.

———. *Fourth Ezra: A Commentary on the Book of Fourth Ezra*. Hermeneia. Minneapolis: Fortress, 1990.

———. "List of Revealed Things in the Apocalyptic Literature." In *Magnalia Dei, The Mighty Acts of God: Essays on the Bible and Archaeology in Memory of G. Ernest Wright*, edited by Frank M. Cross et al., 414–52. Garden City, NY: Doubleday, 1976.

———. "Noah, Books of." In *EncJud* 12:1198.

Strabo. *Geography*. Translated by Horace Leonard Jones. 8 vols. Loeb Classical Library. Cambridge, MA: Harvard University Press, 1917–1932.

Suetonius. *Lives of the Caesars*. Translated by Catharine Edwards. Oxford World's Classics. New York: Oxford University Press, 2000.

Sutherland, C. H. V. *The Cistophori of Augustus*. London: Royal Numismatic Society, 1970.

Tacitus. *The Histories and The Annals*. Translated by C. H. Moore and J. Jackson. 4 vols. Loeb Classical Library. Cambridge, MA: Harvard University Press, 1937.

Tcherikover, Victor A., and Alexander Fuks, eds. *Corpus Papyrorum Judaicarum*. 3 vols. Cambridge, MA: Harvard University Press, 1957–64.

Tertullian. *Apology. De Spectaculis. Minucius Felix: Octavius*. Translated by T. R. Glover. Loeb Classical Library. Cambridge, MA: Harvard University Press, 1931.

Thompson, Leonard L. *The Book of Revelation: Apocalypse and Empire*. Oxford: Oxford University Press, 1990.

Towner, Wayne Sibley. *Daniel*. Interpretation. Atlanta: John Knox, 1984.

VanderKam, James C. *Enoch and the Growth of an Apocalyptic Tradition*. Catholic Biblical Quarterly Monograph Series 16. Washington, DC: Catholic Biblical Association of America, 1984.

———. "Enoch Traditions in Jubilees and Other Second-Century Sources." In *SBL Seminar Papers, 1978*, 1:229–51. 2 vols. Society of Biblical Literature Seminar Papers 15. Missoula, MT: Scholars, 1978.

Bibliography

Varro, Marcus Terentius. *On the Latin Language.* Translated by Roland G. Kent. 2 vols. Loeb Classical Library. Cambridge, MA: Harvard University Press, 1938.

Vawter, Bruce. "Prov 8:22: Wisdom and Creation." *JBL* 99 (1980) 205–16.

Vermes, Geza. "Appendix E: The Use of בר נשא/בר נש in Jewish Aramaic." In *An Aramaic Approach to the Gospels and Acts,* edited by Matthew Black, 310–30. 3rd ed. Oxford: Clarendon, 1967.

Victorin de Poetovio. *Sur l' Apocalypse et autres écrits.* Edited by Martine Dulaey. Source Chrétiennes 423. Paris: Les Éditions du Cerf, 1997.

Virgil. *Aeneid.* Translated by H. Rushton Fairclough. 2 vols. Loeb Classical Library. Cambridge, MA: Harvard University Press, 1999–2001.

Vos, Louis Arthur. *The Synoptic Traditions in the Apocalypse.* Kampen: Kok, 1965.

Weiss, Johannes. *Die Offenbarung des Johannes: Ein Beitrag zur Literatur-und Religionsgeschichte.* Göttingen: Vandenhoeck & Ruprecht, 1904.

Westermann, Claus. *Genesis 1–11.* Translated by John J. Scullion. Continental Commentaries. Minneapolis: Fortress, 1994.

Whitney, K. William. *Two Strange Beasts: Leviathan and Behemoth in Second Temple and Early Rabbinic Judaism.* Harvard Semitic Monographs 63. Winona Lake, IN: Eisenbrauns, 2006.

Willett, Tom W. *Eschatology in the Theodicies of 2 Baruch and 4 Ezra.* Journal for the Study of the Pseudepigrapha: Supplement Series 4. Sheffield: JSOT, 1989.

Wilson, J. Christian. "The Problem of the Domitianic Date of Revelation." *NTS* 39 (1993) 587–605.

Wiseman, Timothy Peter. *Remus: A Roman Myth.* Cambridge: Cambridge University Press, 1995.

Witherington, Ben, III. *Revelation.* Cambridge: Cambridge University Press, 2003.

Wolff, Hans Walter. *Joel and Amos.* Hermeneia. Philadelphia: Fortress, 1977.

Wood, John Turtle. *Discoveries at Ephesus, Including the Site and Remains of the Great Temple of Diana.* 1877. Reprint, New York: Georg Olms, 1975.

Young, Edward J. *Daniel's Vision of the Son of Man.* London: Tyndale, 1958.

www.ingramcontent.com/pod-product-compliance
Lightning Source LLC
Chambersburg PA
CBHW051743230426
43670CB00012B/2139